A BENN STUDY · DRAMA

THE NEW MERMAIDS

Epicoene
or
The Silent Woman

# THE NEW MERMAIDS

*General Editors*

## BRIAN MORRIS
*Professor of English Literature in the University of Sheffield*

## BRIAN GIBBONS
*Senior Lecturer in English in the University of York*

## ROMA GILL
*Senior Lecturer in English Literature in the University of Sheffield*

# Epicoene
## or
# The Silent Woman

## BEN JONSON

*Edited by*

### R. V. HOLDSWORTH

*Lecturer in English*
*University of Manchester*

LONDON/ERNEST BENN LIMITED

NEW YORK/W. W. NORTON AND COMPANY INC.

*First published in this form 1979*
*by Ernest Benn Limited*
*25 New Street Square, Fleet Street, London EC4A 3JA*
*& Sovereign Way, Tonbridge, Kent TN9 1RW*

© *Ernest Benn Limited 1979*

*Published in the United States of America by*
*W. W. Norton and Company Inc.*
*500 Fifth Avenue, New York, N.Y. 10036*

*Distributed in Canada by*
*The General Publishing Company Limited · Toronto*

*Printed in Great Britain*
*by Cox & Wyman Ltd,*
*London, Fakenham and Reading*

**British Library Cataloguing in Publication Data**

Jonson, Ben
  Epicoene, or, The silent woman.
  I. Title   II. Holdsworth, Roger Victor
  822'.3      PR2612

  ISBN 0–510–34154–3
  ISBN 0–393–90040–1 (U.S.A.)

TO
SARA

# CONTENTS

# ACKNOWLEDGEMENTS

I have benefited considerably from the work of earlier editors of *Epicoene*, and owe a particular debt to the commentaries of Henry, Herford and Simpson, and Partridge, and the textual work of Beaurline. In the Introduction the section on the author is taken from G. R. Hibbard's New Mermaid edition of *Bartholmew Fair*.

Many friends and colleagues have generously given assistance: Roma Gill, the General Editor, prevented many errors and omissions; Sara Pearl shared her research on Jonson with me and made many helpful suggestions; D. M. Bain remedied my small Latin and less Greek and in doing so discovered Jonson's probable use of the twenty-seventh declamation of Libanius; F. W. Sternfeld and C. R. Wilson kindly agreed to contribute an appendix on the music for the song in I. i; and on various occasions J. B. Bamborough, Ian Donaldson, Keith Hanley, and D. J. Palmer gave me their time, encouragement, and advice. Finally, I am pleased to thank the Una Ellis-Fermor Memorial Trust for a grant towards the work.

*Manchester*                                                      R.V.H.

# ABBREVIATIONS

## 1. *Texts of* Epicoene

| | |
|---|---|
| F | the edition of 1616, in Jonson's folio *Works* |
| F$^a$ | original setting in F of gathering Yy |
| F$^b$ | second setting in F of gathering Yy |
| Gifford | William Gifford, ed., *The Works of Ben Jonson*, 9 vols., 1816. |
| Henry | Aurelia Henry, ed., *Epicoene or The Silent Woman, Yale Studies in English*, XXXI, New York, 1906. |
| H&S | C. H. Herford and Percy and Evelyn Simpson, eds., *Ben Jonson*, 11 vols., Oxford, 1925–52. |
| Beaurline | L. A. Beaurline, ed., *Epicoene or The Silent Woman*, Regents Renaissance Drama Series, 1967. |
| Partridge | Edward Partridge, ed., *Epicoene*, The Yale Ben Jonson, 1971. |

## 2. *Jonson's works*

| | |
|---|---|
| *Alch.* | *The Alchemist* |
| *B.F.* | *Bartholmew Fair* |
| *Cat.* | *Catiline his Conspiracy* |
| *C.R.* | *Cynthia's Revels* |
| *D. is A.* | *The Devil is an Ass* |
| *Disc.* | *Timber, or Discoveries* |
| *E.M.I.* | *Every Man in his Humour* |
| *E.M.O.* | *Every Man out of his Humour* |
| *Epig.* | *Epigrams* |
| *Hym.* | *Hymenaei* |
| *M.L.* | *The Magnetic Lady* |
| *M.V.* | *Mercury Vindicated from the Alchemists at Court* |
| *N.I.* | *The New Inn* |
| *N.N.W.* | *News from the New World Discovered in the Moon* |
| *N.T.* | *Neptune's Triumph for the Return of Albion* |
| *Poet.* | *Poetaster* |
| *Sej.* | *Sejanus his Fall* |
| *S.N.* | *The Staple of News* |
| *T.T.* | *A Tale of a Tub* |
| *Und.* | *The Underwood* |
| *Volp.* | *Volpone* |

The text used for all quotations and references is that of H&S, with i/j and u/v spellings modernized.

3. *Other works*

| | |
|---|---|
| Nares | Robert Nares, *A Glossary, or Collection of Words, Phrases and Names*, 1822. |
| OED | *The Oxford English Dictionary*. |
| Shakespeare | G. Blakemore Evans, ed., *The Riverside Shakespeare*, Boston, 1974. |
| Sugden | E. H. Sugden, *A Topographical Dictionary to the Works of Shakespeare and his Fellow Dramatists*, Manchester, 1925. |
| Tilley | M. P. Tilley, *A Dictionary of the Proverbs in England in the Sixteenth and Seventeenth Centuries*, Ann Arbor, 1950. |
| Upton | *Remarks on Three Plays of Benjamin Jonson*, 1749. |

In quotations from and references to plays by Jonson's contemporaries, the editions used are, whenever possible, those in the New Mermaids series.

| | |
|---|---|
| corr. | corrected |
| ed. | editor |
| om. | omits |
| s.d. | stage direction |
| s.p. | speech prefix |
| uncorr. | uncorrected |

# INTRODUCTION

## THE AUTHOR

WE KNOW MORE about Jonson's life—some of it from his own lips—than we do about the life of any other major dramatist of the time. Colourful, adventurous, and varied, it conforms, unlike Shakespeare's, to the popular connotation of the word 'Elizabethan', and it brought him into intimate contact with all conditions of men from the lowest to the highest, King James I himself. Born in 1572, either in or near London, he was the posthumous son of a poor gentleman who had eventually become 'a grave minister of the gospel'. Not long after his father's death, his mother took a second husband, a master-bricklayer of Westminster. As a consequence, presumably, of this remarriage, Jonson was 'brought up poorly' in his earliest years, but then had the good fortune to attract the interest of 'a friend', who put him to school at Westminster, where he was taught by the great scholar and historian William Camden. The friendship that grew up between them was one of the main formative influences on Jonson's life. Camden imbued the boy with his own passion for learning; and, later on, the poet acknowledged his debt and repaid it by making his old master the subject of one of his finest epigrams, xiv, in which he addresses him as:

> CAMDEN, most reverend head, to whom I owe
> All that I am in arts, all that I know.

How long Jonson remained at Westminster School we do not know, but it would seem that he did not finish his course there, for he told the Scots poet William Drummond of Hawthornden that he was 'taken from it, and put to ane other Craft'—bricklaying in all probability—'which he could not endure'. His removal from school must have happened about 1588–89. At some time between that date and 1597, he served as a volunteer in the war in Flanders. When he arrived there the war was languishing. Disappointed at the lack of action, he took on some misguided individual on the other side in single combat 'in the face of both the Campes', killed him, stripped him of his arms in the best classical manner, and carried them back with him to his own lines. Having demonstrated in this very practical manner his belief in the Renaissance ideal of the unity of learning and action, Jonson 'betook himself to his wonted studies', whatever that may mean. He also married, at some date between 1592 and 1595, a wife whom he would later describe to Drummond as 'a shrew yet honest'. She bore him two children: a daughter, who died at the age of six months, and a son who survived to the age of seven, 'BEN. IONSON his best piece of *poetrie*', as his father called him in the moving epigram, xlv, which he wrote on the child's death in 1603.

How did Jonson live during this time? The information we have is not altogether reliable, since it comes from Thomas Dekker's play *Satiromastix* (1601) in which Jonson is attacked, but in essence it rings true. From it we learn that he belonged to a troupe of strolling players and that he took the leading role in Thomas Kyd's *The Spanish Tragedy*. From the highway he graduated to the London stage and to trouble. In the summer of 1597 Thomas Nashe had handed over to the players part of an unfinished satirical comedy called *The Isle of Dogs*. It was completed by one of them, the young Ben Jonson, without, according to Nashe, his consent. Its performance, at some time prior to 28 July, resulted in information being laid before the Privy Council to the effect that it was 'a lewd play ... contanynge very seditious and sclandrous matter'. Taking prompt action, the Privy Council had 'some of the Players' apprehended and imprisoned, 'whereof one ... was not only an Actor, but a maker of parte of the said Plaie'. Jonson spent over two months in gaol, and was not released until 8 October. It is a significant beginning to his career as a playwright, for he was to run foul of the authorities again.

On his release, Jonson continued to write plays, and, by September 1598, he was already sufficiently well known to have his name mentioned by Francis Meres, in his *Palladis Tamia*, among those who 'are our best for Tragedie'. In the middle of the same month came his first great success. *Every Man in his Humour* was played by Shakespeare's company, the Lord Chamberlain's Men, to delighted audiences, with Shakespeare himself acting one of the parts. Near-disaster followed. On 22 September, Jonson, pugnacious as ever, quarrelled with an actor called Gabriel Spencer, fought a duel with him, killed him, and was arrested for felony. Tried at the Old Bailey, in October, he pleaded guilty, but managed to escape from the gallows by claiming 'benefit of clergy'. His goods were confiscated and his thumb branded.

At this point in his career, Jonson's urge to experiment, coupled with his readiness to castigate those of his contemporaries whose work he disapproved of, led him into what looks in retrospect something of a blind alley. His romantic comedy *The Case is Altered* did well when it was performed by the Children of the Chapel probably towards the end of 1598, but *Every Man out of his Humour*, put on by the Lord Chamberlain's Men at their new theatre, the Globe, late in 1599 or early in 1600, met with a more mixed reception. Boldly announcing itself as a 'Comicall Satyre' when it was first published in 1600, this comedy is highly original. Dispensing with story almost completely, it depicts fools and gulls in profusion. The audience is taken on an extended tour, as it were, of a great gallery full of living caricatures, exhibited to arouse their derision, and, Jonson would have said, to ensure their edification. The bright young men of the court and the Inns of Court enjoyed it enormously and read it avidly; three quarto editions appeared in 1600. But the ordinary playgoer seems to have been less enthusiastic. He wanted more in the way of story than the dramatist offered him, and may well have sensed that this play was moving away from the central concerns of humanity to matters of a more peripheral and ephemeral kind. It also had the effect of antagonizing some of the other dramatists, especially John Marston, whose bizarre diction it had ridiculed. Not surprisingly, Marston retorted in kind by satirizing Jonson in his *Jack Drum's Entertainment* (1600), and thus precipitated a 'war of the theatres'. Jonson's further contributions to it, *Cynthia's Revels* and *Poetaster*, both performed in 1601 by the Children of the Chapel, are not without their brilliance, but they are 'caviary to the general', because 'the general' have the sense to recognize that one cannot live on caviare and that bread and cheese is a far better diet. Moreover, the pungency of the satire in *Poetaster* had made fresh enemies for Jonson, including men of power and influence. Threatened with prosecution, he retired for a time from the stage.

He returned to it in 1603, when his tragedy *Sejanus* was played by the King's Men, with Shakespeare once again taking one of the parts. Still underrated by many critics, this is, in fact, one of the greatest political plays of the time; but its massive achievement did not save it from the wrath of the groundlings who could not tolerate its long speeches. It was damned, and, to make matters worse, Jonson found himself in trouble over what some took to be satirical allusions to contemporary matters in it. He was called before the Privy Council; but there the matter seems to have ended. Characteristically, he was soon in hot water again. In 1604 he collaborated with Chapman and Marston in the writing of *Eastward Ho!*, a superb send-up of citizen comedy. Unfortunately, the comedy also contained some incidental satire on the Scots and a gibe at King James. Along with his two collaborators, Jonson went to gaol again, but was eventually released.

It was his last brush with authority; he did not go to gaol any more. Instead, he settled down to a decade of high dramatic endeavour, producing a series of superb comedies that no audience could resist. *Volpone* (1605), *Epicoene* (1609–10), *The Alchemist*

(1610), and *Bartholmew Fair* (1614) make up a massive achievement, the great central bastion in the Jonsonian *oeuvre*, estab-
lishing him as the master of the comic mode. In this same period he
composed another Roman tragedy, *Catiline*. Played by the King's
Men in 1611, it was, much to the annoyance of its author, une-
quivocally damned on its first performance. In 1616 came a further
comedy, *The Devil is an Ass*, which leaves one in no doubt about
Jonson's continued grasp on and attitude to the social and
economic realities of the time.

He wrote no play for the next nine years. He did not need to.
Since the Christmas of 1604, he had been composing masques for
the court, and bringing the art of the masque to perfection in the
process. He had also been busy writing the lyrical and ethical
poetry which won him the admiration and the discipleship of
numerous younger poets who liked to think of themselves as
belonging to 'the tribe of Ben'. He was a dominant force in the
many literary activities which had their focus in the London
taverns he loved to frequent, and he found himself a welcome
visitor at the country houses of the great. Oxford University
acknowledged his scholarship by making him a Master of Arts in
1619; and in the previous year he had demonstrated his physical
fitness by walking to Scotland and back. It was in Scotland that he
stayed with Drummond of Hawthornden, who had the good sense
to make a record of what Jonson told him during the course of their
*Conversations*.

By the time *The Staple of News* was first played in 1626, however,
things were going wrong for him. The death of James I, in 1625,
was a serious blow, since Charles I did not share his father's
admiration for Jonson and his work, nor was he as generous as his
father had been. Short of money, the poet, now in his fifties, was
forced to resort to the stage once more. The plays he wrote, though
far from being 'dotages', were out of touch with the taste and the
temper of the time. They did not succeed. Worse still, he was
stricken with paralysis in 1628, and seems not to have left his
chamber thereafter, though he lived on for another nine years. He
died on 6 August 1637, and was buried in Westminster Abbey,
under a tombstone bearing the inscription: 'O rare Ben Jonson'.

G.R.H.

## DATE AND STAGE HISTORY

*Epicoene* was first performed in December 1609 or January 1610.
The former date is suggested by the folio title-page and Jonson's

note at the end of the text, both of which give the year as 1609, and by the fact that in that year the London theatres did not open until 9 December, after an eighteen-month closure because of the plague. Clerimont's 'now, by reason of the sickness' at I.i, 176–7 fixes the time of the action as sometime during this recent epidemic. The latter date is suggested by the folio's calling the company of boy actors who acted the play 'the Children of her Majesties REVELLS', a name it was not officially known by until the granting of its patent on 4 January 1610, and by the Prologue's reference (1. 24) to the Whitefriars, the 'private' playhouse which the company was authorized to use. If December 1609 is right, then the Children must have begun their occupancy of the Whitefriars earlier than their patent indicates, and it must have slipped Jonson's memory that it was not until the following year that they acquired their new name. If January 1610 is right, then the folio must here, exceptionally but not uniquely, be using 'old style' chronology, that is, calculating the year from 25 March, not 1 January.¹ Either way, these limits tell us that *Epicoene* was Jonson's first play since *Volpone*, four years before, that it was written shortly after *The Masque of Queens* (performed February 1609), and was soon to be followed by *The Alchemist* (September 1610).

By February *Epicoene* had been banned by the authorities. The evidence is a despatch of the Venetian ambassador, dated the 8th, concerning the King's cousin Arbella Stuart:

> She complains that in a certain comedy the playwright introduced an allusion to her person and the part played by the Prince of Moldavia. The play was suppressed. Her Excellency is very ill-pleased and shows a determination in this coming Parliament to secure the punishment of certain persons, we don't know who. (H&S, V, 146)

The 'prince' was Stephen Janiculo, a claimant to the throne of the Rumanian province of Moldavia who had visited England in 1607 and afterwards announced (he was in Venice, a safe distance from England, when he did so) that he planned to marry Arbella when he gained his princedom. Arbella's enthusiasm for, and even prior knowledge of, this scheme may be doubted (for one thing, Janiculo was married already), but the subject was anyway a touchy one, since Arbella had a strong claim to the English throne and James did not relish the thought of her marrying and producing children. (Indeed, when she did get married, to William Seymour, later in 1610, James calmed his nerves by having her locked up.) We may be sure that *Epicoene* was the comedy complained of, because Jonson let what was evidently the offending passage remain in the

¹ See W. W. Greg, 'The Riddle of Jonson's Chronology', *The Library* (Fourth Series), VI, (1926), 340–7.

printed text. It occurs at V.i, 17–23, when La Foole tells Clerimont that Daw has a box of writing-materials with which to draw pictures of court celebrities:

> of Nomentack, when he was here, and of the Prince of Moldavia, and of his mistress, Mistress Epicoene.
>
> CLERIMONT
> Away! He has not found out her latitude, I hope.

By 'his mistress' La Foole of course means Daw's mistress, but his (typically) confused syntax also permits 'his' to be taken as referring to the Prince of Moldavia. It is easy to imagine the reaction when these lines were spoken on the Whitefriars stage. William Armstrong observes that

> A favourite intellectual exercise of patrons of private theatres was to try to find points of resemblance between characters in the play and well-known personalities of London . . . some members of the audience came equipped with table-books in order to note down items for scandalous gossip.[2]

In this atmosphere such a meaty ambiguity would be gleefully pounced on. There is, however, no evidence that Arbella's 'certain persons' ever received the punishment she intended.

Was the reference deliberate? Jonson said not. Preparing *Epicoene* for publication, he added a Dedication and second Prologue which protest the author's 'innocency' and round upon the 'hatred' and 'contumely' of those who 'make a libel of which he made a play'. There are grounds for accepting this. Jonson may simply have wanted to tangle La Foole in yet another ludicrous syntactical muddle, and not have fully weighed the alternative sense which the muddle made available. Further, he could claim that the Prince of Moldavia is introduced in the interest not of scandal-mongering but of the thematic concerns of the play, since in 1606 the prince had made a famous escape from a Turkish prison dressed in women's clothes, and is thus another contemporary figure, along with Mistress Mary Ambree and the French hermaphrodite (IV.ii, 110, IV.vi, 27), who suggests ideas of transvestism and the swapping of sexual roles. On the other hand, Jonson certainly did on occasion—despite his loud assertions to the contrary—make covert reference to court personages: in *Cynthia's Revels* and *Eastward Ho!*, both private-theatre plays, this had earned him in the first case royal displeasure, in the second imprisonment. On balance it seems as well to bear in mind Swinburne's

---

[2] 'The Audience of the Elizabethan Private Theatres', *Review of English Studies*, X (1959), 247–8.

remark, 'There is nothing accidental in the work of Ben Jonson'.[3]

It is sometimes argued that our text of *Epicoene* must have been revised by Jonson some years after its first performance. If this were so, it would not be surprising—*Every Man out*, *Sejanus*, and *Volpone* are all cases in point—but the evidence is weak. In June 1611 Arbella Stuart herself played an epicene role when she escaped from the custody of the Bishop of Durham wearing 'a Man's Doublet, a man-lyke Perruque with long Locks over her hair, a blacke Hat, blacke Cloake, russet Bootes with red Tops, and a Rapier by her Syde'.[4] The passage discussed above cannot refer to this incident, however—unless Jonson later added La Foole's explanatory 'Mistress Epicoene' in order to make it do so—since Arbella had already complained about it eighteen months before. Similarly, it has been suggested that the business of Morose's 'divorce'—the protracted wrangling between experts in church law, the discovery of grounds on the twelfth impediment, impotence, and the threat to have Morose 'searched' by a jury of women—is a deliberate parody of the notorious Essex divorce case of 1613, which contained all these features.[5] Certainly later audiences of *Epicoene* would have been strongly reminded of the affair, which was known familiarly as 'the Nullity' (cf. V.iv, 108), but it is difficult to imagine the play's original form without this supposed revision, or to see what Jonson could have expected to accomplish by writing in such a tasteless, and highly dangerous, burlesque. In this matter it is better to believe his statement in the Dedication that 'There is not a line or syllable . . . changed from the simplicity of the first copy', even though bibliographical analysis shows that it is not strictly true, and to regard these later historical parallels as coincidences—proof of life's proclivity to imitate art.

*Epicoene* was plainly written for the type of company and playhouse which presented it. The second prologue assumes an evening performance (1. 5), which only the indoor, artificially lit and heated private theatres could mount, and the play's staging requirements—an upper acting level (IV.ii, 63), and three exits, all visible, at the rear of the lower level, the central one screened by a curtain and the outer two by doors (IV.v, 25–31, V.iii, 5–6)—tally with the little we know about the construction of the private-theatre stage. In style and subject-matter, too, *Epicoene* has the marks of a children's company piece. A concern with upper-

---

[3] A. C. Swinburne, *A Study of Ben Jonson*, 1889, p. 9. Herford and Simpson, II, 71, suggest that Daw, who is often referred to as 'Sir John', is meant as a skit on the courtier and poet Sir John Harington; cf. IV.v, 183 and Appendix I.
[4] Quoted by G. P. V. Akrigg, *Jacobean Pageant*, 1962, p. 121.
[5] Thomas Kranidas, 'Possible Revisions or Additions in Jonson's *Epicoene*', *Anglia*, LXXXIII (1965), 451–3.

class manners, embodied in a sophisticated blend of satire, philosophizing, sexual wit, and literary allusions, was very much the preference in comedy of the largely aristocratic or socially ambitious private-theatre audiences, and this the play supplies in good measure. We are not forced to conclude, however, as critics sometimes do, that Jonson was here for once tamely ministering to the decadent taste and shallow attitudes of a smart coterie public, or that he was offering it, in the three gallants who dominate the action, a wonder-struck idealization of its own values. His deliber-ately—and typically—unco-operative prologue, in which he in effect ticks off the Whitefriars audience for liking snobbish plays and advises them to view his own 'with better thought', is clearly meant as an early warning against such ideas.[6]

At least one Whitefriars patron was not impressed by the play. Jonson told his friend Drummond that

> when his Play of a Silent Woman was first acted, ther was found Verses after on the stage against him, concluding that, that play was well named the Silent Woman. ther was never one man to say plaudite to it. (H&S, I, 151)

But contradicting this not-too-pointed thrust is a mass of refer-ences which indicate the play's early and enduring popularity, including a much-repeated jingle which links it with the mas-terpieces of Jonson's comic art:

> The Fox, The Alchemist, and Silent Woman,
> Done by Ben Jonson and outdone by no man.[7]

Two court performances are recorded in the 1630s (see Appendix I), and *Epicoene* seems to have been the first play to be staged in England when the theatres reopened in June 1660, after Charles

---

[6] Two critics who seem to me to take a damagingly straightforward view of the play's private-theatre auspices are Alfred Harbage and Michael Shapiro. The former thinks that because *Epicoene* is a children's play we are meant to applaud Dauphine's savage dismissal of Morose (V.iv, 199–201) as 'manly bluntness', and to feel no qualms about Cutbeard's betrayal of him (*Shakespeare and the Rival Traditions*, New York, 1952, pp. 258, 278); the latter that the gallants, 'true aristocrats', are 'a flattering representation of the Whitefriars audience', by means of which Jonson 'allowed his spectators to confirm their social identities by basking in the glow of the self-image he offered them'. This writer also thinks that Jonson expects us to be staunchly behind the gallants' treatment of life as a game ('Audience vs. Dramatist in Jonson's *Epicoene* and Other Plays of the Children's Troupes', *English Literary Renaissance*, III (1973), 411–16).

[7] G. E. Bentley, *Shakespeare and Jonson*, Chicago, 1945, II, 273; see also J. F. Bradley and J. Q. Adams, eds., *The Jonson Allusion-Book*, New Haven, 1922; R. V. Holdsworth, 'Early References to Plays by Jonson, Shirley, and Others', *Notes and Queries*, CCXXII (1977), 208–9.

II's return to the capital. Pepys saw it many times, jotting in his diary after one performance 'the best comedy, I think, that ever was wrote', and dwelling after another on his high opinion of Edward Kynaston's part as Epicoene:

> it is an excellent play. Among other things here, Kynaston, the boy, had the good turn to appear in three shapes: first as a poor woman in ordinary clothes, to please Morose; then in fine clothes, as a gallant, and in them was clearly the prettiest woman in the whole house, and lastly, as a man; and then likewise did appear the handsomest man in the house.

Oddly, Pepys was not put out by the absurd decision in later performances to have a woman take the role (a policy which remained in force for the next hundred years); on the contrary, he thought the actress he saw 'did her part mighty well'.[8] In this period the play also enjoyed great, indeed enormous, literary prestige. Dryden thought its construction 'the greatest and most noble of any pure unmixed comedy in any language' and said he preferred it before all other plays;[9] his 'examen' in *An Essay of Dramatic Poesy* (1668) is the first critical discussion in English of a specific literary work. For the Restoration dramatists—attracted, no doubt, by the play's concern with high-society manners and marriage, and its parade of wits, fops, and middle-aged grotesques—*Epicoene* was the great model for comedy. Their plays teem with duplicates of its characters.[10] And even Charles II pressed the play into service: quipping about the henpecked state of his brother, the Duke of York, he christened him Tom Otter.[11]

From about 1750 Jonson's reputation went in decline. He began to be seen as a graceless writer, at once pedantic and coarse, and everything the ever more popular Shakespeare was not. *Epicoene* followed the drift. Garrick's revival of 1752 was a failure, and he did scarcely better in 1776, despite the use of a text revised by George Colman which expurgated the bawdy and softened the torments (omitting, for example, Dauphine's last words to his uncle). Thomas Davies, writing in 1783, passed the judgement of a more sentimental and self-consciously 'refined' age:

---

[8] See entries in the *Diary* for 8 January and 25 May 1661; 1 June 1664; 16 April 1667; 18 and 19 September 1668.

[9] W. P. Ker, ed., *Essays of John Dryden*, New York, 1961, I, 83, 131.

[10] e.g., Heartwell in Congreve's *The Old Bachelor* (Morose); Captain Brazen in Farquhar's *The Recruiting Officer* (La Foole); Sir John Brute in Vanbrugh's *The Provoked Wife* (Otter); Lady Fidget and her companions in Wycherley's *The Country Wife* (the Collegiates); Lady Pliant in Congreve's *The Double Dealer* (Mistress Otter). Truewit's descendants are everywhere. For a discussion of the play's Restoration qualities, see J. B. Bamborough, *Ben Jonson*, 1970, pp. 93–5.

[11] *The Jonson Allusion-Book*, p. 336.

After all the panegyric bestowed upon it, the play is of that number which needs much forgiveness ... The great licentiousness of its dialogue was no obstacle to its success when originally performed; nor in the reign of Charles II when revived. But, as the age advanced in decency of manners, the less could the Silent Woman be tolerated ... The character of Morose, upon whose peevish and perverse humour the plot of the comedy depends, is that of a whimsical recluse, whose disposition can bear no sound but that which he utters himself. If this were the whole of his character, he would still be a good object for comic satire, but the melancholy of Morose degenerates into malice and cruelty ... besides the licentiousness of the manners, and quaintness of expression, in the Silent Woman, the frequent allusions to forgotten customs and characters render it impossible to be ever revived with any probability of success. To understand Jonson's comedies perfectly, we should have before us a satirical history of the age in which he lived ... Mr Colman, after all the pains and skill he could bestow on this comedy, found that it was labour lost; there was no reviving the dead.[12]

In this second revival Garrick restored an essential feature: receiving complaints about the flouting of Jonson's intention, after three nights he took out Sarah Siddons as Epicoene and put in a man.

After 1784 *Epicoene* disappeared from the stage until 1895, when it was acted by an all-male cast at Harvard. Probably this convention of the original staging is necessary for the play's full success. In a review of another all-male production, at Cambridge in 1909, William Poel commented:

if one of the female parts is played by a male, while the others are in the hands of females, it must be very difficult for the audience not to see the difference, and not to know all through that Epicoene is really a boy. Once that feeling is allowed to enter, the point of the joke is lost ... When all the female parts are played by—well, by males, it is quite easy to forget (even if you happen to know it beforehand) that Epicoene is really, both on and off the stage, a boy dressed up, while to know that she is a woman, and to have to pretend when the disclosure is made that you believe her to be a boy, is too violent an effort for the faculty of make-believe. And there is no great loss of femininity. Certainly the Cambridge Lady Haughty was so convincingly feminine as to be a complete puzzle.[13]

To which one may add that in the hermaphrodite world of *Epicoene* 'loss of femininity' is anyway precisely what Jonson intends.

There have been many productions since this time, the best, perhaps, that of the Phoenix Company in 1924, when Godfrey Winn was a convincing Epicoene, Cedric Hardwicke made of Morose 'a tragic figure', and the gallants (Raymond Massey played

---

[12] *Dramatic Miscellanies*, 3 vols., 1783–84, II, 101–3. See also R. G. Noyes, *Ben Jonson on the English Stage 1660–1776*, Cambridge, Mass., 1935, pp. 173ff.

[13] *The Times*, 22 February 1909, p. 10. Anonymous, but attributed to Poel by H&S.

Dauphine) executed their practical jokes with 'fiendish ingenuity'.[14] A different approach was taken in 1948 by the Oxford University Dramatic Society, directed by Frank Hauser. Here Morose was 'a picture of comic senility', and the brutality of Dauphine's dismissal of him was circumvented: he left the stage just at the words 'I'll not trouble you'.[15] In this production Epicoene was again played by a woman. Despite the enthusiasm of student groups, there have been no recent professional revivals. This is a pity, for the play's tightly knit construction and great set speeches, as well as its complex interest in levels of illusion, offer marvellous opportunities to both actors and directors.

## SOURCES

At the start of IV.i, after a climactic scene of torment, Clerimont remarks of Morose's distress, 'I have not read of the like in the chronicles of the land'. This is Jonson's clue to the inquisitive student. Set in England in 1609, *Epicoene* has as the chief sources of its main action two Greek declamations and an Italian comedy.

The declamations are by the fourth-century sophist Libanius. One (XXVI in the standard edition[16]) is spoken by a hater of noise who has been led by a well-meaning friend to marry a supposedly quiet wife, only to discover at the wedding ceremony that she is intolerably rowdy and loquacious; his speech is to the city fathers bewailing his miseries and seeking permission to commit suicide. The other (XXVII) is spoken by a misanthropic recluse whose son has laughed at him on their way to town when he fell down in some mud; in revenge (laughter is this character's special hatred) he has decided to disinherit him. In the Greek the speakers are both named Dyskolos, i.e., 'peevish, difficult', and in the edition which Jonson used, which was equipped with a Latin translation, this is translated as 'Morosus'. The edition must have been the folio of Libanius' works published in Paris in 1606. Declamation XXVI had already been published separately, in 1597, and Jonson had used it: he had borrowed several passages for III.iv of *Volpone*, acted late 1605 or early 1606, where Lady Wouldbe assails Volpone with her barrage of chatter. But XXVII did not appear before the 1606 folio. Here the two declamations are printed a long way apart, but they are placed together in the Contents:

morosus qui uxorem loquacem duxerat se ipsum accusans
morosus pater abdicans filium qui de lapse suo riserat

[14] *The Times*, 19 November 1924, p. 12.
[15] H&S, IX, 222.
[16] R. Foerster, ed., *Libanii Opera*, 8 vols., Leipzig, 1903–15, vol. VI.

It was probably seeing them side-by-side in this way that gave Jonson the idea of combining them into a single story.

The speech of the noise-hating Morosus provided much material. Most important, it provided the central occasion of the play, Morose's bridal, for the Greek speaker is particularly exercised by the horrors of his wedding feast and the behaviour at it of his wife's noisy friends. 'These things were immoderate too,' he moans, 'the amount of applause, the laughter, the unseemly dancing, the senseless marriage-hymn' (XXVI, 11). Further, the speech supplied several passages which are borrowed almost verbatim into the play (see Appendix II), and elsewhere details of action as well as dialogue. Morosus' boast that 'my servants are trained to do nothing which might vex me' (XXVI,9) is turned into the elaborate pantomime in II.i, where Mute communicates with Morose by means of signs, and his announcement that 'I cannot bear anyone snoring or sobbing or hawking and spitting or subject to a cough' (10) gave the cue both for Truewit's needling remark to Morose that his new wife snores like a porpoise (IV.iv, 132) and for the business with the coughing parson who upsets Morose in III.iv. The Greek speaker constantly compares his torments to a flood:

> I fear that the woman may set her tongue on you and overwhelm both you and me ... everything flowed from all sides when I married that fury, like those torrents which crash against each other and make an immense din ... I am soaked by her chatter ... as the sea overwhelms a ship, so the woman's flood has overwhelmed me ... Like those who block up pipes and once they take away the blocking material make the force of the water fiercer, so I, by restraining her voice a little, draw forth a greater stream. (XXVI, 3, 11, 29, 42)

In *Epicoene* this becomes an important dramatic and verbal image. Characters flood on to the stage to persecute Morose in ever-increasing numbers, and Morose harps on the idea in his cries of despair:

> Oh, the sea breaks in upon me! Another flood! An inundation! I shall be o'erwhelmed with noise. It beats already at my shores. I feel an earthquake in myself for't. (III.vi, 2–4)

> Oh no, labour not to stop her. She is like a conduit-pipe that will gush out with more force when she opens again. (IV.iv, 72–3)

Compared with these extensive assimilations, the direct contribution of the second declamation is small. It provided Morose's aim and motive—both he and his Greek counterpart wish to disinherit their son/nephew in revenge for mockery — but only a single phrase: Morose's reiterated intention to 'thrust out' Dauphine from his blood (I.ii, 16–18, II.v, 98–9) is matched by this speaker's desire to 'drive [my son] out of the house . . . thrust out [*eiciam* in the Latin translation] him who opposes me'. Of more significance is the change from son to nephew. This was to some extent forced on Jonson as a means of combining the declamations, since the noise-hating Morosus is not married; but it has interesting repercussions on the conflict in the play, since as a nephew Dauphine's claim on Morose's property (especially to enjoy some of it during his life) is a good deal more tenuous than that of the Greek speaker's son. Of course, Jonson could have invented some additional factors to compensate for this; what is interesting is that he did not choose to do it. Dauphine and his supporters simply treat the claim as an unquestioned right.[17]

The device of the bride who turns out to be a boy comes from *Il Marescalco* (1533), Aretino's comedy about a misogynistic, homosexual gentleman-usher whom a playful nobleman forces to take a wife. In a series of progressively more sadistic scenes the torments of marriage and the awfulness of women are spelled out to the horrified victim, until, at the wedding, he makes a public declaration of impotence to try and escape. At this point the nobleman reveals that the bride is a boy, and the gentleman-usher, understandably gratified by this turn of events, joins in the general mirth. This was clearly Jonson's immediate source. At the back of his mind may have been two other comedies where an old man is tricked by the same device, Machiavelli's *Clizia* and Plautus' *Casina* (a nonce-word is borrowed from this last play at IV.ii, 45), and an anecdote in William Rankins' *Seven Satires Applied to the Week* (1598), in which a foolish gallant — who pretends to learning, writes fatuous poems to women, and has a loud voice very like Sir John Daw — is duped by 'certaine sharkes that upon him fed' who dress up a boy actor as a girl so that the gallant nearly ends up with 'a male-kinde to his wife'.[18]

One other specific source contributed to the play's action: *Twelfth Night*, from III.ii and III.iv of which Jonson took the idea of a near-duel between two reluctant antagonists — Viola and Aguecheek — who are tricked into opposition and then terrified by

[17] Ray L. Heffner Jr suggests that this aspect of the play may owe something to the opposition between Witgood and his uncle Lucre in Middleton's *A Trick to Catch the Old One* (1606), a suggestion which hardly improves one's estimate of Dauphine's conduct; see 'Unifying Symbols in the Comedy of Ben Jonson' in Jonas A. Barish, ed., *Ben Jonson: A Collection of Critical Essays*, Englewood Cliffs, 1963, p. 136.
[18] See Oscar J. Campbell, 'The Relation of *Epicoene* to Aretino's *Il Marescalco*', *PMLA*, XLVI (1931), 752–62; Daniel C. Boughner, '*Clizia* and *Epicoene*', *Philological Quarterly*, XIX (1940), 89–91; H&S, II, 76–9; A. D., 'The Genesis of Jonson's *Epicoene*', *Notes and Queries*, CXCIII (1948), 55–6.

accounts of each other's bloodthirstiness. In Shakespeare the laughter is not all at the victims' expense: the tricksters are not aware that Viola is a girl, and the situation sharpens our sympathy for her, and even for Sir Andrew, from whom Sir Toby Belch intends to profit. In Jonson the divisions are, typically, far more stark. The gallants are total masters of the situation, Daw and La Foole are both equally cowardly knights, and the cool ferocity of Dauphine's on-stage kicks and tweakings is much less comfortable to contemplate than Sir Andrew's off-stage bloody coxcomb. Several features may have led Jonson to remember the play (it was not in print when *Epicoene* was written). It makes use of sexual disguise; in its exposure and correction of characters dominated by *idées fixes* it marks Shakespeare's closest approach to Jonsonian humour comedy; and Malvolio is broadly similar to Morose, who is also an opponent of the principle of cakes and ale, is cruelly baited for his opposition, treated as a madman, and allowed to leave the stage baffled and unredeemed.[19]

Beyond these specific debts, Jonson drew inspiration from a number of comedies and comic traditions. Cutbeard is changed from Libanius' well-intentioned matchmaker to a figure similar to the *servus* of Roman comedy, in the employ of the crotchety *senex* but intriguing against him with the younger generation (indeed, Cutbeard actually calls Morose '*senex*' at II.vi, 12). The Collegiates, versions of the would-be learned female whom Jonson had already portrayed in the comical satires and *Volpone*, resemble the society of ladies in Aristophanes' *Ecclesiazusae*, who live apart from their husbands, boss them about, and seek to usurp male authority generally.[20] They also owe something to the bullying matrons of Plautus, 'those ladies of high station and hauteur and fat dowries, with their shouting and their ordering and their ivory trimmed carriages and their purple and fine linen that cost a husband his liberty'.[21] The play's other grotesques are vigorous copies of earlier Jonsonian types. The downtrodden Captain Otter and his Amazonian spouse, a timeless couple, are anticipated in the similar topsy-turvy partnerships of Fallace and Deliro in *Every Man out* and Chloe and Albius in *Poetaster*; Jonas A. Barish notes that Chloe's verbal idiom in particular, 'a series of scolding rhetorical questions'

---

[19] See below notes to I.iii, 24 and V.i, 58, and P. Mueschke and J. Fleisher, 'Jonsonian Elements in the Comic Underplot of *Twelfth Night*', *PMLA*, XLVIII (1933), 722–40.

[20] See C. G. Thayer, *Ben Jonson: Studies in the Plays*, Norman, Okla., 1963, pp. 83–4; on Jonson and learned women see Juliet Dusinberre, *Shakespeare and the Nature of Women*, 1975, pp. 225–31.

[21] *Aulularia*, 167–9; the lines immediately following in this speech are repeated by Morose at II.v, 87–9. Plautus is also imitated at IV.iv, 50–2 (*Menaechmi*, 828–30).

when speaking to her husband and 'a hodgepodge of vulgarism and pseudo elegance' when among social superiors, was a close model for Mrs Otter's.[22] Daw and La Foole are more triumphantly idiotic versions of the fops in *Cynthia's Revels*. Amorphus has, for example, a sufficiently asinine view of the ancients:

> LUCIAN is absurd, hee knew nothing: I will beleeve mine owne travailes, before all the LUCIANS of *Europe*. He doth feed you with fittons, figments, and leasings. (*C.R.*, I.iv, 20–3)

But this is timid stuff compared with Daw's critical forays:

> Homer, an old, tedious, prolix ass, talks of curriers and chines of beef; Virgil, of dunging of land and bees; Horace, of I know not what. (II.iii, 58–61)

Similarly, Hedon establishes his credentials as a fashion-obsessed ninny with his conviction that 'Your *french ceremonies* are the best' (*C.R.*, V.iv, 84); but La Foole, as his name implies, goes one better: he is actually 'descended lineally of the French La Fooles', and indeed all the La Fooles 'come out of our house' (I.iv, 35–9).

Finally, there is the question of Jonson's numerous literary imitations in the play, examples of what he termed the poet's art of 'quoting an other man fitly' so as 'to convert the substance, or Riches of an other *Poet*, to his owne use' (*Disc.*, 1751, 2468–9). This is a vital principle in Jonson, not a substitute for creative thought. It embodies his belief that the great literature of the past contains truths which speak to all ages, and that every age must be judged by its ability to acknowledge and apply them.[23] Appendix II below presents a sampling of the imitations in *Epicoene*. The *Ars Amatoria*, Ovid's urbane treatise on courtship, and Juvenal's bitter Sixth Satire against women bulk the largest, and the reader may wish to know all the places where they are used:

> Ovid: I.i, 101–27; IV.i, 31–91, 103–21; IV.iii, 28–46, 54–6; V.iv, 220–23.
> Juvenal: II.ii, 16–39, 56–75, 88–134.

In the opinion of Jonas A. Barish, the use of these two poets represents an unresolved clash of attitudes, in which Jonson can be seen fluctuating uncertainly between realistic acceptance of the world (Ovid, Truewit) and outraged rejection of it (Juvenal, Morose).[24] This seems to me forced. Truewit acts as spokesman for both poets, and it is difficult to see Morose as a Juvenalian satirist,

---

[22] *Ben Jonson and the Language of Prose Comedy*, Cambridge, Mass., 1960, pp. 169–72.
[23] For an illuminating discussion of this matter see Ian Donaldson, ed., *Ben Jonson: Poems*, Oxford, 1975, pp. xvi–xviii.
[24] 'Ovid, Juvenal, and *The Silent Woman*', *PMLA*, LXXI (1956), 213–24.

however distorted. Barish's interpretation is challenged by John Ferns.[25] The Latin original of the song 'Still to be neat' (I.i, 87–98) is printed by H&S, X, 6, who note two other English imitations later in the century, including Robert Herrick's 'Delight in Disorder'; Jonson's adaptation is discussed by K. F. Smith.[26] One other borrowing is an imitation in a more literal sense. Cutbeard and Otter's recital of the twelve impediments to marriage at V.iii, 86ff. repeats word-for-word the verse summarizing them in Aquinas's *Summa Theologiae*:

> Error, conditio, votum, cognatio, crimen,
> Cultus disparitas, vis, ordo, ligamen, honestas,
> Si sis affinitas, si forte coire nequibis,
> Haec socianda vetant connubia, facta retractant.

Jonson heightens Morose's agony, as the mock-churchmen plod stolidly through the impediments, by having Otter take the part of a touchy radical, ever ready to intrude his suspicions of such high-church dogma.


## THE PLAY

A silent and loving woman is a gift of the Lord.
(Ecclesiasticus, xxvi, 14)

*Epicoene* is Jonson's most daring departure from comedy's normal direction and purpose. Comedy conventionally leads its characters from sorrow to joy, reuniting couples and families, achieving the triumph of young lovers over the opposition of crabbed age, reaffirming the harmony of the social group through the defeat of splintering, antisocial forces. Its ending is usually a celebration of this new sense of human order and wholeness, symbolized by a dance, a feast, and, almost always, a marriage. *Epicoene* negates this pattern; lack, loss, and disharmony are the qualities it affirms. The play ends not with a marriage, but a divorce, or rather, 'a plain nullity' (V.iv, 108). The bride turns out to be no woman, and the bridegroom confesses to impotence, with the words 'I am no man' (V.iv, 41). There are revels, but the chief guests are either such figures as Sir John Daw, 'a fellow so utterly nothing, as he knows not what he would be' (II.iv, 141–2), or aggressive troublemakers such as Haughty, who points out the lack of proper ceremony in her

---

[25] 'Ovid, Juvenal, and *The Silent Woman*: A Reconsideration', *Modern Language Review*, LXV (1970), 248–53.
[26] 'On the Source of Ben Jonson's Song "Still to be neat"', *American Journal of Philology*, XXIX (1908), 135–55.

fierce complaints to the host: 'No gloves? No garters? No scarfs? No epithalamium? No masque? (III.vi, 81–3). There is no sense of rebirth or joy at the end of the play. Dauphine has won his five hundred pounds per year, but comedy conventionally prefers love to money, using the latter mainly to give its blessing to the former, and Dauphine has no young bride whom he has had to intrigue to secure. What we remember, rather, is his uncle's exit from the stage, terrorized and alone, accompanied only by his nephew's annihilating epitaph:

> Now you may go in and rest, be as private as you will, sir. I'll not trouble you till you trouble me with your funeral, which I care not how soon it come. (V.iv, 199–201)

Now that Morose's non-marriage has been celebrated, death, not birth, is the next 'festival time' (II.iv, 109) to which the play looks forward.

This is a bold and unsettling structure, and it is perhaps not surprising that commentators have sometimes thought the play merely sadistic, or lacking in thematic depth. According to Edmund Wilson, *Epicoene* is 'revolting in its forced barbarity'; in Morose Jonson is 'tormenting himself for what is negative and recessive in his own nature'.[27] In Jonson's own century the dramatic critic John Dennis gave a similar verdict:

> it seems to me, to be without a Moral. Upon which Absurdity, *Ben Johnson* was driven by the Singularity of *Moroses* Character, which is too extravagant for Instruction, and fit, in my opinion only for Farce.[28]

*Epicoene* is certainly a violent play, and fully conscious of this fact, as its hunting and bear-baiting imagery indicates. But this is not simply in the interests of knock-about action. Jonson's 'excellent comedy of affliction' (II.vi, 35–6) is deeply occupied with several interrelated themes and ideas, all of them traditionally treated by the very comic formula which this play inverts.

A pervading concern is sexual decorum. The play asks not only 'what should a man do?' (I.i, 31), but also, how should men and women behave, both as fit examples of their sex, and to one another? The characters furnish a cross-section of wrong answers. Of the women, there is a 'silent woman', which the play insists is an impossibility (I.ii, 34–5; IV.iv, 40–1), and then 'proves' ⌐ ⌐ by turning her into a man; an Amazonian china-woman, ⌐ ⌐ Otter, who beats her husband and thus 'she is Captain O⌐

[27] 'Morose Ben Jonson', in *The Triple Thinkers*, revised edn., New
203–20.
[28] Letter to Congreve, June 1695, in *William Congreve: Letters ⌐
C. Hodges, 1964, p. 175.

# ℭ The deceyte of wo-men.to the instruction

## and ensample of all men, yonge and olde, newly cor-rected.

*I  A Husband-beater*

28); and the college ladies, who live apart from their husbands, are adept in the techniques of contraception and abortion (IV.iii, 51–6), and 'cry down or up what they like or dislike in a brain or a fashion with most masculine or rather hermaphroditical authority' (I.i, 75–7). Centaure, in particular, 'has immortalized herself with taming of her wild male' (IV.iii, 25–6). Of the men, there are two effeminate knights who, appropriately, claim to have slept with the silent 'woman' (V.i); a henpecked bearward who is 'his wife's subject ... calls her princess', but rails on her most desperately behind her back (II.vi, 67); and Clerimont's 'boy', who Truewit suggests — whether jokingly or not it is impossible to say — is Clerimont's 'ingle' (I.i, 23), who is 'the welcom'st thing' 'under' and 'above' a man (I.i, 9–10), and whom the Collegiates dress in women's clothes (I.i, 12–17). As Edward Partridge notes, 'Nearly everyone in the play is epicene in some way'.[29]

Mannish women and womanish men were, of course, familiar satirical targets, condemned in Deuteronomy, fulminated against by Puritan writers, and ridiculed in any number of Jacobean plays.[30] What makes Jonson's treatment distinctive is not only the sheer range of presentation, but the way in which these sexually aberrant characters are used to comment on the play's central instance of sexual indecorum, Morose's marriage to a silent woman, not through a desire to marry, but solely for the purpose of disinheriting his nephew. In III.vi, after the wedding, the sexual monsters pour into Morose's house and start to function like the disorderly satyrs in a masque: not, in this case, in order to set off by contrast the harmonious union of the new couple, but to emphasize the discord and indecorum which their union represents.[31]

Morose violates the traditional purposes of marriage, and the irony of his punishment is that he suffers the very griefs and injuries which marriage was traditionally regarded as enabling people to avoid. Henry Smith, the Elizabethan churchman, states

[29] *The Broken Compass*, 1958, p. 162.

[30] See Deuteronomy, xxii, 5; Philip Stubbes, *Anatomy of Abuses*, 1583, ed. F. J. Furnivall, 1877–79, pp. 68ff.; Zeal-of-the-Land Busy's objections to the puppets in *B.F.*, V.v; *Troilus and Cressida*, III.iii, 217–19; Middleton's *A Mad World, My Masters*, III.iii, 99ff. and *More Dissemblers Besides Women*, I.iv, 68ff. (ed. A. H. Bullen, 1885–86). On Mrs Otter, cf. Ecclesiasticus, xxv, 22: 'A woman, if she maintains her husband, is full of anger, impudency, and much reproach'.

[31] See Ian Donaldson's comparison of *Epicoene* with Jonson's masque *Hymenaei* in *The World Upside-Down*, Oxford, 1970, pp. 37–45. Donaldson notes that several features of this and later scenes — for example the jarring noise of '*Music of all sorts*' and the threat to have Morose blanketed — are meant to remind us of such social rituals as the *charivari* and the skimmington, which were conducted to mock various types of marital aberration, such as henpecked husbands or couples of widely different ages. I am indebted to Donaldson's fine essay.

# *HÆC-VIR:*
## Oʀ
# The Womanish-Man:

### Being an Answere to a late Booke intituled *Hic-Mulier*.

### Exprest in a briefe Dialogue betweene *Hæc-Vir* the Womanish-Man, and *Hic-Mulier* the Man-Woman.

London printed for *I.T.* and are to be fold at Chrift Church gate. 1620.

*II Jacobean Examples of Sexual Topsy-turviness*

that among the most important reasons why a man should marry is so that he may

> avoid the inconvenience of solitarines, signified in these words, *It is not good for man to be alone* [Genesis, ii, 18], as though [this text] had said, this life would be miserable & irksome and unpleasant to man, if the Lord had not given him a wife to company his troubles. If it be not good for man to be alone, then it is good for man to have a fellow: therfore, as God created a paire of all other kinds, so he created a paire of this kind.
>   We say that one is none, because he cannot be fewer than one, he cannot be lesser than one, he cannot be weaker than one, and therfore the wise man saith, *Woe to him which is alone*, that is, he which is alone, shall have woe. Thoughtes and cares, and feares, will come to him, because he hath none to comfort him, as theeves steale in when the house is emptie; like a Turtle, which has lost his mate, like one legge when the other is cut off, like one wing when the other is clipt, so had the man bin, if the woman had not bene joyned to him: therfore for mutuall societie, God coupled two togither, that the infinit troubles which lie upon us in this world, might be eased, with the comfort and helpe one of another.[32]

Smith's analogies are biblical commonplaces, so Jonson need not have known his book, but the frequent points of agreement between this passage and the play indicate how closely Morose's woes illustrate those conventionally visited on the solitary man. 'Thoughtes and cares, and feares' do come to him, and 'he hath none to comfort him'; 'theeves' — at least of his peace of mind — do 'steale in' to his house; and dismemberment comes to be precisely the fate he yearns for: 'Would I could redeem it with the loss of an eye', he laments to Dauphine, 'a hand, or any other member' (IV.iv, 8–9). Smith's 'one is none' is also matched in the play: we have Sir John Daw's madrigal, which contains the couplet 'No noble virtue ever was alone,/But two in one' (II.iii, 26–7). Daw's proud repetition of the lines indicates his vanity; it also enables Jonson to emphasize their point.

The above could be called Morose's subsidiary woes; the main one is his discovery that his ideal silent wife is apparently the opposite kind of sexual monster, a shrieking termagant, full of 'masculine and loud commanding' and 'Amazonian impudence' (IV.i, 8–9; III.v, 39). This punishment is again linked ironically to biblical advice. Smith comments, immediately after the passage quoted above:

> But as it is not good to be alone, so Salomon sheweth *That it is better to be alone, than to dwell with a froward wife*, which is like a quotidian ague, to keep his patience in ure [i.e., practice]. Such furies do haunt some men, like *Sauls* spirit, as though the divell had put a sword into their hands to

---

[32] *A Preparative to Marriage*, 1591, pp. 18–19.

kil themselves, therfore choose whom thou maist enjoy, or live alone stil, & thou shalt not repent thy bargain.

Reference to Smith's text here, Proverbs, xxi, 9, shows that in this instance Jonson intends a specific parallel with Solomon's persecuted husband. The text reads:

It is better to dwell in a corner of the housetop, than with a brawling woman in a wide house.[33]

This is exactly what Morose elects to do. Dauphine tells the gallants:

He has got on his whole nest of night-caps, and locked himself up i' the top o' the house, as high as ever he can climb from the noise. I peeped in at a cranny and saw him sitting over a cross-beam o' the roof, like him o' the saddler's horse in Fleet Street, upright; and he will sleep there. (IV.i, 18–23)

Apart from the general irony of the perverter of marriage ending up with a perverted marriage, but not the one he intends, this picture adds another nice touch: Morose, the fussy traditionalist much given to citing learned precedents to justify his behaviour, has himself become a traditional emblem of his own worst punishment.

Morose's obsession with noise and silence also gives him a central place in the play's other main concern, decorum of speech. It is important to remember here that Morose's desire for a wife who is as near silent as possible had a long, and perfectly respectable, ancestry. Volpone was telling the truth when he attempted to fend off the chattering Lady Wouldbe with the observation 'The Poet,/As old in time, as PLATO, and as knowing,/Say's that your highest female grace is silence',[34] and Henry Smith's remarks suggest the strength of the idea in the Christian tradition:

[The sign of a good wife] is her speech, or rather her silence: for the ornament of a woman is silence ... As the Eccho answereth but one for many which are spoken to her; so a maydes answere should be in a word, for she which is full of talke, is not likelie to proove a quyet wife. The eye and the speech are the mindes Glasses.[35]

By identifying this notion with the monomaniac Morose—who wants to induce silence in others while talking constantly himself, just as he wants to live in the middle of the city yet silence its economic life — Jonson indicates the degree of his antagonism to it.

---

[33] The Geneva Bible, which Jonson would have used in 1609, has 'contentious' for 'brawling'.

[34] *Volpone*, III.iv, 76–8; the poet is Sophocles, *Ajax*, 293.

[35] op. cit., pp. 29–30. Jonson shares this last (traditional) image: 'No glasse renders a mans forme, or likenesse, so true as his speech' (*Disc.*, 2033–5).

T ʜɪs reprefentes the vertues of a wife,
  Her finger, ftaies her tonge to runne at large.

*III The Perfect Wife*

It is not merely that Morose is being unrealistic because, as
Truewit points out to him, women are naturally talkative: 'you
would be friends with your wife upon unconscionable terms, her
silence' (IV.iv, 40–1); a more important level of suggestion in the
play (and indeed in Truewit's words) is that it is impossible for
anyone, male or female, to be silent and fully human at the same
time.[36] '*Language* most shewes a man: speake that I may see thee'
Jonson remarks in *Discoveries* (2031–2), and the play places the
same stress on the humanizing power of speech by regularly
associating silence with unnaturalness, disease, and death. The
name of the (apparently) most silent character is 'Epicoene', suggesting an impossible aberration, and when 'she' begins to use her
tongue, and Morose cries out, appalled, 'She can talk!', she
promptly reminds him that she is neither a statue, a marionette,
nor an imbecile (III.iv, 34–8). Similarly, Dauphine's first words
in the play are to ask his friends 'What ail you, sirs? Dumb?' (I.ii,
1), and almost his last to dismiss his uncle to the silence of the grave
(V.iv, 201). Moreover, silence is anticomic, and in two senses:
comedy naturally backs the vital and expressive, and, more funda-
mentally, without speakers there would be no play; *Epicoene* would
be the 'dumb piece' Jonson describes it as in his Dedication. Only

[36] This point is developed in Terence Hawkes' excellent study in *Shakespeare's
Talking Animals*, 1973, pp. 158ff.

after it is over can it return its audience to 'silence' — the play's concluding word.

Jonson does not suggest, however, that the more one talks the more human one is. His view is that 'too much talking is ever the *Indice* of a foole ... to speake, and to speake well, are two things' (*Discoveries*, 367, 1865–6), and if language threatens in some parts of the play to disappear into silence, in far more it threatens to degenerate into mere noise and nonsense, as groups of disorderly chatterers throng on to the stage and clamour to be heard. Like Wittgenstein, who held that 'to imagine a language means to imagine a form of life', Jonson was deeply interested in the ways in which a society's use of words serves as an index of its values and manners. 'Wheresoever, manners, and fashions are corrupted', he notes in *Discoveries*,

*IV  A Talking Fool*

Language is. It imitates the publicke riot. The excesse of Feasts, and apparrell, are the notes of a sick State; and the wantonnesse of language, of a sick mind. (954–8)

*Epicoene* vividly elaborates this idea, matching each of its socially disruptive characters with an appropriate mode of disorderly speech. The range of styles is extraordinary. It includes the meandering, breathless incoherence of La Foole (I.iv, 35ff.), the staccato chatter of Daw (exhibited also in his 'madrigals'), and Mistress Otter's ludicrous attempts at courtly idiom ('mark her language' Truewit advises his friends). Morose's speech is, appropriately, particularly impressive from this point of view. It takes three sharply different forms: a preening, 'literary' style, that of a man who has spent his life with books, not living speakers; the extraordinary, contorted tirade at II.v, 96ff., in which grammar seems to collapse under the pressure of feeling; and the sound of Morose in distress, which is characterized by a tendency to lament in duplicate ('cut his throat, cut his throat', 'Oh, my torment, my torment', 'Compliment! Compliment!'), then quadruplicate ('Oh, a plot, a plot, a plot, a plot upon me!'), and later simply by meaningless yelps of pain ('Oh, oh, oh!', 'Oh, oh, oh!').[37] Of all the characters, Dauphine comes closest to embodying the Jonsonian norm of linguistic straightforwardness, clarity, and restraint; at least, while not exactly straightforward, either in his actions or words (notice the way in which he equivocates at Truewit's expense at IV.i, 127), he is in full accord with Jonson's axiom that 'A *wise tongue* should not be licentious, and wandring; but mov'd, and (as it were) govern'd with certaine raines from the heart and bottome of the brest' (*Discoveries*, 330–2). And it is fitting that, having stunned the whole cast into silence with his final disclosure, which has been four months in the planning, he should leave the summing-up to Truewit, the play's most loquacious character, who, appropriately, is the first to recover his full powers of speech.

The play's imagery, visual and verbal, also insists on the ideas of social division and 'publicke riot'. Most obviously, there is a preoccupation with doors as boundaries of one's private territory, dividing the world without from the world within. In the first scene, Clerimont chats with his page about Lady Haughty's door being 'kept shut against your master, when the entrance is so easy to you' (I.i, 18–19), while his own door is standing open for Truewit to enter by, unannounced, at I.i, 21. Truewit proceeds to expatiate on the 'public' and 'private' doings of ladies, with the caution 'nor when the doors are shut should men be inquiring'.

[37] See Jonas A. Barish's brilliant analysis of this aspect of the play in *Ben Jonson and the Language of Prose Comedy*, pp. 142ff.

Immediately afterwards, the idea is applied to Morose, with more ominous overtones:

> This youth practised on him one night like the bellman, and never left till he had brought him down to the door with a long sword, and there left him flourishing with the air. (157–60)

As soon as he appears, Morose shows an intense concern about his door (II.i, 8, 11, 24–6); later, when the public world begins to invade and overwhelm his privacy, it develops into a positive fixation (II.ii, 144–5; III.v, 31–3). Finally, tormented by Otter's drums and trumpets, he imagines his whole house collapsing: 'They have rent my roof, walls, and all my windows asunder, with their brazen throats' (IV.ii, 116–17). Houses are torn apart and so, a related train of imagery suggests, are people. Morose and Daw are both prepared to have limbs or other parts of themselves cut off (IV.iv, 8–9; IV.v, 112ff.), and the Collegiates carry out an admiring vivisection of Dauphine:

> CENTAURE
> I could love a man for such a nose!
> MAVIS
> Or such a leg!
> CENTAURE
> He has an exceeding good eye, madam!
> MAVIS
> And a very good lock!    (IV.vi, 33–6)

But the prize for human decomposability must go to Mistress Otter, who quite literally comes to bits:

> All her teeth were made i' the Blackfriars, both her eyebrows i' the Strand, and her hair in Silver Street. Every part o' the town owns a piece of her . . . She takes herself asunder still when she goes to bed, into some twenty boxes, and about next day noon is put together again, like a great German clock. (IV.ii, 84–90)

Elsewhere, rather than coming apart, human beings solidify into stones, posts, statues, dummies, puppets, and machines, and in the general unsticking of normal associations drinking-tankards become animals and animals receive men's names (III.i, 45–6). Disunity and indecorum are thus the main burden of the imagery, as they are of the play's larger action.[38]

If the above discussion goes some way in answering Dennis' charge that *Epicoene* is 'without a Moral', it ought not to imply that Jonson's perspective is wholly or simply moralistic. To see the full complexity of the play's attitude to the fragmented society it

---

[38] For a discussion of Jonson's 'imagery of division' see Ian Donaldson, 'Language, Noise, and Nonsense: *The Alchemist*', in *Seventeenth-Century Imagery*, ed. Earl Miner, Berkeley and Los Angeles, 1971, pp. 69ff.

creates, it is helpful to compare Jonson's epistle 'To Katherine, Lady Aubigny' (*Forest*, XIII), where Jonson eloquently praises his subject's composed detachment from the public world:

> wisely you decline your life,
> Farre from the maze of custome, error, strife,
> And keepe an even, and unalter'd gaite;
> Not looking by, or backe (like those, that waite
> Times, and occasions, to start forth, and seeme)
> Which though the turning world may dis-esteeme,
> Because that studies spectacles, and showes,
> And after varyed, as fresh objects goes,
> Giddie with change, and therefore cannot see
> Right, the right way: yet must your comfort bee
> Your conscience, and not wonder, if none askes
> For truthes complexion, where they all weare maskes.   (59–70)

This outer world of shifting superficies, 'turning ... Giddie with change', is precisely the one dramatized in the play. It is the world of La Foole, whose horse is 'rid into a foam with posting from place to place and person to person' (II.iv, 96–7), of the Collegiates, who urge Epicoene to obtain a 'coach and four horses ... And go with us to Bedlam, to the china-houses, and to the Exchange' (IV.iii, 19–23), of Clerimont, who likes to talk 'of pins, and feathers, and ladies, and rushes, and such things' (I.i, 61–2), and of Truewit, who thinks a lady should 'vary every hour' (I.i, 101–2). It is also a world where 'all weare maskes'. Ladies have their perukes and cosmetics, La Foole his motley colours, Daw his pseudo learning, Truewit his bewildering sequence of poses, Dauphine his secret plans. The crucial difference is that *Epicoene* has no Lady Aubigny. It has instead Morose, a grotesque parody of the self-sufficient and detached personality, whose answer to the swirling turbulence of the life outside his house is to 'devise a room with double walls and treble ceilings, the windows close shut and caulked, and there he lives by candlelight' (I.i, 178–80). Forced to join this life, his reaction is mental collapse: 'a torrent of evil! My very house turns round with the tumult! I dwell in a windmill! The perpetual motion is here, and not at Eltham' (V.iii, 59–62). A more suitable alternative, the play seems to imply, is to find some *modus vivendi* with the muddle and deceptiveness of things; the sort of attitude which will enable one to 'leave to live i' your chamber, then, a month together', as Truewit advises Dauphine (who seems to be developing a family trait), 'and come abroad where the matter is frequent, to court, to tiltings, public shows and feasts, and church sometimes' (IV.i, 51–5). Certainly one should not hope to reduce this chaos to order. To do that would mean turning back the endless procession of La Fooles who seem in his description to

*V The Devil Applying Cosmetics*

troop out of a quite literal family 'house' to flood the world with folly ('the La Fooles o' the north, the La Fooles of the west, the La Fooles of the east and south'), or curing such a congenital solipsist as Morose ('how if he do *convalere*?', Cutbeard asks Otter; 'He cannot *convalere*, it is impossible', Otter explains). Finally, one should not be too glib in one's demands for 'truthes complexion'. As Jonson warns us, with calculated irony, before his play begins:

> On forfeit of yourselves, think nothing true,
>   Lest so you make the maker to judge you.

It is a fact that human appearances — like plays — benefit from the 'adulteries of art' (I.i, 97), however much comparison with the 'simplicity' of Nature might seem to expose such procedures as untruthful. As readers and spectators of a play — this play — we too are admitting that we depend on, and delight in, the false appearances of 'spectacles, and showes'; and to underline our inescapable relationship with the sort of world the play depicts, Jonson ends by overturning our assumptions about the boundaries between actual and fictional truth and illusion. Dauphine takes off Epicoene's peruke, to reveal not a less beautiful version of the same lady, but a boy, who is also the boy-actor taking the role: something we have 'known' all along. In many ways, the implications are those of the final lines of Jonson's next great prose comedy, *Bartholmew Fair*:

> lead on . . . and bring the *Actors* along, wee'll ha' the rest o' the *Play* at home.

# A NOTE ON THE TEXT

THE EARLIEST-KNOWN text, and the only one with authority, is that contained in the folio *Works* of 1616, printed by William Stansby. The present edition is based on a copy of this text in the Bodleian Library, shelfmark Douce I, 302, collated against the editions of Herford and Simpson, Beaurline, and Partridge.

There is a faint possibility that the folio was preceded by a quarto of 1612, which has since been lost. Gifford said he had seen such a quarto in his edition of Jonson in 1816, and his claim is lent some colour by the Stationers' Register, which has an entry dated 28 September 1612 transferring the publishing rights in the play from John Brown and John Busby to Walter Burre. Burre may then have brought out a quarto, as he did with *The Alchemist* in the same year. It seems more likely, however, that Gifford was mistaken. Recent textual scholars have argued, very plausibly, that the folio *Epicoene* was set from manuscript rather than printed copy, and this would have been an odd choice had a quarto been available.[1]

Stansby's manuscript was clearly authorial. The Dedication, the style of act and scene division imitated from editions of classical dramatists, the carefully explanatory stage-directions (e.g., II.i, 9, IV.vi, 1, IV.vii, 1), all point to the same meticulous preparation of copy which Jonson carried out for the other plays in the folio. The printing was, after a shaky start, equally careful. The compositors introduced a thin scattering of errors, but scarcely any of any substance. The most serious to escape notice were 'Thy' for 'They' at I.i, 98, and 'alwaies' for 'all ways' at IV.i, 84. Unlike most previous editors, I think F is correct at II.ii, 133, III.iii, 32, and IV.v, 157; I am not quite so sure about V.iv, 187. At I.ii, 19, 'more', the General Editor suggests emending to 'mere', an attractive reading, but I can parallel this use of 'more' but not the use of 'portent' which the emendation requires. Conversely, F's *'came'* at IV.v, 117 s.d., which I emend to *'come'*, may be correct: an instance, as at IV.vii, 1, of Jonson slipping into the past-tense style of direction he employs in his masques.

One major irregularity in the printing needs to be noted. Gathering Yy (the prologues and the play to II.ii, 60) exists in two states, the second a resetting in entirely new type. What seems to have

---

[1] Beaurline, pp. xx–xxi; Johan Gerritsen, 'Stansby and Jonson Produce a Folio: A Preliminary Account', *English Studies*, XL (1959), 54. For a full review of the problem, see W. W. Greg, 'Was there a 1612 Quarto of *Epicene*?', *The Library* (Fourth Series), XV (1935), 306–15.

happened was that Stansby and/or Jonson noticed, after a number of sheets of the gathering had been printed, both that the compositors had made many blunders, and that the speech-prefix DAV., for Dauphine, was liable to be confused with DAW. for Daw, who was due to appear in the next scene. They decided to scrap all twelve type-pages and set them up afresh, with DAV. altered to DAVP. Jonson also took the opportunity to make some substantial local changes. He added an explanatory comment beneath the title of the second prologue and a marginal gloss at I.i, 34. In the text of the play he added words at I.ii, 32 and substituted them at I.i, 171 and II.ii, 33. These last three revisions, together with the variant at I.i, 98 (see Appendix I) and the stop-press corrections at II.iii, 53 and IV.iv, 13, contradict his statement in the Dedication that 'There is not a line or a syllable . . . changed from the simplicity of the first copy'. Only major discrepancies between the two states are noted below. H&S, IX, 21–30, give a complete list, but the wrong way round, since, as Gerritsen and Beaurline have shown, their identification of which of the two settings is the later was mistaken.

In the present edition Jonson's marginal stage-directions have been incorporated into the text, and additions to them enclosed in square brackets. Departures from the copy text, in readings which affect sense, have been noted at the foot of the page. Two of Jonson's conventions of presentation in the folio have been silently removed: the custom of not supplying a speech-prefix for the character who speaks first in the scene, and 'massed' entries, i.e., the listing at the start of each scene of all the characters who appear in it, irrespective of whether they enter at that point or not. F's frequent use of brackets, indicating either an aside, or an interjected remark, or a temporary diversion of thought within a speech, has been considerably reduced. Spelling has been modernized, but occasionally — as in other New Mermaid editions of Jonson — an obsolete form has been retained in order to preserve some special intention of the author. Thus, the consciously odd spelling 'modestee' at II.iii, 36 points up Daw's 'chiming' rhymes; 'kastrils' (IV.iv, 174) puns on 'cast'; and 'vellet' is distinguished in F from 'velvet', for reasons of colloquialism or euphony. Jonson's deliberate signalling of a Latin root (e.g., 'porcpisce', 'moniments', 'tyrans') has also been preserved. Punctuation is a more difficult problem. Jonson's rhetorical style of pointing, marking stresses and pauses rather than units of meaning, is likely to seem intolerably heavy to a modern reader, particularly in a prose text. What a modernizing editor must therefore do, it seems to me, is judge every case separately and decide when an important nuance is in danger of being lost. Following this principle, I have, for example, retained the comma after 'it' at V.iv, 47 and the exclamation mark after 'worsts' at V.iv, 138, since they help convey the speakers' breathless outrage; and removed the comma after 'marriage' at IV.iv, 147—after some hesitation, since a portentous emphasis may be intended. The result is probably superior to the blanket imposition of a lighter system, but a degree of arbitrariness is an inevitable penalty.

# ILLUSTRATIONS

I A Tudor husband-beater, putting her spouse 'under correction' (IV.ii, 105) and 'taming . . . her wild male' (IV.iii, 25–6). Title-page of an anonymous pamphlet, undated (mid-16th century). 'Newly corrected' puns on the common printing formula advertising a later edition.

II Title-page of an anonymous pamphlet, published the same year as *Hic Mulier: or, The Man-Woman: being a medicine to cure the coltish disease of the staggers in the masculine–feminine of our times*. The 'man' has a moustache.

III From Geoffrey Whitney, *A Choice of Emblemes*, 1586, p. 93. Emblem entitled 'Uxoriae Virtutes'. The verse continues:
> The modest lookes, doe shewe her honest life.
> The keys, declare shee hathe a care, and chardge,
> Of husbandes goodes: let him goe where he please.
> The Tortyse warnes, at home to spend her daies.

IV From Sebastian Brandt's *The Ship of Fools*, trans. Alexander Barclay, 1509, f. li. Woodcut illustrating poem entitled 'Of to moche spekynge or blabynge' which exhorts the reader to 'take example by the chatrynge pye./Whiche doth hyr nest and byrdes also betray'. Cf. 'The only talking sir i' th' town! Jack Daw' (I.ii, 65).

V The devil applying cosmetics. Woodcut from a Jacobean ballad entitled *Householde Talke, or: Good Councell for a Married Man* (Roxburghe Collection, I, 149).

# FURTHER READING

Anderson, Mark A., 'The Successful Unity of *Epicoene*: A Defense of Ben Jonson', *Studies in English Literature 1500–1900*, X (1970), 349–66.

Barish, Jonas A., 'Ovid, Juvenal, and *The Silent Woman*', *PMLA*, LXXI (1956), 213–24.

Barish, Jonas A., *Ben Jonson and the Language of Prose Comedy*, Cambridge, Mass., 1960, pp. 142–86.

Barish, Jonas A., 'Feasting and Judging in Jonsonian Comedy', *Renaissance Drama*, n.s. V (1972), 3–35.

Camden, Carroll, *The Elizabethan Woman*, 1952.

Donaldson, Ian, *The World Upside-Down*, Oxford, 1970, pp. 24–45.

Dryden, John, *An Essay of Dramatic Poesy*, 1668.

Hallahan, Huston D., 'Silence, Eloquence, and Chatter in Jonson's *Epicoene*', *Huntington Library Quarterly*, XL (1977), 117–27.

Hawkes, Terence, *Shakespeare's Talking Animals*, 1973, pp. 157–65.

Heffner, Ray L., Jr, 'Unifying Symbols in the Comedy of Ben Jonson', in *Ben Jonson: A Collection of Critical Essays*, ed. Jonas A. Barish, Englewood Cliffs, N. J., 1963, pp. 133–46.

Jones, Dorothy, 'Th' Adulteries of Art: A Discussion of *The Silent Woman*', in *Shakespeare and Some Others*, ed. Alan Brissenden, Adelaide, 1976, pp. 83–103.

Kay, W. David, 'Jonson's Urbane Gallants: Humanistic Contexts for *Epicoene*', *Huntington Library Quarterly*, XXXIX (1976), 251–66.

Kelso, Ruth, *The Doctrine of the English Gentleman in the Sixteenth Century*, Urbana, Ill., 1929.

Kernan, Alvin B., *The Cankered Muse*, New Haven, 1959, pp. 156–91.

Leggatt, Alexander, 'Morose and His Tormentors', *University of Toronto Quarterly*, XLV (1976), 221–35.

Nichols, Marianna Da Vinci, 'Truewit and Sir Epicure Mammon: Jonson's Creative Accidents', *Ariel*, VII, no. 4 (1976), 4–21.

Partridge, Edward B., *The Broken Compass*, 1958.

Paster, Gail Kern, 'Ben Jonson's Comedy of Limitation', *Studies in Philology*, LXXII (1975), 51–71.

Salingar, L. G., 'Farce and Fashion in *The Silent Woman*', *Essays and Studies*, n.s. XX (1967), 29–46.

Slights, William W. E., '*Epicoene* and the Prose Paradox', *Philological Quarterly*, XLIX (1970), 178–87.

Wilson, Edmund, 'Morose Ben Jonson', in *The Triple Thinkers*, revised edn., New York, 1948, pp. 203–20.

# EPICOENE,

## OR

# The silent VVoman.

*A Comœdie.*

Acted in the yeere 1609. By
the Children of her Maiesties
R E V E L L S.

## The Author B. I.

H O R A T.

*Vt sis tu similis Cæli, Byrrhiĝ, latronum,*
*Non ego sim Capri, neĝ, Sulci. Cur metuas me?*

---

L O N D O N,

Printed by VVILLIAM STANSBY.

---

M. DC. XVI.

*EPICOENE*. Having the characteristics of both sexes. Jonson is fond of the word; cf. *N.N.W.*, 276, and *N.T.*, 260; in 'An Epigram on the Court Pucelle' (*Und.*, XLIX), 7, it is used of masculine behaviour in a woman: see note to II.ii, 110. The play's title and the name of the character are Jonson's only clue to the audience as to the real sex of the supposed heroine. He spoils the joke for the reader: see The Persons of the Play, 5.

*The silent Woman*. The play's second title, by which it has always been better known, can be seen as a tongue-in-cheek version of a popular type of play-title in the period, the title which offers an arresting paradox; e.g. *The Honest Whore, The Honest Lawyer, A Chaste Maid in Cheapside, Wit in a Constable*. Coupled with '*Epicoene*' the effect is to imply that a silent woman is a contradiction: sexual abnormality must be what makes such a creature possible.

*Ut . . . me*. From Horace's defence of satire in *Satires*, I.iv, 69–70: 'Though you are like Caelius and Birrius, the robbers, I need not be like Caprius or Sulcius [described earlier as professional informers, hoarse from bawling their accusations in the courts]: why should you fear me?'

Sir Francis Stuart:

Sir,                                                                                      5
    My hope is not so nourished by example, as it will conclude this
dumb piece should please you by cause it hath pleased others
before, but by trust, that when you have read it, you will find it
worthy to have displeased none. This makes that I now number
you not only in the names of favour but the names of justice to what    10
I write, and do presently call you to the exercise of that noblest and
manliest virtue, as coveting rather to be freed in my fame by the
authority of a judge than the credit of an undertaker. Read therefore, I pray you, and censure. There is not a line or syllable in it
changed from the simplicity of the first copy. And, when you shall   15
consider, through the certain hatred of some, how much a man's
innocency may be endangered by an uncertain accusation, you
will, I doubt not, so begin to hate the iniquity of such natures as I
shall love the contumely done me, whose end was so honourable as
to be wiped off by your sentence.                                    20

                              Your unprofitable but true lover,
                                                BEN JONSON

 6 *example* authorizing instances in the past
 7 *by cause* because
 9 *makes* is the reason
11 *presently* at this time
12 *fame* reputation (Latin *fama*)
14 *censure* judge

---

 4 *Sir Francis Stuart*. 'He was a learned gentleman, and one of the club at the
   Mermayd, in Fryday street, with Sir Walter Ralegh, etc., of that sodalitie:
   heroes and witts of that time' (John Aubrey, *Brief Lives*, ed. A. Clark, 2 vols.,
   Oxford, 1898, II, 239).
 7 *dumb piece*. (i) silent play (because the authorities had suppressed *Epicoene* in
   1610); (ii) silent woman (regarded sexually; cf. *Troilus and Cressida*, IV.ii, 63,
   where Helen is called 'a flat and tamed piece').
13 *undertaker*. Guarantor, sponsor: according to *OED*, sb., 7, a sense first used by
   Jonson (in the dedication to *Poet.*); here with the pejorative associations of a
   political 'fixer' who influences voting in Parliament (see *OED*, sb., 4.b).
15 *simplicity*. Openness, straightforwardness, ingenuousness (Latin *simplicitas*).
   But perhaps Jonson himself is being covertly disingenuous, since *Epicoene* is a
   highly sophisticated play, in which simplicity is itself a leading theme; see I.i, 94
   and Introduction, p. xliii.

# THE PERSONS OF THE PLAY

MOROSE, *a gentleman that loves no noise*
DAUPHINE EUGENIE, *a knight, his nephew*
CLERIMONT, *a gentleman, his friend*
TRUEWIT, *another friend*
EPICOENE, *a young gentleman, supposed the silent woman*     5
JOHN DAW, *a knight, her servant*
AMOROUS LA FOOLE, *a knight also*
THOMAS OTTER, *a land and sea captain*
CUTBEARD, *a barber*

---

6 *servant* lover devoted to the service of his lady

---

1 MOROSE. Latin *morosus* means 'peevish, stubborn' (from *mos*, custom, habit), which is the sense here; see above, p. xxiii. *OED* has only one example of the word, from a Latin-English dictionary of 1565, before this one.

2 DAUPHINE EUGENIE. The immediate meaning is 'well-born heir', but Dauphine's name also associates him with the ideas of effeminate fashionableness and sexual ambivalence embodied in the more obviously satirized characters. It connects him with things French (since the Dauphin was the heir apparent to the King of France), and in the play France, fashion, and sexual unnaturalness are linked (cf. II.ii, 57, II.v, 71, IV.iii, 21, IV.vi, 27, and the name 'La Foole'); also, it is given an 'incorrect', indeed impossible, feminine form by the addition of the *e* (cf. 'La Foole' and 'Centaure'). As well as representing the Greek for 'well-born', *Eugenie* points to *génie*, French for 'wit'.

3 CLERIMONT. Another French name; cf. Marlowe, *Edward II*, V.v, 68–9. Partridge suggests an echo of French *clairement*, clearly, plainly, in view of Clerimont's championing of simplicity against artifice in the debate with Truewit in I.i.

6 JOHN DAW. The daw is the jackdaw, a bird 'noted for its loquacity and thievish propensities' (*OED*), and *daw* commonly meant 'noodle, dolt'; cf. the proverb 'As wise as a daw' (Tilley, D50).

7 AMOROUS LA FOOLE. Cf. Thomas Overbury's character 'An Amorist': 'his fashion exceeds the worth of his weight. He is never without verses, and muske comfects: and sighes to the hazard of his buttons . . . His imagination is a foole . . . shortly hee is translated out of a man into folly; his imagination is the glasse of lust, and himselfe the traitor to his own discretion' (*Characters*, 1614, sig. E1ʳ).

8 OTTER. '*Animal amphibium*' (I.iv, 24), which suits with Otter's captaincy of 'land and sea'. The Otters' name also suggests their sexual topsy-turviness, since the creature was a byword for the unclassifiable: '[is the otter] a beast or a fish? . . . I have heard, the question hath been debated among many great Clerks, and they seem to differ about it; yet most agree that his tail is Fish' (Izaac Walton, *The Complete Angler*, 1653, chap. ii). Cf. Falstaff on the Hostess in *1 Henry IV*, III.iii, 123–8: she is 'an otter . . . she's neither fish nor flesh, a man knows not where to have her'.

MUTE, *one of Morose his servants*                              10
MADAME HAUGHTY ⎤
MADAME CENTAURE ⎬ *ladies collegiates*
MISTRESS MAVIS ⎦
MISTRESS TRUSTY, *the Lady Haughty's woman* ⎤ *pretenders*
MISTRESS OTTER, *the Captain's wife* ⎦                  15
*Parson, Pages, Servants, [Musicians]*

### The Scene

## LONDON

14–15 *pretenders* aspirants (to membership of the college)

---

12 CENTAURE. The classical monster, half human, half horse, characteristically
   savage and lustful. 'For the Greeks Centaurs are representative of wild life,
   animal desires, and barbarism' (*Oxford Classical Dictionary*). Despite IV.v, 43,
   and Zeuxis' famous painting of a Centaur family scene, female Centaurs do not
   exist in classical mythology. Centaurs mated with mares, or, usually by raping
   them, women.
   *collegiates*. Belonging to a college (=collective body, society). For the plural
   adjective in official phrases cf. 'letters patents'.
13 MAVIS. 'Song-thrush', adding another to the multitude of birds in the play,
   though in this case the name is comically inappropriate to its owner. A more
   learned sense, Italian 'Maviso, *for* Malviso, *an ill face*' (J. Florio, *Queen Anna's
   New World of Words*, 1611, p. 304), is punned on at V.ii, 34.

*feastisp + writing*  *commercial fair (for?)*
                       *the theatre*

# PROLOGUE

Truth says, of old the art of making plays
 Was to content the people, and their praise
 Was to the Poet money, wine, and bays.
But in this age a sect of writers are,
 That only for particular likings care                    5
 And will taste nothing that is popular.
With such we mingle neither brains nor breasts;
 Our wishes, like to those make public feasts,
 Are not to please the cook's tastes, but the guests'.
Yet if those cunning palates hither come,                  10
 They shall find guests' entreaty and good room;
 And though all relish not, sure there will be some
That, when they leave their seats, shall make 'em say,
 Who wrote that piece could so have wrote a play,

 8 *those make* those who make
10 *cunning* learned, sophisticated
11 *entreaty* entertainment (*OED*'s first example of this sense)
12 *all relish not* everything is not to their taste
 *some* some parts (of the play)

---

 1 *Truth says*. In particular Terence, in the opening lines of the prologue to *Andria*,
   which Jonson is echoing.
 3 *bays*. Acclaim, fame (from the bay laurel, the leaves of which formed the poet's
   garland).
 4 *sect of writers*. Possibly Jonson had in mind such dramatists as George Chapman
   and John Marston, his collaborators in *Eastward Ho!* (1604), who wrote exclu-
   sively for the private-theatre companies.
 5 *particular*. Restricted to a set of persons; cf. 'these domestic and particular broils'
   (*King Lear*, V.i, 30).
 6 *popular*. Pertaining to the common people, or the people as a whole.
 9 *not ... guests'*. The comparison is common, deriving from Martial, *Epigrams*,
   IX.lxxxi, though it is interesting that it is developed with similar elaborateness
   in the epilogue to another Queen's Revels' play, Chapman's *All Fools* (*c.* 1604).
   Jonson, who was intensely interested in food, and fond of describing literary and
   moral discrimination in terms of culinary, no doubt found the simile especially
   significant and appealing; cf. *C.R.*, Induction, 185–8; the dialogue between the
   Poet and Cook in *N.T.*
14 *so*. i.e. making every piece to the taste of the 'cunning palates'; cf. *Volp.*,
   Dedication, 111–14.

7

But that he knew this was the better way.                    15
For to present all custard or all tart
    And have no other meats to bear a part,
    Or to want bread and salt, were but coarse art.
The Poet prays you, then, with better thought
    To sit, and when his cates are all in brought,        20
    Though there be none far-fet, there will dear-bought
Be fit for ladies; some for lords, knights, squires,
    Some for your waiting-wench and city-wires,
    Some for your men and daughters of Whitefriars.
Nor is it only while you keep your seat                     25
    Here that his feast will last, but you shall eat
    A week at ord'naries on his broken meat,
                    If his Muse be true,
                    Who commends her to you.

16 *custard* open pie containing meat or fruit
17 *meats* dishes
20 *cates* choice victuals, usually bought
27 *ord'naries* eating-houses, taverns
   *broken meat* fragments of food left after a meal
29 *her* herself

---

15 *this . . . way.* The opposite of Jonson's earlier attitude; cf. the revised conclusion
   in the quarto text of *E.M.O.* (H&S, III, 603–4): 'We know (and we are pleas'd to
   know so much)/The Cates that you have tasted were not season'd/For every
   vulgar Pallat, but prepar'd/To banket pure and apprehensive eares:/Let then
   their Voices speake for our desert'; also *Disc.*, 409–12.
18 *coarse.* Punning on '(food) course', the spelling in F.
21–2 *none . . . ladies.* Proverbial: 'dear bought and far fetched are dainties for ladies'
   (Tilley, D12).
23 *city-wires.* Fashionable gentlewomen of the city, who used wire to support their
   ruffs and hair.
24 *men . . . Whitefriars.* Both the audience of the Whitefriars theatre, where the play
   was performed, and the residents of the district between Fleet Street and the
   Thames where the theatre was situated. The sense implied by this latter reference is 'thieves and prostitutes', since Whitefriars at this date, because it enjoyed
   privilege of sanctuary, was a notorious centre of crime and vice. It is a haunt of
   Lieutenant Shift, the pimp of *Epig.*, XII, and in *Volp.*, IV.ii, 51 Lady Wouldbe
   calls Peregrine one of 'your *white-Friers* nation' when she mistakes him for 'a
   lewd harlot'.

# ANOTHER

*Occasioned by some person's impertinent exception*

The ends of all who for the scene do write
  Are, or should be, to profit and delight.
And still 't hath been the praise of all best times,
  So persons were not touched, to tax the crimes.
Then, in this play which we present tonight,          5
  And make the object of your ear and sight,
On forfeit of yourselves, think nothing true,
  Lest so you make the maker to judge you.
For he knows, poet never credit gained
  By writing truths, but things like truths well feigned.   10

---

*impertinent* probably 'inappropriate, irrelevant', or more loosely 'absurd, silly' (*OED*, a., 2, 3), rather than the modern sense, which is not common before the eighteenth century
*exception* objection, faultfinding
1 *scene* stage (Latin *scena*)
3 *still* always
  *praise* subject of praise
4 *So* provided
7 *true* real, describing an actual occurrence

---

Occasioned ... *exception* F^b (om. F^a). See Introduction, pp. xvii–xix.
1–2 *The ... delight*. The Horatian maxim (*Ars Poetica*, 343–4). It was 'a fixed article in Jonson's literary creed: he is never tired of repeating it' (H&S, IX, 420, who cite numerous examples).
4 *So ... crimes*. Another favourite maxim of Jonson's, from Martial, *Epigrams*, X.xxxiii; cf. *Und*., XII, 28, and the Apologetical Dialogue appended to *Poet*., 84–5: 'My Bookes have still been taught/To spare the persons, and to speake the vices'.
7 *On ... yourselves*. Cf. the stage-keeper's agreement with the audience in *B.F.*, Induction, 145–8, concerning anyone caught associating the characters with real people: 'that such person, or persons so found, be left discovered to the mercy of the *Author*, as a forfeiture to the *Stage*, and your laughter, aforesaid'.
8 *maker*. 'A *Poet* is that, which by the *Greeks* is call'd κατ ' 'εξοχὴν, ὁ Ποιητὴς, a Maker, or a fainer' (*Disc*., 2347–8).
9–10 *poet ... feigned*. From Horace, *Ars Poetica*, 338; often echoed by Jonson: e.g. *Disc*., 2351–4; The Prologue for the Court in *S.N.*, 11–14.

9

If any yet will, with particular sleight
  Of application, wrest what he doth write,
And that he meant or him or her will say,
  They make a libel which he made a play.

---

11 *sleight* cunning device, jugglery
12 *wrest* twist, misinterpret
13 *or ... or* either ... or

---

11–14 The standard protest of the Elizabethan and Jacobean satirist. The *locus classicus* is Marston's 'To Him that hath Perused Me', appended to *The Scourge of Villainy* (1598): 'If thou hast perused me, what lesser favour canst thou graunt then not to abuse me with unjust application? Yet I feare me, I shall be much, much injuried by two sorts of readers: the one being ignorant, not knowing the nature of Satyre, (which is under fained private persons, to note generall vices,) will needes wrest each fayned name to a private unfained person. The other too subtile, bearing a private malice to some greater personage then he dare in his owne person seeme to maligne, will strive by a forced application of my generall reproofes to broach his private hatred ... Let this protestation satisfie our curious readers'. Jaques makes the same disclaimer in *As You Like It*, II.vii, 70ff., and Jonson, at considerable length, in Chorus II of *M.L.*, where he explicitly recalls the present prologue (H&S, VI, 544).

11 *particular*. Personal, relating in detail to an individual; cf. *Volp.*, Dedication, 56–7: '*Where have I beene particular? Where personall?*'

# EPICOENE

## OR

## THE SILENT WOMAN

### Act I, Scene i

*[Enter]* CLERIMONT. *He comes out making himself
ready, [followed by]* BOY

CLERIMONT
Ha' you got the song yet perfect I ga' you, boy?
BOY
Yes, sir.
CLERIMONT
Let me hear it.
BOY
You shall, sir, but i' faith let nobody else.
CLERIMONT
Why, I pray?                                                      5
BOY
It will get you the dangerous name of a poet in town, sir,
besides me a perfect deal of ill will at the mansion you wot
of, whose lady is the argument of it, where now I am the
welcom'st thing under a man that comes there.
CLERIMONT
I think, and above a man too, if the truth were racked out of    10
you.

---

s.d. *making ... ready* dressing
  1 *perfect* perfectly memorized
  7 *wot* know
  8 *argument* subject
    *where* whereas

---

  6 *dangerous ... poet*. Because poets (at this time the term included playwrights)
    satirize folly and vice, and were regarded, in Jonson's view, with scorn: 'now,
    letters onely make men vile. Hee is upbraidingly call'd a *Poet*, as if it were a most
    contemptible *Nick-name*' (*Disc.*, 280–2).
  9 *under a man*. With a sexual pun; cf. 'ingle' (1. 23) and 'Mistress Underman' in
    Middleton's *A Chaste Maid in Cheapside*, II.iii, 17.
 10 *above*. (i) better than; (ii) taller than (as a result of being stretched on the rack);
    (iii) continuing the sexual joke in *under*.

11

BOY

No, faith, I'll confess before, sir. The gentlewomen play
with me and throw me o' the bed, and carry me in to my
lady, and she kisses me with her oiled face, and puts a
peruke o' my head, and asks me an' I will wear her gown,      15
and I say no; and then she hits me a blow o' the ear and calls
me innocent, and lets me go.

CLERIMONT

No marvel if the door be kept shut against your master,
when the entrance is so easy to you. Well, sir, you shall go
there no more, lest I be fain to seek your voice in my lady's   20
rushes a fortnight hence. Sing, sir.

BOY *sings*


[*Enter* TRUEWIT]

TRUEWIT

Why, here's the man that can melt away his time, and never
feels it! What between his mistress abroad and his ingle at
home, high fare, soft lodging, fine clothes, and his fiddle,
he thinks the hours ha' no wings or the day no post-horse.      25
Well, sir gallant, were you struck with the plague this
minute or condemned to any capital punishment
tomorrow, you would begin then to think and value every
article o' your time, esteem it at the true rate, and give all
for't.                                                          30

CLERIMONT

Why, what should a man do?

TRUEWIT

Why, nothing, or that which, when 'tis done, is as idle.
Hearken after the next horse-race, or hunting-match; lay


15 *an'* if
17 *innocent* simpleton
20 *fain* obliged
21 *rushes* green rushes strewn on the floor of houses
23 *abroad* away from home
   *ingle* boy kept for homosexual purposes, catamite
29 *article o' your time* moment (Latin *articulus temporis*)
32 *idle* vain, useless
33 *Hearken* inquire

18–19 *door . . . entrance.* For the innuendo see note to V.i, 71.
21 s.d. The song is that at l.87. Jonson delays printing it until then so that it can be
   read in conjunction with Truewit's disquisition on artifice.

wagers, praise Puppy, or Peppercorn, Whitefoot, *Horses o'*
Franklin; swear upon Whitemane's party; spend *the time*      35
aloud that my lords may hear you; visit my ladies at night
and be able to give 'em the character of every bowler or
bettor o' the green. These be the things wherein your
fashionable men exercise themselves, and I for company.

CLERIMONT
Nay, if I have thy authority, I'll not leave yet. Come, the    40
other are considerations when we come to have grey heads
and weak hams, moist eyes and shrunk members. We'll
think on 'em then; then we'll pray and fast.

TRUEWIT
Ay, and destine only that time of age to goodness which our
want of ability will not let us employ in evil?               45

CLERIMONT
Why then 'tis time enough.

TRUEWIT
Yes, as if a man should sleep all the term and think to effect
his business the last day. Oh, Clerimont, this time,
because it is an incorporeal thing and not subject to sense,
we mock ourselves the fineliest out of it, with vanity and     50
misery indeed, not seeking an end of wretchedness, but
only changing the matter still.

CLERIMONT
Nay, thou'lt not leave now—

TRUEWIT
See but our common disease! With what justice can we
complain that great men will not look upon us nor be at        55
leisure to give our affairs such dispatch as we expect, when
we will never do it to ourselves, nor hear nor regard ourselves.

---

34–5 *Horses ... time* F^b (om. F^a)                    36 *aloud* ostentatiously
40 *leave* leave off
45 *ability* capacity, or perhaps 'bodily power, strength' (*OED*, sb., 3)
47 *term* one of the four periods of the year during which the London law-courts
   were in session
52 *still* ever, continually                    57 *nor hear* F^b (not heare F^a)

---

38 *bettor*. *OED*'s first example of the word.
50 *fineliest*. Most perfectly. Partridge suggests that this old-fashioned form of the
   adverb, used only by Truewit (cf. II.ii, 97), may be Jonson's way of calling
   attention to his elaborate language.
54 *common disease*. 'Discontent, the nobleman's consumption' (*The Revenger's
   Tragedy*, I.i, 126), caused by lack of patronage and neglect at court; *common*=
   common to all.

CLERIMONT

Foh, thou hast read Plutarch's *Morals* now, or some such
tedious fellow, and it shows so vilely with thee, 'fore God,          60
'twill spoil thy wit utterly. Talk me of pins, and feathers,
and ladies, and rushes, and such things, and leave this
stoicity alone till thou mak'st sermons.

TRUEWIT

Well, sir, if it will not take, I have learned to lose as little of
my kindness as I can. I'll do good to no man against his          65
will, certainly. When were you at the college?

CLERIMONT

What college?

TRUEWIT

As if you knew not!

CLERIMONT

No, faith, I came but from court yesterday.

TRUEWIT

Why, is it not arrived there yet, the news? A new foun-          70
dation, sir, here i' the town, of ladies that call themselves
the Collegiates, an order between courtiers and country
madams, that live from their husbands and give entertainment to all the Wits and Braveries o' the time, as they
call 'em, cry down or up what they like or dislike in a          75
brain or a fashion with most masculine or rather
hermaphroditical authority, and every day gain to their
college some new probationer.

CLERIMONT

Who is the president?

TRUEWIT

The grave and youthful matron, the Lady Haughty.          80

63 *stoicity* stoicism (Clerimont's coinage)
64 *sir, if* ed. (sir. If F)
   *take* take effect
73 *from* apart from
75 *cry down or up* decry or extol

---

59 *Plutarch.* In fact the stoic philosopher Seneca, *De Brevitate Vitae*, III.v; see
   II.iii, 40–1.
62 *rushes.* Suggesting triviality; cf. 'Not worth a rush' (Tilley, S918).
72 *Collegiates.* *OED*'s first example of the noun.
74 *Wits and Braveries.* i.e. gallants who set the fashion in talk and dress respectively.
   Cf. *Und.*, XLII, 33–6: '[I] Have eaten with the Beauties, and the wits,/And
   braveries of Court . . . and came so nigh to know/Whether their faces were their
   owne, or no'.

CLERIMONT

A pox of her autumnal face, her pieced beauty! There's no
man can be admitted till she be ready nowadays, till she has
painted and perfumed and washed and scoured, but the
boy here, and him she wipes her oiled lips upon like a
sponge. I have made a song, I pray thee hear it, o' the          85
subject.

[BOY *sings*]

SONG

Still to be neat, still to be dressed,
As you were going to a feast;
Still to be powdered, still perfumed:
Lady, it is to be presumed,                                      90
Though art's hid causes are not found,
All is not sweet, all is not sound.

Give me a look, give me a face,
That makes simplicity a grace;
Robes loosely flowing, hair as free:                            95
Such sweet neglect more taketh me
Than all th' adulteries of art:
They strike mine eyes, but not my heart.

TRUEWIT

And I am clearly o' the other side: I love a good dressing
before any beauty o' the world. Oh, a woman is then like a      100
delicate garden; nor is there one kind of it: she may vary
every hour, take often counsel of her glass and choose the

82 *ready* properly attired, having finished one's toilet (*OED*, a., 1.b); cf. I.i, 1 s.d.
87 *Still* always
98 *They* F$^a$ (*Thy* F$^b$)
99 *dressing* pun on (i) attire; (ii) ornamentation (used of technical processes in arts
   and manufactures)

---

81 *pieced*. (i) mended, patched; (ii) made up of pieces (cf. ll. 112–14, IV.ii, 86).
83 *scoured* F$^b$ (sour'd F$^a$). Scrubbed, with the idea of the hard rubbing of stone or
   metal with detergent. The first of several such associations in the play; cf. V.ii,
   33. Clerimont's list reverses the order of the stages of preparation, as though
   stripping off the layers of artifice.
94 *simplicity*. Absence of ornament or decoration (*OED*'s first example), and
   suggesting also, in view of 'adulteries', the moral senses of the Dedication, 15.
96 *taketh*. Captivate, catch the fancy of; a sense coined by Jonson in *Volp*., I.ii, 56.
97 *adulteries*. Adulterations. The first of *OED*'s two instances, the second being a
   reminiscence of this one.

best. If she have good ears, show 'em; good hair, lay it out;
good legs, wear short clothes; a good hand, discover it
often; practise any art to mend breath, cleanse teeth, repair    105
eyebrows, paint, and profess it.

CLERIMONT

How! publicly?

TRUEWIT

The doing of it, not the manner: that must be private.
Many things that seem foul i' the doing, do please, done. A
lady should indeed study her face when we think she    110
sleeps; nor when the doors are shut should men be inquiring; all is sacred within, then. Is it for us to see their
perukes put on, their false teeth, their complexion, their
eyebrows, their nails? You see gilders will not work but
enclosed. They must not discover how little serves with the    115
help of art to adorn a great deal. How long did the canvas
hang afore Aldgate? Were the people suffered to see the
city's *Love* and *Charity* while they were rude stone, before
they were painted and burnished? No. No more should
servants approach their mistresses but when they are com-    120
plete and finished.

CLERIMONT

Well said, my Truewit.

TRUEWIT

And a wise lady will keep a guard always upon the place,
that she may do things securely. I once followed a rude
fellow into a chamber, where the poor madam, for haste,    125
and troubled, snatched at her peruke to cover her baldness
and put it on the wrong way.

104  *discover* reveal, as at l. 115
106  *profess* declare, acknowledge
107  *How* exclamation of surprise
115  *enclosed* shut up in a room
120  *servants* lovers

---

113  *complexion.* A deft play on two senses: (i) natural colour, texture, and appear-
     ance of the face; (ii) cosmetic application; cf. *Alch.*, I.i, 29, and J. Bullokar, *An
     English Expositor*, 1616, sig. D8ᵛ: '*Complexion* ... painting used by women'.
116–19  *How ... burnished.* Aldgate, the main eastern gate in the old city wall, was
     pulled down in 1606 and rebuilt. On the new gate, completed in 1609, were set
     'two Feminine personages, the one South-ward, appearing to be Peace, with a
     silver Dove upon her one hand, and a guilded wreath or Garland in the other.
     On the North side standeth Charity, with a child at her brest, and another led in
     her hand. Implying (as I conceive) that where Peace, and Love or Charity do
     prosper, and are truely embraced, that Citie shall be for ever blessed' (J. Stow's
     *Survey of London*, continued by A. Munday, 1618, p. 231). Cf. Appendix II.

CLERIMONT

Oh prodigy!

TRUEWIT

And the unconscionable knave held her in compliment an
hour, with that reversed face, when I still looked when she   130
should talk from the tother side.

CLERIMONT

Why, thou shouldst ha' relieved her.

TRUEWIT

No, faith, I let her alone, as we'll let this argument, if you
please, and pass to another. When saw you Dauphine
Eugenie?                                                      135

CLERIMONT

Not these three days. Shall we go to him this morning? He
is very melancholic, I hear.

TRUEWIT

Sick o' the uncle, is he? I met that stiff piece of formality,
his uncle, yesterday, with a huge turban of nightcaps on his
head, buckled over his ears.                                 140

CLERIMONT

Oh, that's his custom when he walks abroad. He can
endure no noise, man.

TRUEWIT

So I have heard. But is the disease so ridiculous in him as it
is made? They say he has been upon divers treaties with the
fishwives and orange-women, and articles propounded        145
between them. Marry, the chimney-sweepers will not be
drawn in.

CLERIMONT

No, nor the broom-men: they stand out stiffly. He cannot
endure a costardmonger, he swoons if he hear one.

TRUEWIT

Methinks a smith should be ominous.                          150

131 *tother* common form of other
133 *argument* topic
144 *made* made out to be
    *been* entered
149 *costardmonger* fruit-seller

---

129 *compliment*. 'Courtiers ... do nothing but sing the gamuth A-re of com-
    plementall courtesie' (T. Dekker, *The Gull's Horn Book*, 1609, p. 2). The stock
    expressions are listed in *King John*, I.i,184ff.
138 *Sick ... uncle*. Adapting 'sick of the mother' (hysteria).
139 *nightcaps*. Worn in the daytime by the elderly and infirm.
148 *broom-men*. Either 'street-sweepers' (*OED*'s only sense) or 'broom-sellers'
    (Henry, H&S, who quote their cries).

CLERIMONT

Or any hammerman. A brazier is not suffered to dwell in
the parish, nor an armourer. He would have hanged a
pewterer's 'prentice once upon a Shrove Tuesday's riot for
being o' that trade, when the rest were quit.

TRUEWIT

A trumpet should fright him terribly, or the hau'boys?    155

CLERIMONT

Out of his senses. The waits of the city have a pension of
him not to come near that ward. This youth practised on
him one night like the bellman, and never left till he had
brought him down to the door with a long sword, and there
left him flourishing with the air.                        160

BOY

Why, sir, he hath chosen a street to lie in so narrow at both
ends that it will receive no coaches nor carts nor any of
these common noises, and therefore we that love him
devise to bring him in such as we may, now and then, for
his exercise, to breathe him. He would grow resty else in   165
his ease. His virtue would rust without action. I entreated a

---

151 *hammerman* metal-worker
    *brazier* worker in brass
153 *upon* vp/on F$^b$ (on F$^a$)
154 *quit* acquitted
155 *hau'boys* oboes (French *hautbois*)
156 *waits* band of street musicians maintained at the public charge
157 *ward* district of the city
    *This youth* Clerimont's boy
    *practised* played a trick, imposed
158 *bellman* night-watchman, who called the hours, ringing a bell
161 *lie* live
164 *in* F$^b$ (om. F$^a$)
165 *breathe* exercise briskly (said of horses)
    *resty* sluggish (said of horses that refuse to go forward)
166 *virtue* special quality, and glancing at the sense 'manly vigour' (Latin *virtus*)

---

153 *pewterer*. Cf. Middleton's *Women Beware Women*, III.i, 77–9: 'she hates the
    name of pewterer/More than sick men the noise, or diseased bones/That quake
    at fall o'th'hammer'.
    *Shrove Tuesday*. When the apprentices went on the rampage, wrecking brothels
    and sometimes playhouses. The authorities reacted sharply if the fun got out of
    hand: in 1617 'The Prentizes on Shrove Tewsday last, to the nomber of 3. or
    4000 comitted extreame insolencies ... such of them as are taken his Majestie
    hath commaunded shal be executed for example sake' (quoted by A. Gurr, *The
    Shakespearean Stage 1574–1642*, Cambridge, 1970, pp. 13–14).
155 *trumpet*. Anticipating Truewit's device in II.ii.

bearward one day to come down with the dogs of some four
parishes that way, and I thank him he did, and cried his
games under Master Morose's window till he was sent
crying away with his head made a most bleeding spectacle      170
to the multitude. And another time a fencer, marching to
his prize, had his drum most tragically run through for
taking that street in his way, at my request.

TRUEWIT

A good wag. How does he for the bells?

CLERIMONT

Oh, i' the Queen's time he was wont to go out of town every      175
Saturday at ten o'clock or on holiday eves. But now, by
reason of the sickness, the perpetuity of ringing has made
him devise a room with double walls and treble ceilings,
the windows close shut and caulked, and there he lives by
candlelight. He turned away a man last week for having a      180
pair of new shoes that creaked, and this fellow waits on him
now in tennis-court socks, or slippers soled with wool, and
they talk each to other in a trunk.—See who comes here!


## Act I, Scene ii

### [*Enter*] DAUPHINE

DAUPHINE

How now! What ail you, sirs? Dumb?

171 *marching* F$^b$ (going F$^a$)
174 *wag* mischievous boy
177 *sickness* plague
180 *turned away a man* dismissed a servant
183 *trunk* speaking-tube (see note to II.i, 2)

---

167 *bearward*. Keeper of a bear for baiting by dogs. Henry quotes the bearward of
   W. Cavendish's *The Humorous Lovers* (1667), V.i: 'fetch me a Bag-pipe, we will
   walk the streets in triumph, and give the people notice of our sport'.
172 *prize*. Fencing-match. Fencers were often drummed through the streets to
   publicize their matches.
176–7 *now ... sickness*. An up-to-date allusion. In 1609 the virulence of the plague
   'was far more severe than in any other year between 1603 and 1625, and the
   total mortality was [4,240,] greater by 2,000 than in any year from 1604 to 1623'
   (F. P. Wilson, *The Plague in Shakespeare's London*, Oxford, 1927, p. 121).
177 *ringing*. London was famous for its bells, and their sound was impossible to
   escape during time of plague, when the city's 114 churches tolled for their dead.
   Cf. Volpone on Lady Wouldbe's voice: 'The bells, in time of pestilence, ne're
   made/Like noise, or were in that perpetuall motion;/The cock-pit comes not
   neere it' (*Volp.*, III.v, 5–7).

TRUEWIT

Struck into stone almost, I am here, with tales o' thine
uncle! There was never such a prodigy heard of.

DAUPHINE

I would you would once lose this subject, my masters, for
my sake. They are such as you are that have brought me 5
into that predicament I am with him.

TRUEWIT

How is that?

DAUPHINE

Marry, that he will disinherit me, no more. He thinks I and
my company are authors of all the ridiculous acts and
moniments are told of him. 10

TRUEWIT

'Slid, I would be the author of more to vex him; that
purpose deserves it: it gives thee law of plaguing him. I'll
tell thee what I would do. I would make a false almanac,
get it printed, and then ha' him drawn out on a coronation
day to the Tower-wharf, and kill him with the noise of the 15
ordinance. Disinherit thee! He cannot, man. Art not thou
next of blood, and his sister's son?

DAUPHINE

Ay, but he will thrust me out of it, he vows, and marry.

TRUEWIT

How! That's a more portent. Can he endure no noise, and
will venture on a wife? 20

CLERIMONT

Yes. Why, thou art a stranger, it seems, to his best trick
yet. He has employed a fellow this half year all over Eng-

2 *I am here* as I stand here
4 *once* once for all
11 *'Slid* God's (eye)lid, a common oath
11–12 *that purpose* Morose's purpose to disinherit Dauphine
12 *gives thee law* authorizes you
16 *ordinance* ordnance, cannon (the original form and pronunciation)
17 *next* nearest
20 *venture on* dare to take (*OED*, v., 9.b)

9–10 *acts and moniments*. The first English edition (1563) of John Foxe's *The Book
of Martyrs* was entitled *Acts and Monuments*; 'moniments' follows Latin *monimen-
tum*. Cf. III.vii,11.
14–15 *coronation day*. Anniversary of James I's coronation, 24 March, when the
Tower guns fired a salute.
19 *more*. Greater. Marriage might produce children, whereas disinheriting seems
illegal (Partridge). This archaic usage, appropriate to a conservative stylist like
Truewit, is paralleled in *Cat.*, IV, 46.

land to hearken him out a dumb woman, be she of any form
or any quality, so she be able to bear children. Her silence
is dowry enough, he says.                                      25

TRUEWIT
But I trust to God he has found none.

CLERIMONT
No, but he has heard of one that's lodged i' the next street
to him, who is exceedingly soft-spoken, thrifty of her
speech, that spends but six words a day. And her he's about
now and shall have her.                                        30

TRUEWIT
Is't possible! Who is his agent i' the business?

CLERIMONT
Marry, a barber, one Cutbeard, an honest fellow, one that
tells Dauphine all here.

TRUEWIT
Why, you oppress me with wonder! A woman, and a
barber, and love no noise!                                     35

CLERIMONT
Yes, faith. The fellow trims him silently and has not the
knack with his shears or his fingers, and that continence in
a barber he thinks so eminent a virtue as it has made him
chief of his counsel.

TRUEWIT
Is the barber to be seen? or the wench?                        40

CLERIMONT
Yes, that they are.

TRUEWIT
I pray thee, Dauphine, let's go thither.

DAUPHINE
I have some business now; I cannot i' faith.

TRUEWIT
You shall have no business shall make you neglect this, sir.
We'll make her talk, believe it; or if she will not, we can   45
give out at least so much as shall interrupt the treaty. We
will break it. Thou art bound in conscience, when he
suspects thee without cause, to torment him.

---

23 *hearken ... out* find by inquiry                       24 *quality* rank
32 *one Cutbeard* F$^b$ (om. F$^a$)              34 *oppress* overwhelm (Latin *opprimere*)
46 *give out* report, put about
   *interrupt the treaty* hinder the negotiation (the legal metaphors continue to l. 52)

---

37 *knack*. (i) know-how, trick; (ii) sharp snap, crack: cf. J. Cooke, *Greene's Tu
Quoque*, 1614, sig. D3$^r$: 'the Barber ... can snacke his fingers with dex-
teritie'.

DAUPHINE

Not I, by any means. I'll give no suffrage to't. He shall
never ha' that plea against me that I opposed the least 50
fant'sy of his. Let it lie upon my stars to be guilty, I'll be
innocent.

TRUEWIT

Yes, and be poor, and beg; do, innocent, when some
groom of his has got him an heir, or this barber, if he
himself cannot. Innocent!—I pray thee, Ned, where lies 55
she? Let him be innocent still.

CLERIMONT

Why, right over against the barber's, in the house where
Sir John Daw lies.

TRUEWIT

You do not mean to confound me!

CLERIMONT

Why? 60

TRUEWIT

Does he that would marry her know so much?

CLERIMONT

I cannot tell.

TRUEWIT

'Twere enough of imputation to her, with him.

CLERIMONT

Why?

TRUEWIT

The only talking sir i' th' town! Jack Daw! And he teach 65
her not to speak—God b' w' you. I have some business too.

CLERIMONT

Will you not go thither then?

49 *suffrage* consent
51 *Let ... stars* though I be fated
53 *innocent* playing on the sense of I.i,17
54 *groom* servant
   *got* begot
57 *over against* opposite
59 *confound* dumbfound
63 *to her* against her (that she is talkative)
65 *only* pre-eminent

51 *fant'sy*. Fancy; and so pronounced, but full contraction obscures the range of
   meaning available: e.g. caprice, amorous passion, delusion (Partridge).
65 *sir*. Mockingly for 'gentleman'; cf. 'a proud, and spangled sir', *C.R.*, III.iv,12.

TRUEWIT

Not with the danger to meet Daw, for mine ears.

CLERIMONT

Why? I thought you two had been upon very good terms.

TRUEWIT

Yes, of keeping distance.                                        70

CLERIMONT

They say he is a very good scholar.

TRUEWIT

Ay, and he says it first. A pox on him, a fellow that
pretends only to learning, buys titles, and nothing else of
books in him.

CLERIMONT

The world reports him to be very learned.                        75

TRUEWIT

I am sorry the world should so conspire to belie him.

CLERIMONT

Good faith, I have heard very good things come from him.

TRUEWIT

You may. There's none so desperately ignorant to deny
that: would they were his own. God b' w' you, gentlemen.

*[Exit]*

CLERIMONT

This is very abrupt!                                             80


## Act I, Scene iii

DAUPHINE

Come, you are a strange open man to tell everything thus.

CLERIMONT

Why, believe it, Dauphine, Truewit's a very honest fellow.

DAUPHINE

I think no other, but this frank nature of his is not for
secrets.

CLERIMONT

Nay, then, you are mistaken, Dauphine. I know where he          5

---

73 *pretends ... to* makes a claim to

---

73 *titles.* Cf. J. Earle's 'A Pretender to Learning', *Microcosmography*, 1628, sig.
G2$^r$: 'Hee is a great Nomen-clator of Authors, which hee has read in generall in
the Catalogue, and in particular in the Title, and goes seldome so farre as the
Dedication'.

has been well trusted, and discharged the trust very truly
and heartily.

DAUPHINE

I contend not, Ned, but with the fewer a business is
carried, it is ever the safer. Now we are alone, if you'll go
thither, I am for you.                                             10

CLERIMONT

When were you there?

DAUPHINE

Last night, and such a *Decameron* of sport fallen out!
Boccace never thought of the like. Daw does nothing but
court her, and the wrong way. He would lie with her, and
praises her modesty; desires that she would talk and be      15
free, and commends her silence in verses, which he reads
and swears are the best that ever man made. Then rails at
his fortunes, stamps, and mutines why he is not made a
councillor and called to affairs of state.

CLERIMONT

I pray thee, let's go. I would fain partake this.—Some      20
water, boy.

[*Exit* BOY]

DAUPHINE

We are invited to dinner together, he and I, by one that
came thither to him, Sir La Foole.

CLERIMONT

Oh, that's a precious manikin!

DAUPHINE

Do you know him?                                                  25

CLERIMONT

Ay, and he will know you too, if e'er he saw you but once,
though you should meet him at church in the midst of

---

7 *heartily* earnestly
8 *contend not* do not dispute it
9 *carried* managed
10 *thither* i.e. to visit Epicoene
12 *fallen out* come about, happened
18 *mutines why* mutinies because

---

12 *Decameron*. Boccaccio's collection of a hundred tales, much concerned with
amorous folly.
20 *fain partake*. Gladly have some of. *OED*, v., 1.b, has no example before 1617,
but in view of the gallants' detachment, and the frequency with which Jonson
images folly as a feast, this sense is preferable to 'take part in'.
24 *manikin*. Little model of a man, puppet; perhaps suggested by *Twelfth Night*,
III.ii, 53, where Sir Andrew Aguecheek is called 'a dear manikin'.

prayers. He is one of the Braveries, though he be none o'
the Wits. He will salute a judge upon the bench and a
bishop in the pulpit, a lawyer when he is pleading at the    30
bar, and a lady when she is dancing in a masque, and put
her out. He does give plays and suppers, and invites his
guests to 'em aloud out of his window as they ride by in
coaches. He has a lodging in the Strand for the purpose, or
to watch when ladies are gone to the china-houses or the    35
Exchange, that he may meet 'em by chance and give 'em
presents, some two or three hundred pounds' worth of
toys, to be laughed at. He is never without a spare banquet
or sweetmeats in his chamber, for their women to alight at
and come up to, for a bait.                                 40

DAUPHINE
Excellent! He was a fine youth last night, but now he is
much finer! What is his christian name? I ha' forgot.

[*Enter* BOY]

CLERIMONT
Sir Amorous La Foole.
BOY
The gentleman is here below that owns that name.
CLERIMONT
'Heart, he's come to invite me to dinner, I hold my life.    45
DAUPHINE
Like enough. Pray thee, let's ha' him up.

---

31–2 *put her out* make her forget her part; cf. V.iii, 182
34 *purpose, or* ed. (purpose: or F$^a$ purpose. Or F$^b$)
38 *toys* trifles, trumpery
39 *for their* F$^b$ (om. for F$^a$)
   *their women* the maidservants of the ladies of l. 35
   *alight* descend from their coaches
40 *bait* (i) refreshment, snack; (ii) food as a lure (using the women to catch the ladies)
44 *below* F$^b$ (om. F$^a$)
   *owns* F$^b$ (owes F$^a$)

---

34 *Strand.* Where many of the gentry lived.
35 *china-houses.* Shops selling oriental goods, fashionable meeting-places.
36 *Exchange.* The New Exchange on the south side of the Strand, opened in 1609; its milliners' shops made it a fashionable resort for ladies (Sugden).
38 *to ... at.* i.e. (i) the toys; (ii) La Foole. The pun is repeated at V.iv, 225.
   *banquet.* Course of sweetmeats, fruit, and wine. Overbury's Amorist is never without comfits; see p. 4.

CLERIMONT

Boy, marshal him.

BOY

With a truncheon, sir?

CLERIMONT

Away, I beseech you. [*Exit* BOY]—I'll make him tell us his
pedigree now, and what meat he has to dinner, and who are          50
his guests, and the whole course of his fortunes, with a
breath.


### Act I, Scene iv

[*Enter*] LA FOOLE

LA FOOLE

'Save, dear Sir Dauphine, honoured Master Clerimont.

CLERIMONT

Sir Amorous! You have very much honested my lodging
with your presence.

LA FOOLE

Good faith, it is a fine lodging, almost as delicate a lodging
as mine.                                                            5

CLERIMONT

Not so, sir.

LA FOOLE

Excuse me, sir, if it were i' the Strand, I assure you. I am
come, Master Clerimont, to entreat you wait upon two or
three ladies to dinner today.

CLERIMONT

How, sir! Wait upon 'em? Did you ever see me carry           10
dishes?

LA FOOLE

No, sir, dispense with me; I meant to bear 'em company.


47 *marshal him* show him in
48 *truncheon* (i) marshal's baton; (ii) cudgel
50 *meat* food
 1 *'Save* affectedly for 'God save you'
12 *dispense with me* affectedly for 'excuse me'

 2 *honested*. Honoured (Latin *honestare*); becoming archaic at this date, and used
   by Clerimont to mock La Foole's affected courtliness.

CLERIMONT

Oh, that I will, sir. The doubtfulness o' your phrase,
believe it, sir, would breed you a quarrel once an hour with
the terrible boys, if you should but keep 'em fellowship a      15
day.

LA FOOLE

It should be extremely against my will, sir, if I contested
with any man.

CLERIMONT

I believe it, sir. Where hold you your feast?

LA FOOLE

At Tom Otter's, sir.      20

DAUPHINE

Tom Otter? What's he?

LA FOOLE

Captain Otter, sir; he is a kind of gamester, but he has had
command both by sea and by land.

DAUPHINE

Oh, then he is _animal amphibium_?

LA FOOLE

Ay, sir. His wife was the rich china-woman that the cour-      25
tiers visited so often, that gave the rare entertainment. She
commands all at home.

CLERIMONT

Then she is Captain Otter?

LA FOOLE

You say very well, sir. She is my kinswoman, a La Foole by
the mother side, and will invite any great ladies for my      30
sake.

DAUPHINE

Not of the La Fooles of Essex?

13 _phrase_ way of talking
15 _but_ F<sup>b</sup> (om. F<sup>a</sup>)
22 _gamester_ player of a game (here, bear-baiting)
30 _mother side_ mother's side

---

13 _that I will_. Referring to La Foole's 'dispense with me' as well as what he says
    next, and playing on the sense 'do away with' or 'do without'.
15 _terrible boys_. Gangs of swaggering bullies, Kastril's 'angry boys' in _Alch._, usually
    called roarers or roaring boys; an amusingly unlikely fellowship for the per-
    fumed and affected La Foole.
25 _china-woman_. Owner of a china-house, but through 'doubtfulness of phrase' (cf.
    _visited, entertainment_) La Foole manages to imply that his kinswoman was a
    high-class prostitute.
26 _rare_. Excellent, but (because of _often_) suggesting 'infrequent, scant'. Cf. II.iii,
    30, where Dauphine uses the same pun consciously.

LA FOOLE

No, sir, the La Fooles of London.

CLERIMONT

[*Aside to* DAUPHINE] Now h'is in.

LA FOOLE

They all come out of our house, the La Fooles o' the north,  35
the La Fooles of the west, the La Fooles of the east and
south—we are as ancient a family as any is in Europe—but
I myself am descended lineally of the French La Fooles—
and we do bear for our coat yellow, or or, checkered
azure and gules, and some three or four colours more,  40
which is a very noted coat and has sometimes been sol-
emnly worn by divers nobility of our house—but let that
go, antiquity is not respected now—I had a brace of fat
does sent me, gentlemen, and half a dozen of pheasants, a
dozen or two of godwits, and some other fowl, which I  45
would have eaten while they are good, and in good company—there will be a great lady or two, my Lady
Haughty, my Lady Centaure, Mistress Dol Mavis—and
they come a' purpose to see the silent gentlewoman, Mistress Epicoene, that honest Sir John Daw has promised to  50
bring thither—and then Mistress Trusty, my Lady's
woman, will be there too, and this honourable knight, Sir
Dauphine, with yourself, Master Clerimont—and we'll be
very merry and have fiddlers and dance—I have been a
mad wag in my time, and have spent some crowns since I  55

34 *in* underway
35 *house* family, lineage
39 *for* F[b] (om. F[a])
   *coat* coat-of-arms
39–40 *or ... gules* yellow ... red (in heraldry)
41 *sometimes* in former times (with an unfortunate ambiguity)
45 *godwits* marsh-birds, a delicacy

40 *some ... more*. Like Sogliardo in *E.M.O.*, III.iv, 57, La Foole unwittingly
suggests the motley coat of the fool or jester.
44 *does*. 'Doves' has been proposed as the correct reading, but 'does' is confirmed by
III.iii, 79 and IV.v, 181 (a typical example of Jonson's attentiveness to the
smallest and apparently most random detail of his design). For comment on La
Foole's extravagant feast, and the moral and social failings it symbolizes, see W.
Trimpi, *Ben Jonson's Poems: A Study of the Plain Style* (Stanford, 1962), pp.
187–8.

was a page in court to my Lord Lofty, and after my Lady's
gentleman-usher, who got me knighted in Ireland, since it
pleased my elder brother to die—I had as fair a gold jerkin
on that day as any was worn in the Island Voyage or at
Caliz, none dispraised, and I came over in it hither,      60
showed myself to my friends in court and after went down
to my tenants in the country and surveyed my lands, let
new leases, took their money, spent it in the eye o' the land
here, upon ladies—and now I can take up at my pleasure.

DAUPHINE

Can you take up ladies, sir?                               65

CLERIMONT

Oh, let him breathe, he has not recovered.

DAUPHINE

Would I were your half in that commodity—

LA FOOLE

No, sir, excuse me: I meant money, which can take up
anything. I have another guest or two to invite and say as
much to, gentlemen. I'll take my leave abruptly, in hope   70
you will not fail—Your servant.

                              [*Exit* LA FOOLE]

---

57 *gentleman-usher* gentleman who serves a person of high rank
63 *eye* centre
64 *take up* borrow (at interest)
67 *half* partner
68 s.p. LA FOOLE F$^b$ (CLE. F$^a$)
    *take up* purchase

---

56 *after*. i.e. after that I was; *who* presumably='my Lady'. Throughout this speech
   La Foole's verbal ineptness continually leaves his sense open to ludicrous
   misinterpretations; e.g. 'that day', which could mean the day of his brother's
   death.
57 *Ireland*. A dubious place to be knighted. In 1599, during his Irish campaign, the
   Earl of Essex had been sharply criticized for cheapening the title by bestowing it
   too liberally.
59 *Island Voyage*. Another unfortunate boast. Gallants had flocked to join the
   disastrous expedition led by Essex, Howard, and Raleigh against the Spanish in
   the Azores in 1597, many of them dressed, according to one English captain,
   'rather like Maskers then Souldiers' (H&S).
60 *Caliz*. Cadiz, captured by Essex and Howard in 1596.
65–7 *take up . . . commodity*. Referring to money-lenders' practice, in order to
   circumvent the rates of interest fixed by the government, of making clients
   accept part of their loan in goods. These would either be greatly overpriced, or
   would be bought back by the money-lender much more cheaply than he parted
   with them.

**DAUPHINE**

We will not fail you, sir precious La Foole; but she shall
that your ladies come to see, if I have credit afore Sir Daw.

**CLERIMONT**

Did you ever hear such a wind-fucker as this?

**DAUPHINE**

Or such a rook as the other, that will betray his mistress to     75
be seen! Come, 'tis time we prevented it.

**CLERIMONT**

Go.                                                  [*Exeunt*]

---

73 *have credit afore* take precedence to (the metaphor refers back to ll. 64–5)
75 *rook* gull, simpleton (as often, but here glancing at Daw's name)

---

74 *wind-fucker*. 'The kistrilles or windfuckers that filling themselves with winde, fly
against the winde evermore' (T. Nashe, *Lenten Stuff*, 1599, sig. H1$^r$).

## Act II, Scene i

[*Enter*] MOROSE, MUTE

MOROSE

Cannot I yet find out a more compendious method than by
this trunk to save my servants the labour of speech and
mine ears the discord of sounds? Let me see. All discourses
but mine own afflict me, they seem harsh, impertinent,
and irksome. Is it not possible that thou shouldst answer          5
me by signs, and I apprehend thee, fellow? Speak not,
though I question you. You have taken the ring off from
the street door, as I bade you? Answer me not by speech
but by silence, unless it be otherwise.—Very good.
     *At the breaches, still the fellow makes legs or signs*
And you have fastened on a thick quilt or flock-bed on the        10
outside of the door, that if they knock with their daggers or
with brickbats, they can make no noise? But with your leg,
your answer, unless it be otherwise.—Very good. This is
not only fit modesty in a servant, but good state and
discretion in a master. And you have been with Cutbeard,            15
the barber, to have him come to me?—Good. And he will
come presently? Answer me not but with your leg, unless it
be otherwise; if it be otherwise, shake your head or
shrug.—[MUTE *makes a leg*] So. Your Italian and Spaniard
are wise in these, and it is a frugal and comely gravity. How      20
long will it be ere Cutbeard come? Stay, if an hour, hold up
your whole hand; if half an hour, two fingers; if a quarter,
one.—[MUTE *holds up one finger bent*] Good; half a quarter?
'Tis well. And have you given him a key to come in without

1 *compendious* expeditious, direct
4 *impertinent* irrelevant
7 *ring* (circular) door-knocker
9 s.d. *breaches* breaks (in the text)
  s.d. *makes legs* bows (by drawing back one leg and bending the other)
10 *flock-bed* mattress stuffed with wool or cotton waste
12 *brickbats* pieces of brick
14 *state* dignity of demeanour
15 *discretion* judgement
22 *your* F$^b$ (you F$^a$)

2 *trunk*. A pipe in the wall for communicating with different parts of the house,
  such as Dol uses in *Alch.*, I.iv, 5.

knocking?—Good. And is the lock oiled, and the hinges, 25
today?—Good. And the quilting of the stairs nowhere
worn out and bare?—Very good. I see by much doctrine
and impulsion, it may be effected. Stand by. The Turk in
this divine discipline is admirable, exceeding all the poten-
tates of the earth; still waited on by mutes, and all his 30
commands so executed, yea, even in the war, as I have
heard, and in his marches, most of his charges and directions given by signs and with silence: an exquisite art! And
I am heartily ashamed and angry oftentimes that the
princes of Christendom should suffer a barbarian to trans- 35
cend 'em in so high a point of felicity. I will practise it
hereafter.

*One winds a horn without*

How now? Oh! oh! What villain, what prodigy of mankind
is that?—Look. [*Exit* MUTE. *Horn sounds*]*again*—Oh! cut
his throat, cut his throat! What murderer, hell-hound, 40
devil can this be?

[*Enter* MUTE]

MUTE
It is a post from the court—
MOROSE
Out, rogue! And must thou blow thy horn too?
MUTE
Alas, it is a post from the court, sir, that says he must speak
with you, pain of death— 45
MOROSE
Pain of thy life, be silent!

27 *doctrine* teaching (Latin *doctrina*)
28 *impulsion* influence, instigation
   *by* to one side
29 *discipline* branch of instruction
30 *still* always
32–3 *charges ... directions* orders ... instructions for the deployment of troops
37 s.d. *winds* blows
38 *prodigy* monster
42 *post* express messenger (who often announced his arrival by blowing a horn)
43 *Out* exclamation expressing reproach
45 *with* F$^b$ (om. F$^a$)

26 *quilting*. Padding (*OED* has no example before 1710). Another sign of Morose's
oddity: floor carpets did not begin to be widely used in England before the
eighteenth century.

## Act II, Scene ii

[*Enter*] TRUEWIT [*carrying a post-horn and a halter*]

TRUEWIT

By your leave, sir—I am a stranger here—is your name
Master Morose?—[*To* MUTE] Is your name Master Morose? Fishes, Pythagoreans all! This is strange! What say
you, sir? Nothing? Has Harpocrates been here with his
club among you?—Well, sir, I will believe you to be the        5
man at this time; I will venture upon you, sir. Your friends
at court commend 'em to you, sir—

MOROSE

[*Aside*] Oh men! Oh manners! Was there ever such an
impudence?

TRUEWIT

And are extremely solicitous for you, sir.                     10

MOROSE

Whose knave are you?

TRUEWIT

Mine own knave and your compeer, sir.

MOROSE

Fetch me my sword—

TRUEWIT

You shall taste the one half of my dagger if you do, groom,
and you the other if you stir, sir. Be patient, I charge you in   15
the King's name, and hear me without insurrection. They
say you are to marry? To marry! Do you mark, sir?

MOROSE

How then, rude companion!

6 *venture upon* hazard an approach to
11 *knave* menial
12 *compeer* equal
18 *companion* fellow (expressing contempt)

---

3 *Fishes*. 'As mute as a fish' (Tilley, F300).
  *Pythagoreans*. Ironically inappropriate to Morose. The religious society founded
  by Pythagoras vowed itself to silence for the purpose of self-examination.
4 *Harpocrates*. The god of silence, represented with a finger over his mouth, and
  occasionally with a club (acquired from Hercules, by confusion).
8 *Oh men! Oh manners!* Echoing Cicero's fámous 'O tempora, O mores' (*In
  Catilinam*, I.2). An ironic self-identification, in view of Cicero's reputation as
  the paragon of learned eloquence.
9 *impudence*. Probably '(instance of) shamelessness' (Latin *impudentia*) rather
  than the modern sense, which is not common before the eighteenth century.

TRUEWIT

Marry, your friends do wonder, sir, the Thames being so
near, wherein you may drown so handsomely; or London        20
Bridge at a low fall with a fine leap, to hurry you down the
stream; or such a delicate steeple i' the town as Bow, to
vault from; or a braver height as Paul's; or if you affected to
do it nearer home and a shorter way, an excellent garret
window into the street; or a beam in the said garret, with     25
this halter (*he shows him a halter*), which they have sent,
and desire that you would sooner commit your grave head
to this knot than to the wedlock noose; or take a little
sublimate and go out of the world like a rat, or a fly, as one
said, with a straw i' your arse: any way rather than to follow  30
this goblin matrimony. Alas, sir, do you ever think to find a
chaste wife in these times? Now? When there are so many
masques, plays, Puritan preachings, mad folks, and other
strange sights to be seen daily, private and public? If you
had lived in King Etheldred's time, sir, or Edward the       35
Confessor's, you might perhaps have found in some cold
country hamlet, then, a dull frosty wench would have been
contented with one man; now, they will as soon be pleased
with one leg or one eye. I'll tell you, sir, the monstrous
hazards you shall run with a wife.                           40

MOROSE

Good sir! Have I ever cozened any friends of yours of their
land? bought their possessions? taken forfeit of their

---

23 *braver* more splendid, more excellent
29 *sublimate* mercury sublimate (mercuric chloride, used as rat-poison)
33 *preachings* F^b (parleys F^a)
37 *would* who would
41 *cozened* cheated

---

19 *Marry*. Quibbling on the exclamation of surprise; as if the verb 'to marry' were
   itself an expression of surprise, indignation, and 'wonder' (Partridge).
21 *at . . . fall*. At a low ebb-tide, when it would be difficult to drown from the bank.
   The water gushed with great force from under the bridge, because of the
   bridge-piers which impeded the stream.
22 *Bow*. St Mary-le-Bow, in Cheapside.
29–30 *fly . . . arse*. In fly and spider fights, a popular diversion, a straw was thrust
   into the fly's tail.
33 *mad folks*. Viewing the inmates of Bedlam was a popular amusement; a small fee
   was charged.
35 *Etheldred*. Ethelred the Unready (978–1016), the father of Edward the Confessor (1042–66). Cf. Appendix II.

mortgage? begged a reversion from 'em? bastarded their
issue? What have I done that may deserve this?

TRUEWIT

Nothing, sir, that I know, but your itch of marriage.                45

MOROSE

Why, if I had made an assassinate upon your father,
vitiated your mother, ravished your sisters—

TRUEWIT

I would kill you, sir, I would kill you if you had.

MOROSE

Why, you do more in this, sir. It were a vengeance cen-
tuple for all facinorous acts that could be named, to do that   50
you do—

TRUEWIT

Alas, sir, I am but a messenger: I but tell you what you
must hear. It seems your friends are careful after your
soul's health, sir, and would have you know the
danger—but you may do your pleasure for all them; I    55
persuade not, sir. If after you are married your wife do run
away with a vaulter, or the Frenchman that walks upon
ropes, or him that dances the jig, or a fencer for his skill at
his weapon, why, it is not their fault; they have discharged
their consciences when you know what may happen. Nay,   60
suffer valiantly, sir, for I must tell you all the perils that
you are obnoxious to. If she be fair, young, and vegetous,
no sweetmeats ever drew more flies; all the yellow doublets
and great roses i' the town will be there. If foul and
crooked, she'll be with them and buy those doublets and   65
roses, sir. If rich and that you marry her dowry, not her,
she'll reign in your house as imperious as a widow. If

43 *reversion* right of succession to an office
   *from* away from
   *bastarded* rendered illegitimate
46 *assassinate* murderous attack
47 *vitiated* corrupted
50 *facinorous* wicked, infamous
57–9 *vaulter ... jig ... weapon* with sexual innuendoes
59 *discharged* relieved
62 *obnoxious* open, liable (Latin *obnoxius*)
   *to* ed. (too F)
   *vegetous* lively (Latin *vegetus*)
65 *be with them and buy* seek *their* company and pay for

---

58 *ropes*. The skill of the French at tightrope-walking is mentioned in *Women
   Beware Women*, III.iii, 122.
64 *roses*. Rosettes, worn on shoes by gallants, often very ornate.

noble, all her kindred will be your tyrans. If fruitful, as
proud as May and humorous as April; she must have her
doctors, her midwives, her nurses, her longings every          70
hour, though it be for the dearest morsel of man. If
learned, there was never such a parrot; all your patrimony
will be too little for the guests that must be invited to hear
her speak Latin and Greek, and you must lie with her in
those languages too, if you will please her. If precise, you   75
must feast all the silenced brethren once in three days,
salute the sisters, entertain the whole family or wood of
'em, and hear long-winded exercises, singings, and
catechizings, which you are not given to and yet must give
for, to please the zealous matron your wife, who for the       80
holy cause will cozen you over and above. You begin to
sweat, sir? But this is not half, i' faith; you may do your
pleasure notwithstanding, as I said before; I come not to
persuade you.—

                          *The* MUTE *is stealing away*
Upon my faith, master servingman, if you do stir, I will       85
beat you.

MOROSE

Oh, what is my sin, what is my sin?

TRUEWIT

Then, if you love your wife, or rather dote on her, sir, oh,
how she'll torture you and take pleasure i' your torments!
You shall lie with her but when she lists; she will not hurt   90
her beauty, her complexion; or it must be for that jewel or
that pearl when she does; every half hour's pleasure must

68  *tyrans* tyrants (Latin *tyrannus*)
69  *humorous* capricious
71  *morsel* with a sexual innuendo
75  *precise* a Puritan
78  *exercises* religious observances
81  *over and above* into the bargain
83  *before*; ed. (before, F)
91  *complexion* face make-up, as at I.i, 113

---

69  *proud*. (i) exuberant (cf. Shakespeare's Sonnet 98 and *Hamlet*, III.iii, 81, 'as
    flush as May'); (ii) haughty, arrogant; (iii) sexually excited, said of 'a female . . .
    in her heate' (example dated 1615 in *OED*, a., 8.b). Cf. 1. 109.
72  *parrot*. Cf. the learned Lady Wouldbe, wife of Sir Pol, in *Volp*.
76  *silenced brethren*. Puritan clergy who refused to conform to the canons passed at
    the Hampton Court conference of 1604 and lost their licenses to preach;
    Tribulation Wholesome's 'silenced saints' in *Alch.*, III.i, 38.
77  *wood*. Latin *silva* could mean a crowd or collection of anything, not only trees.
    Punning on *wood* = 'mad', as in *Alch.*, III.ii, 95.

be bought anew, and with the same pain and charge you
wooed her at first. Then you must keep what servants she
please, what company she will; that friend must not visit      95
you without her license; and him she loves most she will
seem to hate eagerliest, to decline your jealousy; or feign to
be jealous of you first, and for that cause go live with her
she-friend or cousin at the college, that can instruct her in
all the mysteries of writing letters, corrupting servants,      100
taming spies; where she must have that rich gown for such
a great day, a new one for the next, a richer for the third; be
served in silver; have the chamber filled with a succession
of grooms, footmen, ushers, and other messengers,
besides embroiderers, jewellers, tire-women, sempsters,        105
feathermen, perfumers; while she feels not how the land
drops away, nor the acres melt, nor foresees the change
when the mercer has your woods for her velvets; never
weighs what her pride costs, sir, so she may kiss a page or a
smooth chin that has the despair of a beard; be a states-      110

---

93 *pain and charge* trouble and cost
97 *eagerliest* most fiercely
   *decline* avert
105 *tire-women* dressmakers
   *sempsters* men or women who sew
106 *feathermen* dealers in feathers and plumes
107 *change* punning on 'exchange'
108 *mercer* dealer in fabrics, especially silk and velvet
109 *so* as long as

---

 99 *she-friend or cousin.* Both terms could mean 'mistress' or 'strumpet', and *cousin*
    was also a euphemism for 'lover'; Jonson's substitution for Juvenal's 'wife's
    mother'.
101 *spies.* Cf. Volpone to Celia: 'Cannot we delude the eyes/Of a few poore
    household-spies?' (*Volp.*, III.vii, 176–7).
103 *silver.* A mark of Bianca's finicky upper-classness in *Women Beware Women*,
    III.i, 76, is the demand to be 'served all in silver' rather than the normal
    household pewter.
104 *and . . . messengers.* Implying that all these servants would be there to act as
    go-betweens in amorous intrigues.
110 *despair of a beard.* See Appendix II. The accusations of sexual unnaturalness
    here and down to 1. 119 are paralleled in Jonson's attack on Cecilia Bulstrode
    (d. 1609), 'An Epigram on the Court Pucelle', 7–12: 'What though with
    Tribade [=lesbian] lust she force a Muse,/And in an Epicoene fury can write
    newes/Equall with that, which for the best newes goes,/. . . What though she
    talke, and can at once with them,/Make State, Religion, Bawdrie, all a theame?'
110–11 *stateswoman.* Jonson's satiric coinage for a Jacobean impossibility: a female
    politician.

woman, know all the news; what was done at Salisbury,
what at the Bath, what at court, what in progress; or so she
may censure poets and authors and styles, and compare
'em, Daniel with Spenser, Jonson with the tother youth,
and so forth; or be thought cunning in controversies or the          115
very knots of divinity, and have often in her mouth the
state of the question, and then skip to the mathematics and
demonstration, and answer in religion to one, in state to
another, in bawdry to a third.

MOROSE

Oh, oh!          120

TRUEWIT

All this is very true, sir. And then her going in disguise to
that conjuror and this cunning woman, where the first
question is, how soon you shall die? next, if her present
servant love her? next that, if she shall have a new servant?
and how many? which of her family would make the best          125
bawd, male or female? what precedence she shall have by
her next match? And sets down the answers, and believes
'em above the scriptures. Nay, perhaps she'll study the art.

112 *progress* monarch's state visit to the provinces
113 *censure* judge
115 *cunning* skilful
116 *knots* essential (and most difficult) points
117 *state* in rhetoric, the principal point at issue (Latin *status*); cf. V.iii, 35
118 *demonstration* making evident by reasoning
     *state* politics
122 *conjuror* wizard, astrologer
     *cunning woman* or wise woman, who told fortunes
124 *servant* in the amatory sense of The Persons of the Play, l. 6
126 *bawd* pander
     *precedence* right of preceding others at formal social occasions
127 *match* marriage
128 *study* i.e. practice (the art of fortune-telling)

111–12 *Salisbury ... Bath*. Fashionable places for race-meetings and medicinal
   bathing respectively.
114 *Daniel ... Spenser*. H&S cite several instances of contemporaries comparing
   them, and Jonson reviews them together, very uncomplimentarily, in a con-
   versation with Drummond (H&S, I, 132).
   *tother youth*. Probably Shakespeare: by 1609 it must have been as commonplace
   to compare the two leading dramatists of the time as it became after the
   Restoration. Jonson had much to say about Shakespeare, who had acted in two
   of his plays and may have assisted the start of his career; here he humorously
   makes Truewit unable to remember his name. However, the joke is affec-
   tionate, not hostile: neither Shakespeare nor Jonson was a 'youth' in 1609. In
   Juvenal the comparison is between Virgil and Homer.

MOROSE

Gentle sir, ha' you done? Ha' you had your pleasure o' me?
I'll think of these things.                                    130

TRUEWIT

Yes, sir; and then comes reeking home of vapour and sweat
with going afoot, and lies in a month of a new face, all oil
and birdlime, and rises in asses' milk, and is cleansed with a
new fucus. God b' w' you, sir. One thing more, which I
had almost forgot. This too, with whom you are to marry    135
may have made a conveyance of her virginity aforehand, as
your wise widows do of their states, before they marry, in
trust to some friend, sir. Who can tell? Or if she have not
done it yet, she may do, upon the wedding day, or the night
before, and antedate you cuckold. The like has been heard   140
of in nature. 'Tis no devised, impossible thing, sir. God b'
w' you. I'll be bold to leave this rope with you, sir, for a
remembrance.—Farewell, Mute.

> [*Exit*]

MOROSE

Come, ha' me to my chamber, but first shut the door.
> *The horn again*

Oh, shut the door, shut the door. Is he come again?       145

[*Enter* CUTBEARD]

CUTBEARD

'Tis I, sir, your barber.


136 *conveyance* legal transference of property from one person to another
137 *states* estates
138 *friend* punning on the sense 'lover'
141 *devised* invented, contrived
143 *remembrance* reminder (*OED*, sb., 8.c; earliest example, 1617)

---

131 *reeking*. (i) steaming; (ii) stinking (a sense not recorded in *OED* before 1710,
  but cf. Appendix II).
132 *lies ... of*. i.e. before giving birth to.
133 *birdlime*. 'i.e. viscous and glutinous unguents and cataplasms for beautifying
  the face' (Upton).
  *rises*. Like Venus rising from the waves at her birth. Many editors have
  suppressed this ironic parallel by emending to 'rinses', on the grounds that this
  is the sense in Juvenal, but Juvenal's *fovetur* does not clearly mean this (see
  Appendix II), and anyway Jonson is not tied in this pedestrian way to his
  sources. Cf. Belinda's toilet in *The Rape of the Lock*, 140: 'The fair each moment
  rises in her charms'.
134 *fucus*. Wash or colouring for the face (Latin *fucus*), coined by Jonson in *C.R.*,
  V.ii, 391.

MOROSE

Oh, Cutbeard, Cutbeard, Cutbeard! here has been a cutthroat with me: help me in to my bed, and give me physic with thy counsel.

[*Exeunt*]

### Act II, Scene iii

[*Enter*] DAW, CLERIMONT, DAUPHINE, EPICOENE

DAW

Nay, and she will, let her refuse at her own charges; 'tis nothing to me, gentlemen. But she will not be invited to the like feasts or guests every day.

CLERIMONT

Oh, by no means, she may not refuse—(*they dissuade her privately*) to stay at home if you love your reputation. 5 'Slight, you are invited thither o' purpose to be seen and laughed at by the lady of the college and her shadows. This trumpeter hath proclaimed you.

DAUPHINE

You shall not go; let him be laughed at in your stead, for not bringing you, and put him to his extemporal faculty of 10 fooling and talking loud to satisfy the company.

CLERIMONT

He will suspect us, talk aloud.—Pray, Mistress Epicoene, let's see your verses; we have Sir John Daw's leave; do not conceal your servant's merit and your own glories.

EPICOENE

They'll prove my servant's glories if you have his leave so 15 soon.

DAUPHINE

[*Aside to* EPICOENE] His vainglories, lady!

DAW

Show 'em, show 'em, mistress, I dare own 'em.

EPICOENE

Judge you what glories!

1 *and* if
  *charges* cost
7 *shadows* parasites, toadies
7–8 *This trumpeter* Daw
11 *fooling* acting foolishly
  *satisfy* i.e. with an explanation
15 *glories* (i) triumphs; (ii) boasts
18 *own* acknowledge as my own

DAW

Nay, I'll read 'em myself too: an author must recite his own          20
works. It is a madrigal of modesty.
   'Modest and fair, for fair and good are near
     Neighbours, howe'er'—

DAUPHINE

Very good.

CLERIMONT

Ay, is't not?                                                        25

DAW

   'No noble virtue ever was alone,
     But two in one.'

DAUPHINE

Excellent!

CLERIMONT

That again, I pray, Sir John.

DAUPHINE

It has something in't like rare wit and sense.                       30

CLERIMONT

Peace.

DAW

   'No noble virtue ever was alone,
     But two in one.
  Then, when I praise sweet modesty, I praise
     Bright beauty's rays:                   35
  And having praised both beauty' and modestee,
     I have praised thee.'

DAUPHINE

Admirable!

CLERIMONT

How it chimes, and cries tink i' the close, divinely!

---

21 *madrigal of* love lyric concerning
36 *beauty'* indicating the elision of a syllable
 *modestee* see above, p. xliii

---

22ff. Daw's 'own works' in fact comprise two platitudes; cf. P. Charron, *Of
 Wisdom*, 1612, p. 18, '*Faire* and good are neere neighbours', and Anon.,
 *England's Parnassus, or The Choicest Flowers of our Modern Poets*, 1600, p. 292,
 'The simple vertue may consist alone,/But better are two vertues joynd in one'.
39 *chimes*. The word suggested for Jonson the mechanical and overemphatic rhy-
 mes of ballads; in *N.T.*, 162, contrasting poetry and ballads, he compares
 'Musick with the vulgars chime'.
 *close*. Conclusion of a musical phrase, continuing the ballad comparison; cf. the
 prisoners' drinking-song in W. Cartwright's *The Royal Slave* (1636), I.i, 19:
 'And make our hard Irons cry clinke in the Close'.

DAUPHINE

Ay, 'tis Seneca. 40

CLERIMONT

No, I think 'tis Plutarch.

DAW

The dor on Plutarch, and Seneca, I hate it: they are mine own imaginations, by that light. I wonder those fellows have such credit with gentlemen!

CLERIMONT

They are very grave authors. 45

DAW

Grave asses! Mere essayists! A few loose sentences, and that's all. A man would talk so his whole age; I do utter as good things every hour, if they were collected and observed, as either of 'em.

DAUPHINE

Indeed, Sir John! 50

CLERIMONT

He must needs, living among the Wits and Braveries too.

DAUPHINE

Ay, and being president of 'em as he is.

DAW

There's Aristotle, a mere commonplace fellow; Plato, a discourser; Thucydides and Livy, tedious and dry;

43 *imaginations* inventions
  *by that light* variant of 'By God's light' (cf. "Slight', 1. 6)
45 *grave* weighty (Latin *gravis*)
46 *sentences* maxims (Latin *sententiae*)
53 *There's* F corr. (There is F uncorr.)
  *commonplace fellow* ed. (common place-fellow F)

40–1 *Seneca ... Plutarch.* Whose essays were regarded as storehouses of moral wisdom. Part of the joke lies in the suggestion that the poem is prosaic enough to be mistaken for a prose essay (Partridge).
42 *The dor on.* I scoff at, a set phrase. An audience could also understand *daw*, as though Daw were using his own name as a term of abuse.
46 *essayists.* Jonson himself voices a low opinion of modern essayists, 'even their Master *Mountaigne*', in *Disc.*, 719ff. Punning on 'asses'.
53–6 As Partridge notes, Daw's comments have an appositeness of which he is unaware. Aristotle, whom Jonson hails in *Disc.*, 2569, as one who 'understood the Causes of things', could be accurately described as the great philosopher of the 'common place' (Latin *locus communis*), the universal truth; Plato wrote dialogues which exemplified the art of learning through discourse; 'tedious' is close in sound to 'Thucydides'; 'Livy' suggests 'livid' (Latin *liveo*), the colour of melancholy, the 'dry' humour; *tacitus* in Latin means 'secret, hidden', which goes well with 'knot' in the sense at II.ii, 116.

Tacitus, an entire knot, sometimes worth the untying,   55
very seldom.

CLERIMONT

What do you think of the poets, Sir John?

DAW

Not worthy to be named for authors. Homer, an old,
tedious, prolix ass, talks of curriers and chines of beef;
Virgil, of dunging of land and bees; Horace, of I know not   60
what.

CLERIMONT

I think so.

DAW

And so Pindarus, Lycophron, Anacreon, Catullus, Seneca
the tragedian, Lucan, Propertius, Tibullus, Martial,
Juvenal, Ausonius, Statius, Politian, Valerius Flaccus,   65
and the rest—

CLERIMONT

What a sackful of their names he has got!

DAUPHINE

And how he pours 'em out! Politian with Valerius Flaccus!

CLERIMONT

Was not the character right of him?

DAUPHINE

As could be made, i' faith.   70

DAW

And Persius, a crabbed coxcomb not to be endured.

DAUPHINE

Why, whom do you account for authors, Sir John Daw?

---

69 *character* character sketch (at I.ii, 65ff.)

---

59 *curriers and chines*. Groomers of horses and backbones (because horses figure
prominently in *The Iliad*, and at VII, 321 Agamemnon gives Ajax 'the whole
length of the chine' of an ox). Daw's slack syntax also permits the senses
'groomers of cattle' and 'makers of beef curry'.

60 *dunging ... bees*. In *Georgics*, I, 79–81 and IV respectively; there are also some
famous similes concerning bees in the *Aeneid*. More ambiguous syntax.

60–1 *of ... what*. Appropriately, in view of Jonson's description of Horace as 'the
best master, both of vertue, and wisdome' (*Disc.*, 2592).

63–5 A chaotic jumble of major, minor, and very obscure classical poets, with an
Italian humanist, Politian (Angelo Poliziano, 1454–94), absurdly included.
'Seneca the tragedian' implies that Daw thinks this writer is different from the
Seneca of ll. 40–4.

67–70 Probably spoken ironically in Daw's hearing.

DAW

Syntagma juris civilis, Corpus juris civilis, Corpus juris canonici, the King of Spain's Bible.

DAUPHINE

Is the King of Spain's Bible an author?	75

CLERIMONT

Yes, and Syntagma.

DAUPHINE

What was that Syntagma, sir?

DAW

A civil lawyer, a Spaniard.

DAUPHINE

Sure, Corpus was a Dutchman.

CLERIMONT

Ay, both the Corpuses, I knew 'em: they were very cor-	80
pulent authors.

DAW

And then there's Vatablus, Pomponatius, Symancha; the
other are not to be received within the thought of a scholar.

DAUPHINE

'Fore God, you have a simple learned servant, lady, in
titles.	85

CLERIMONT

I wonder that he is not called to the helm and made a
councillor!

DAUPHINE

He is one extraordinary.

CLERIMONT

Nay, but in ordinary! To say truth, the state wants such.

DAUPHINE

Why, that will follow.	90

77 *What* who
84 *simple* purely, absolutely (with an ironic pun)
88 *extraordinary* outside the regular staff (with an ironic pun)
89 *in ordinary* full-time, belonging to the regular staff
   *wants* requires, punning ironically on 'lacks'

73–4 *Syntagma ... Bible.* Titles which Daw has seen on the spines of books and
mistaken for names of authors. The first two are the same book, the standard
collection of Roman law, since *syntagma* is Greek for *corpus*; the third is the
collection of canon law, the fourth the polyglot Bible sponsored by Philip II,
known as the *Biblia Regia*.
79 *Dutchman.* The English thought of the Dutch as chronically fat, due to a diet
largely composed of butter and alcohol.
82 *Vatablus, Pomponatius, Symancha.* Minor 16th-century continental scholars.

CLERIMONT

I muse a mistress can be so silent to the dotes of such a
servant.

DAW

'Tis her virtue, sir. I have written somewhat of her silence
too.

DAUPHINE

In verse, Sir John?    95

CLERIMONT

What else?

DAUPHINE

Why, how can you justify your own being of a poet, that so
slight all the old poets?

DAW

Why, every man that writes in verse is not a poet; you have
of the Wits that write verses and yet are no poets: they are    100
poets that live by it, the poor fellows that live by it.

DAUPHINE

Why, would not you live by your verses, Sir John?

CLERIMONT

No, 'twere pity he should. A knight live by his verses? He
did not make 'em to that end, I hope.

DAUPHINE

And yet the noble Sidney lives by his, and the noble family    105
not ashamed.

CLERIMONT

Ay, he professed himself; but Sir John Daw has more
caution: he'll not hinder his own rising i' the state so much!
Do you think he will? Your verses, good Sir John, and no
poems.    110

---

91 *dotes* natural gifts, endowments (Latin *dotes*), glancing at *dote*, 'to act stupidly'
107 *professed* openly declared

---

99–101 *every . . . it*. Daw is making a standard distinction between two sorts of poet,
the professional, such as Spenser, Drayton, and Jonson himself, who made a
living from his pen by having his work printed, and the gentleman amateur,
such as Sidney or Greville, who wrote for a small circle of friends and shunned
print as socially lowering. However, Daw fogs the issue by combining with it
his own topsy-turvy distinction between the poet and the verser. For Daw,
who, like Hedon in *C.R.*, II.i, 48–9, regards himself as 'a rimer, and thats a
thought better then a poet', 'poets' are contemptible fellows who get a living
from their work, whereas those who just write verse are your true wits.
105 *lives by*. Sidney had died in 1586, and his work had been published, with his
family's permission, during the 1590s.

DAW

> 'Silence in woman is like speech in man,
> Deny't who can.'

DAUPHINE

Not I, believe it; your reason, sir.

DAW

> 'Nor is't a tale
> That female vice should be a virtue male,                    115
> Or masculine vice, a female virtue be:
> You shall it see
> Proved with increase,
> I know to speak, and she to hold her peace.'

Do you conceive me, gentlemen?                                 120

DAUPHINE

No, faith; how mean you 'with increase', Sir John?

DAW

Why, 'with increase' is when I court her for the common cause of mankind, and she says nothing, but *consentire videtur*, and in time is *gravida*.

DAUPHINE

Then this is a ballad of procreation?                          125

CLERIMONT

A madrigal of procreation; you mistake.

EPICOENE

Pray give me my verses again, servant.

DAW

If you'll ask 'em aloud, you shall.

> [*Walks apart with* EPICOENE]

CLERIMONT

See, here's Truewit again!

114 s.p. DAW ed. (DAV. F)
123–4 *consentire videtur* she seems to consent
124 *gravida* pregnant
128 *you'll* ed. (you you'll F)

---

114–20 *tale ... peace ... conceive*. Unconscious sexual puns.
125 *ballad*. Jonson, like many of his literary contemporaries, detested 'th' abortive, and extemporall dinne/Of balladrie' (*N.T.*, 163–4).

## Act II, Scene iv

[*Enter*] TRUEWIT [*with his post-horn*]

CLERIMONT

Where hast thou been, in the name of madness, thus
accoutred with thy horn?

TRUEWIT

Where the sound of it might have pierced your senses with
gladness had you been in ear-reach of it. Dauphine, fall
down and worship me: I have forbid the banns, lad. I have          5
been with thy virtuous uncle and have broke the match.

DAUPHINE

You ha' not, I hope.

TRUEWIT

Yes, faith; and thou shouldst hope otherwise, I should
repent me. This horn got me entrance, kiss it. I had no
other way to get in but by feigning to be a post; but when I        10
got in once, I proved none, but rather the contrary, turned
him into a post or a stone or what is stiffer, with thund'ring
into him the incommodities of a wife and the miseries of
marriage. If ever Gorgon were seen in the shape of a
woman, he hath seen her in my description. I have put him           15
off o' that scent forever. Why do you not applaud and adore
me, sirs? Why stand you mute? Are you stupid? You are
not worthy o' the benefit.

DAUPHINE

Did not I tell you? mischief!—

CLERIMONT

I would you had placed this benefit somewhere else.                 20

TRUEWIT

Why so?

CLERIMONT

'Slight, you have done the most inconsiderate, rash, weak
thing that ever man did to his friend.

DAUPHINE

Friend! If the most malicious enemy I have had studied to
inflict an injury upon me, it could not be a greater.               25

2 *accoutred* equipped
5 *forbid the banns* made a formal objection to the intended marriage
13 *incommodities* hurtful disadvantages
17 *stupid* stupefied (Latin *stupidus*), glancing also at the current sense

14 *Gorgon*. One of the three female monsters of classical legend; anyone who met
their gaze was turned to stone.

TRUEWIT

Wherein, for God's sake? Gentlemen, come to yourselves again.

DAUPHINE

But I presaged thus much afore to you.

CLERIMONT

Would my lips had been soldered when I spake on't. 'Slight, what moved you to be thus impertinent?                30

TRUEWIT

My masters, do not put on this strange face to pay my courtesy; off with this visor. Have good turns done you and thank 'em this way?

DAUPHINE

'Fore heav'n, you have undone me. That which I have plotted for and been maturing now these four months, you      35 have blasted in a minute. Now I am lost, I may speak. This gentlewoman was lodged here by me o' purpose, and, to be put upon my uncle, hath professed this obstinate silence for my sake, being my entire friend, and one that for the requital of such a fortune as to marry him, would have       40 made me very ample conditions; where now all my hopes are utterly miscarried by this unlucky accident.

CLERIMONT

Thus 'tis when a man will be ignorantly officious, do services and not know his why. I wonder what courteous itch possessed you! You never did absurder part i' your    45 life, nor a greater trespass to friendship, to humanity.

DAUPHINE

Faith, you may forgive it best; 'twas your cause principally.

CLERIMONT

I know it; would it had not.

[*Enter* CUTBEARD]

DAUPHINE

How now, Cutbeard, what news?                                 50

28 *presaged* gave warning of (see I.iii, 1–9)
38 *put upon* combining two senses: to trick, by being imposed upon him
39–40 *for … him* in return for the fortune she would gain by marrying him
41 *conditions* provisions, settlement
45 *did* played      47 *your cause* i.e. your fault

34–6 *That … minute.* The metaphor is provided by *plot* = 'plot out land', as in Marvell's 'An Horatian Ode', 31.
36 *Now … speak.* 'Give losers leave to speak' (Tilley, L458).

CUTBEARD

The best, the happiest that ever was, sir. There has been a
mad gentleman with your uncle this morning—[*seeing*
TRUEWIT] I think this be the gentleman—that has almost
talked him out of his wits with threat'ning him from mar-
riage—							55

DAUPHINE

On, I pray thee.

CUTBEARD

And your uncle, sir, he thinks 'twas done by your pro-
curement; therefore he will see the party you wot of
presently, and if he like her, he says, and that she be so
inclining to dumb as I have told him, he swears he will		60
marry her today, instantly, and not defer it a minute
longer.

DAUPHINE

Excellent! Beyond our expectation!

TRUEWIT

Beyond your expectation? By this light, I knew it would be
thus.							65

DAUPHINE

Nay, sweet Truewit, forgive me.

TRUEWIT

No, I was 'ignorantly officious, impertinent'; this was the
'absurd, weak part.'

CLERIMONT

Wilt thou ascribe that to merit now, was mere fortune?

TRUEWIT

Fortune? Mere providence. Fortune had not a finger in't. I	70
saw it must necessarily in nature fall out so: my genius is
never false to me in these things. Show me how it could be
otherwise.

DAUPHINE

Nay, gentlemen, contend not; 'tis well now.

TRUEWIT

Alas, I let him go on with 'inconsiderate', and 'rash', and	75
what he pleased.

58 *wot* know
59 *presently* immediately
60 *dumb* dumbness (a common idiom)
69 *was* which was
70 *Mere* nothing short of, sheer
   *providence* foreknowledge
71 *genius* attendant spirit

CLERIMONT

Away, thou strange justifier of thyself, to be wiser than
thou wert by the event.

TRUEWIT

Event! By this light, thou shalt never persuade me but I
foresaw it as well as the stars themselves.                    80

DAUPHINE

Nay, gentlemen, 'tis well now. Do you two entertain Sir
John Daw with discourse while I send her away with
instructions.

TRUEWIT

I'll be acquainted with her first, by your favour.
                              [*They approach* EPICOENE *and* DAW]

CLERIMONT

Master Truewit, lady, a friend of ours.                    85

TRUEWIT

I am sorry I have not known you sooner, lady, to celebrate
this rare virtue of your silence.

CLERIMONT

Faith, an' you had come sooner, you should ha' seen and
heard her well celebrated in Sir John Daw's madrigals.
                    [*Exeunt* DAUPHINE, EPICOENE, *and* CUTBEARD]

TRUEWIT

Jack Daw, God save you, when saw you La Foole?                    90

DAW

Not since last night, Master Truewit.

TRUEWIT

That's miracle! I thought you two had been inseparable.

DAW

He's gone to invite his guests.

TRUEWIT

Gods so, 'tis true! What a false memory have I towards that
man! I am one: I met him e'en now upon that he calls his                    95
delicate fine black horse, rid into a foam with posting from
place to place and person to person to give 'em the cue—

CLERIMONT

Lest they should forget?

TRUEWIT

Yes; there was never poor captain took more pains at a
muster to show men than he at this meal to show friends.                    100

78 *event* outcome
87 *rare* (i) excellent; (ii) very uncommon     96 *delicate* exquisite

99 *poor*. The corruptness of officers' recruiting methods at this time, for motives of
profit, was notorious.

DAW

It is his quarter-feast, sir.

CLERIMONT

What, do you say so, Sir John?

TRUEWIT

Nay, Jack Daw will not be out, at the best friends he has, to
the talent of his wit. Where's his mistress, to hear and
applaud him? Is she gone?                                    105

DAW

Is Mistress Epicoene gone?

CLERIMONT

Gone afore with Sir Dauphine, I warrant, to the place.

TRUEWIT

Gone afore! That were a manifest injury, a disgrace and a
half, to refuse him at such a festival time as this, being a
Bravery and a Wit too.                                       110

CLERIMONT

Tut, he'll swallow it like cream: he's better read in *jure
civili* than to esteem anything a disgrace is offered him
from a mistress.

DAW

Nay, let her e'en go; she shall sit alone and be dumb in her
chamber a week together, for Sir John Daw, I warrant her.    115
Does she refuse me?

CLERIMONT

No, sir, do not take it so to heart: she does not refuse you,
but a little neglect you. Good faith, Truewit, you were too
blame to put it into his head that she does refuse him.

TRUEWIT

She does refuse him, sir, palpably, however you mince it.    120
An' I were as he, I would swear to speak ne'er a word to her
today for't.

DAW

By this light, no more I will not.

TRUEWIT

Nor to anybody else, sir.

115 *for* as far as . . . is concerned
120 *mince* make light of

---

101 *quarter-feast*. Daw's sarcastic coinage from *quarter-day*, one of the four days of
the year on which rents fall due; cf. I.iv, 61ff.

103–4 *out . . . wit*. 'he wil sooner lose his best friend, then his least jest' (*Poet.*,
IV.iii, 110–11).

111–12 *jure civili*. Civil law, one of Daw's 'authors' at II.iii, 73.

118–19 *too blame*. The phrase was commonly understood as adverb plus adjective.

DAW

Nay, I will not say so, gentlemen.                               125

CLERIMONT

It had been an excellent happy condition for the company
if you could have drawn him to it.

DAW

I'll be very melancholic, i' faith.

CLERIMONT

As a dog, if I were as you, Sir John.

TRUEWIT

Or a snail or a hog-louse: I would roll myself up for this    130
day; in troth, they should not unwind me.

DAW

By this picktooth, so I will.

CLERIMONT

'Tis well done: he begins already to be angry with his teeth.

DAW

Will you go, gentlemen?

CLERIMONT

Nay, you must walk alone if you be right melancholic, Sir    135
John.

TRUEWIT

Yes, sir, we'll dog you, we'll follow you afar off.

                                                    [*Exit* DAW]

CLERIMONT

Was there ever such a two yards of knighthood, measured
out by time, to be sold to laughter?

TRUEWIT

A mere talking mole! Hang him, no mushroom was ever so     140

126 *condition* (i) item in an agreement; (ii) state
130 *hog-louse* wood-louse
131 *day; in troth*, ed. (day, introth, F)
137 *dog* follow, covertly implying 'hound, torment'
140 *mere* absolute

---

126–7, 133 Spoken ironically in Daw's hearing.
129 *dog*. Using the proverb 'As melancholy as a dog' (Tilley, D438) to screen the
   common term of abuse; cf. IV.ii, 5–6.
132 *picktooth*. Toothpick, a mark of the affected gallant; Fastidious Brisk, the
   fashion-fixated courtier of *E.M.O.*, has a case-full (IV.i, 39).
133 *teeth*. Glancing at the proverb 'Good that the teeth guard the tongue' (Tilley,
   T424).
140 *mole*. Cf. 'As blind as a mole' (Tilley, M1034).
   *mushroom*. Cf. 'these mushrompe gentlemen,/That shoot up in a night to place,
   and worship' (*E.M.O.*, I.ii, 162–3). Jonson often likens social climbers to
   fungi; cf. *Cat.*, II, 136, and the character Fungoso in *E.M.O.*

fresh. A fellow so utterly nothing, as he knows not what he
would be.

CLERIMONT

Let's follow him, but first let's go to Dauphine; he's hov-
ering about the house to hear what news.

TRUEWIT

Content.                                              [*Exeunt*]  145

## Act II, Scene v

[*Enter*] MOROSE, EPICOENE, CUTBEARD, MUTE

MOROSE

Welcome, Cutbeard; draw near with your fair charge, and
in her ear softly entreat her to unmask. [CUTBEARD *whispers
to* EPICOENE, *who removes her mask*] So. Is the door shut? —
[MUTE *makes a leg*] Enough. Now, Cutbeard, with the same
discipline I use to my family, I will question you. As I           5
conceive, Cutbeard, this gentlewoman is she you have
provided and brought, in hope she will fit me in the place
and person of a wife? Answer me not but with your leg,
unless it be otherwise.—Very well done, Cutbeard. I conceive besides, Cutbeard, you have been pre-acquainted           10
with her birth, education, and qualities, or else you would
not prefer her to my acceptance, in the weighty consequence of marriage.—This I conceive, Cutbeard. Answer
me not but with your leg, unless it be otherwise. — Very
well done, Cutbeard. Give aside now a little, and leave me       15
to examine her condition and aptitude to my affection. (*He
goes about her and views her*) She is exceeding fair and of a
special good favour; a sweet composition or harmony of
limbs; her temper of beauty has the true height of my
blood. The knave hath exceedingly well fitted me without:       20
I will now try her within.—Come near, fair gentlewoman;
let not my behaviour seem rude, though unto you, being

1 *your* ed. (you F)
5 *family* household servants (Latin *familia*)
12 *prefer* recommend
18 *favour* comeliness, beauty

19–20 *her . . . blood.* A roundabout, and distinctly unpassionate way of saying 'her
  beauty is of exactly the sort which excites my passion'.
21 *try her within.* Morose's courtly idiom is continually slipping unconsciously into
  crude sexual innuendo; cf. ll. 28–9, 65–6.

rare, it may haply appear strange. (*She curtsies*) Nay, lady,
you may speak, though Cutbeard and my man might not:
for of all sounds only the sweet voice of a fair lady has the          25
just length of mine ears. I beseech you, say, lady; out of the
first fire of meeting eyes, they say, love is stricken: do you
feel any such motion suddenly shot into you from any part
you see in me? Ha, lady? (*Curtsy*) Alas, lady, these answers
by silent curtsies from you are too courtless and simple. I          30
have ever had my breeding in court, and she that shall be
my wife must be accomplished with courtly and audacious
ornaments. Can you speak, lady?

EPICOENE

Judge you, forsooth.                              *She speaks softly*

MOROSE

What say you, lady? Speak out, I beseech you.                       35

EPICOENE

Judge you, forsooth.

MOROSE

O' my judgement, a divine softness! But can you naturally,
lady, as I enjoin these by doctrine and industry, refer
yourself to the search of my judgement and, not taking
pleasure in your tongue, which is a woman's chiefest          40
pleasure, think it plausible to answer me by silent gestures,
so long as my speeches jump right with what you conceive?
(*Curtsy*) Excellent! Divine! If it were possible she should
hold out thus! Peace, Cutbeard, thou art made forever, as
thou hast made me, if this felicity have lasting; but I will          45
try her further. Dear lady, I am courtly, I tell you, and I
must have mine ears banqueted with pleasant and witty
conferences, pretty girds, scoffs, and dalliance in her that I
mean to choose for my bed-fere. The ladies in court think it

23  *rare* of uncommon excellence
     *haply* perhaps
30  *courtless* affectedly for 'uncourtly' (*OED*'s only example)
38  *these* Cutbeard and Mute
     *doctrine* instruction
41  *plausible* pleasantly acceptable
42  *jump right* agree
48  *girds* gibes
49  *bed-fere* bedfellow

---

32  *audacious*. 'Spirited, confident', but suggesting inadvertently 'shameless, bra-
    zen'.
37  *softness*. Cf. *King Lear*, V.iii, 273–4: 'Her voice was ever soft,/Gentle, and low,
    an excellent thing in woman'.

a most desperate impair to their quickness of wit and good    50
carriage if they cannot give occasion for a man to court 'em,
and when an amorous discourse is set on foot, minister as
good matter to continue it as himself; and do you alone so
much differ from all them that what they, with so much
circumstance, affect and toil for, to seem learned, to seem    55
judicious, to seem sharp and conceited, you can bury in
yourself with silence, and rather trust your graces to the
fair conscience of virtue than to the world's or your own
proclamation?

EPICOENE

I should be sorry else.    60

MOROSE

What say you, lady? Good lady, speak out.

EPICOENE

I should be sorry, else.

MOROSE

That sorrow doth fill me with gladness! Oh, Morose, thou
art happy above mankind! Pray that thou mayst contain
thyself. I will only put her to it once more, and it shall be    65
with the utmost touch and test of their sex. — But hear me,
fair lady; I do also love to see her whom I shall choose for
my heifer to be the first and principal in all fashions,
precede all the dames at court by a fortnight, have her
council of tailors, lineners, lace-women, embroiderers,    70
and sit with 'em sometimes twice a day upon French
intelligences, and then come forth varied like Nature, or

50 *impair* impairment, injury
51 *carriage* demeanour
52 *minister* supply
55 *circumstance* ceremony, to do
   *affect* aim at
56 *conceited* witty
58 *conscience* inward knowledge    64 *happy* fortunate
66 *touch* trial    70 *lineners* linen-drapers

---

68 *heifer*. A young cow that has not had a calf, hence 'yoke-mate, bride'. *OED*'s only
   example, apart from the proverb 'To plow with another's heifer' (Tilley, H395).

71–2 *French intelligences*. i.e. news of the latest fashions. Fitzdottrel in *D. is A.*
   wishes to be rich enough to allow his wife 'to sit with your foure women/In
   councell, and receive intelligences,/From forraigne parts, to dress you at all
   pieces' (II.vii, 35–7).

72–4 *and . . . servant*. Sir Epicure Mammon really desires this transformation for
   Dol: 'thou shalt ha' thy wardrobe,/Richer then *Natures*, still, to change thy
   selfe,/And vary oftener, for thy pride, then shee:/Or *Art*, her wise, and almost-
   equall servant' (*Alch.*, IV.i, 166–9).

oft'ner than she, and better by the help of Art, her emulous
servant. This do I affect. And how will you be able, lady,
with this frugality of speech, to give the manifold, but 75
necessary, instructions for that bodice, these sleeves, those
skirts, this cut, that stitch, this embroidery, that lace, this
wire, those knots, that ruff, those roses, this girdle, that
fan, the tother scarf, these gloves? Ha? What say you, lady?

EPICOENE

I'll leave it to you, sir. 80

MOROSE

How, lady? Pray you, rise a note.

EPICOENE

I leave it to wisdom and you, sir.

MOROSE

Admirable creature! I will trouble you no more; I will not
sin against so sweet a simplicity. Let me now be bold to
print on those divine lips the seal of being mine. [*Kisses* 85
*her*] Cutbeard, I give thee the lease of thy house free; thank
me not, but with thy leg. — I know what thou wouldst say,
she's poor and her friends deceased: she has brought a
wealthy dowry in her silence, Cutbeard, and in respect of
her poverty, Cutbeard, I shall have her more loving and 90
obedient, Cutbeard. Go thy ways and get me a minister
presently, with a soft, low voice, to marry us, and pray him
he will not be impertinent, but brief as he can; away;
softly, Cutbeard. [*Exit* CUTBEARD] Sirrah, conduct your
mistress into the dining room, your now-mistress. [*Exeunt* 95
MUTE *and* EPICOENE] Oh my felicity! How I shall be
revenged on mine insolent kinsman and his plots to fright
me from marrying! This night I will get an heir and thrust
him out of my blood like a stranger. He would be knighted,
forsooth, and thought by that means to reign over me, his 100
title must do it: no, kinsman, I will now make you bring me
the tenth lord's and the sixteenth lady's letter, kinsman,
and it shall do you no good, kinsman. Your knighthood
itself shall come on its knees, and it shall be rejected; it

---

74 *affect* love
77 *cut* ornamental slash in a garment exposing the lining
78 *wire* frame of wire to support the hair or the ruff
   *roses* shoe-roses; see II.ii, 64
   *girdle* belt
92 *presently* at once
93 *impertinent* irrelevant
102 *letter* i.e. letter of commendation, character reference

shall be sued for its fees to execution, and not be redeemed;  105
it shall cheat at the twelvepenny ordinary, it knighthood,
for its diet all the term time, and tell tales for it in the
vacation, to the hostess; or it knighthood shall do worse,
take sanctuary in Coleharbour, and fast. It shall fright all it
friends with borrowing letters, and when one of the four-  110
score hath brought it knighthood ten shillings, it knighthood shall go to the Cranes or the Bear at the Bridge-foot
and be drunk in fear; it shall not have money to discharge
one tavern-reckoning, to invite the old creditors to forbear
it knighthood, or the new that should be, to trust it knight-  115
hood. It shall be the tenth name in the bond, to take up the
commodity of pipkins and stone jugs, and the part thereof
shall not furnish it knighthood forth for the attempting of a
baker's widow, a brown baker's widow. It shall give it
knighthood's name for a stallion to all gamesome citizens'  120
wives, and be refused, when the master of a dancing school
or—how do you call him?—the worst reveller in the town
is taken; it shall want clothes, and by reason of that, wit, to
fool to lawyers. It shall not have hope to repair itself by

---

105 *to execution* as far as execution of the writ of seizure of debtors' goods
107 *term time* see I.i, 47
110 *borrowing* i.e. begging
117 *pipkins* small earthenware pots

---

106 *twelvepenny ordinary*. One of the more expensive London eating-houses fre-
    quented by gallants, where gambling was common (hence 'cheat').
    *it*. Archaic form of *its*, *his*, used in talking to babies.
107 *tell tales*. 'The wife of the ordinarie gives him his diet, to maintaine her table in
    discourse' (*C.R.*, II.iii, 93–4).
109 *Coleharbour*. Or Coldharborough, a seedy maze of tenements on Upper
    Thames Street. 'In some obscure way it had acquired the right of sanctuary'
    (Sugden).
112 *Cranes . . . Bear*. The Three Cranes on Upper Thames Street and the Bear at
    the Southwark end of London Bridge, well-known taverns.
116–17 *tenth . . . jugs*. See I.iv, 65–7 and note. As tenth in the list of borrowers
    forced to accept their loan in the form of worthless goods, Dauphine could
    expect to receive only a small share ('part') of the cash when they were sold.
119 *brown*. (i) coarse and inferior bread; (ii) of (unfashionable) dark complexion,
    ill-favoured; cf. 'brown wench' in *Henry VIII*, III.ii, 295.
122 *how* (*How* F). F's capital and italics indicate a reference to Edmund Howes, the
    public chronicler. Jonson repeats the joke in *S.N.*, I.v, 32.
124 *fool to*. Probably 'play the fool in front of', as at IV.v, 12, with the idea of 'make
    up to', rather than 'deceive'.

Constantinople, Ireland, or Virginia; but the best and last   125
fortune to it knighthood shall be to make Dol Tearsheet or
Kate Common a lady, and so it knighthood may eat.

          [*Exit*]


### Act II, Scene vi

[*Enter*] TRUEWIT, DAUPHINE, CLERIMONT

TRUEWIT
Are you sure he is not gone by?
DAUPHINE
No, I stayed in the shop ever since.
CLERIMONT
But he may take the other end of the lane.
DAUPHINE
No, I told him I would be here at this end; I appointed him
hither.                                                            5
TRUEWIT
What a barbarian it is to stay then!

[*Enter* CUTBEARD]

DAUPHINE
Yonder he comes.
CLERIMONT
And his charge left behind him, which is a very good sign,
Dauphine.
DAUPHINE
How now, Cutbeard, succeeds it or no?                              10
CUTBEARD
Past imagination, sir, *omnia secunda*; you could not have
prayed to have had it so well. *Saltat senex*, as it is i' the
proverb; he does triumph in his felicity, admires the party!
He has given me the lease of my house too! And I am now
going for a silent minister to marry 'em, and away.               15

4 *appointed him hither* arranged to meet him here
6 *it* i.e. he

---

125 *Constantinople, Ireland, or Virginia.* Places where younger brothers, wastrels,
and criminals might go to rescue their fortunes or escape the law (Partridge).
126–7 *Dol Tearsheet or Kate Common.* Type names for whores; cf. Dol Tearsheet in
2 *Henry IV* and Dol Common in *Alch.*
6 *barbarian.* A bad pun on 'barber'.
11–12 *omnia secunda ... Saltat senex.* Roman proverb, here meant literally: 'All's
well, the old boy is cutting capers' (H&S).

TRUEWIT

'Slight, get one o' the silenced ministers; a zealous brother
would torment him purely.

CUTBEARD

*Cum privilegio*, sir.

DAUPHINE

Oh, by no means; let's do nothing to hinder it now; when
'tis done and finished, I am for you, for any device of        20
vexation.

CUTBEARD

And that shall be within this half hour, upon my dexterity,
gentlemen. Contrive what you can in the meantime, *bonis
avibus*.

                                                            [*Exit*]

CLERIMONT

How the slave doth Latin it!                                   25

TRUEWIT

It would be made a jest to posterity, sirs, this day's mirth, if
ye will.

CLERIMONT

Beshrew his heart that will not, I pronounce.

DAUPHINE

And for my part. What is't?

TRUEWIT

To translate all La Foole's company and his feast hither        30
today, to celebrate this bridal.

DAUPHINE

Ay, marry, but how will't be done?

TRUEWIT

I'll undertake the directing of all the lady guests thither,
and then the meat must follow.

---

17 *purely* (i) perfectly; (ii) in the true Puritan manner
18 *Cum privilegio* with authority
19 *now; when* ed. (now when F)
23–4 *bonis avibus* the omens being favourable
30 *translate* transfer
34 *meat* food

---

16 *silenced ministers*. Cf. II.ii, 76.
22 *upon my dexterity*. A suitable oath for a barber (H&S); see note to I.ii, 37.
25 *Latin it*. Lard his talk with scraps of Latin; no doubt a common affectation
among barbers at this time, since they were also surgeons; cf. Middleton's
Sweetball in *Anything for a Quiet Life*.

CLERIMONT

For God's sake, let's effect it; it will be an excellent comedy  35
of affliction, so many several noises.

DAUPHINE

But are they not at the other place already, think you?

TRUEWIT

I'll warrant you for the college-honours: one o' their faces
has not the priming colour laid on yet, nor the other her
smock sleeked.  40

CLERIMONT

Oh, but they'll rise earlier than ordinary to a feast.

TRUEWIT

Best go see and assure ourselves.

CLERIMONT

Who knows the house?

TRUEWIT

I'll lead you. Were you never there yet?

DAUPHINE

Not I.  45

CLERIMONT

Nor I.

TRUEWIT

Where ha' you lived then? Not know Tom Otter!

CLERIMONT

No. For God's sake, what is he?

TRUEWIT

An excellent animal, equal with your Daw or La Foole, if
not transcendent, and does Latin it as much as your  50
barber. He is his wife's subject; he calls her princess, and at
such times as these follows her up and down the house like
a page, with his hat off, partly for heat, partly for rever-
ence. At this instant he is marshalling of his bull, bear, and
horse.  55

DAUPHINE

What be those, in the name of Sphinx?

36 *several* different
37 *the other place* Otter's house
38 *I'll warrant you for* I can guarantee you about  40 *sleeked* smoothed

---

39 *priming*. As though painting a house. *OED*'s first example of *priming* applied to painting.

40 *smock*. Apart from the suggestion of female sexuality which this word often carries (cf. V.i, 48 and *Alch.*, V.iv, 126, where Dol is called a 'smock-rampant'), the point is that many layers of clothing would remain to go over the smock.

56 *Sphinx*. Who asked riddles.

TRUEWIT

Why, sir, he has been a great man at the Bear Garden in his
time, and from that subtle sport has ta'en the witty
denomination of his chief carousing cups. One he calls his
bull, another his bear, another his horse. And then he has　60
his lesser glasses, that he calls his deer and his ape, and
several degrees of 'em too, and never is well, nor thinks any
entertainment perfect, till these be brought out and set o'
the cupboard.

CLERIMONT

For God's love, we should miss this if we should not go!　65

TRUEWIT

Nay, he has a thousand things as good that will speak him
all day. He will rail on his wife, with certain commonplaces, behind her back, and to her face—

DAUPHINE

No more of him. Let's go see him, I petition you.

　　　　　　　　　　　　　　　　　　　　[*Exeunt*]

---

62 *degrees* sizes
　　*well* content
66 *speak* describe, reveal

---

57 *Bear Garden*. Next to Paris Garden on the Bankside, the centre for bull- and
　　bear-baiting; 'the sport was as popular as football is now' (Sugden).
59 *cups*. Their lids are in the shape of the animals' heads; cf. IV.ii, 125–6.

## Act III, Scene i

[*Enter*] OTTER, MISTRESS OTTER. TRUEWIT, CLERIMONT,
DAUPHINE [*presently follow, unobserved*]

OTTER

Nay, good princess, hear me *pauca verba*.

MISTRESS OTTER

By that light, I'll ha' you chained up with your bull-dogs
and bear-dogs, if you be not civil the sooner. I'll send you
to kennel, i' faith. You were best bait me with your bull,
bear, and horse! Never a time that the courtiers or col-        5
legiates come to the house, but you make it a Shrove
Tuesday! I would have you get your Whitsuntide velvet
cap and your staff i' your hand to entertain 'em; yes, in
troth, do.

OTTER

Not so, princess, neither, but under correction, sweet        10
princess, gi' me leave—these things I am known to the
courtiers by. It is reported to them for my humour, and
they receive it so, and do expect it. Tom Otter's bull, bear,
and horse is known all over England, in *rerum natura*.

MISTRESS OTTER

'Fore me, I will 'na-ture' 'em over to Paris Garden and        15
'na-ture' you thither too, if you pronounce 'em again. Is a
bear a fit beast, or a bull, to mix in society with great ladies?
Think i' your discretion, in any good polity?

4 *were best* had best
  *with* along with
10 *under correction* subject to correction (common expression of deference)
15 *'Fore me* before me, a common asseveration
18 *discretion* judgement
  *good polity* affectedly for 'well-run community' (*OED* has no example of this
  sense of *polity* before 1650)

---

1 *pauca verba*. Few words, a catch-phrase; appropriate to Otter, since it was 'the
  Benchers [=bar-fly's] phrase' (*E.M.I*, IV.ii, 40), meaning 'drink more, and talk
  less'.
6–7 *Shrove Tuesday*. See I.i, 153 and note.
7–8 *velvet cap*. Worn during holidays, such as Whitsun-week.
12 *humour*. Characteristic oddity, special trick of disposition; here an affectation of
  a humour, as Jonson distinguishes it in *E.M.O.*, Induction, 75ff.
14 *rerum natura*. The phrase often meant 'the universe, the world', but here a more
  literal sense seems intended: 'the natural order of things'.

OTTER

The horse then, good princess.

MISTRESS OTTER

Well, I am contented for the horse; they love to be well          20
horsed, I know. I love it myself.

OTTER

And it is a delicate fine horse this. *Poetarum Pegasus.*
Under correction, princess, Jupiter did turn himself into
a—*taurus*, or bull, under correction, good princess.

MISTRESS OTTER

By my integrity, I'll send you over to the Bankside, I'll         25
commit you to the master of the Garden, if I hear but a
syllable more. Must my house, or my roof, be polluted
with the scent of bears and bulls, when it is perfumed for
great ladies? Is this according to the instrument when I
married you? That I would be princess and reign in mine          30
own house, and you would be my subject and obey me?
What did you bring me, should make you thus peremptory? Do I allow you your half-crown a day to spend where
you will among your gamesters, to vex and torment me at
such times as these? Who gives you your maintenance, I           35
pray you? Who allows you your horse-meat and man's
meat? Your three suits of apparel a year? Your four pair of
stockings, one silk, three worsted? Your clean linen, your
bands and cuffs, when I can get you to wear 'em? 'Tis mar'l
you ha' 'em on now. Who graces you with courtiers or great        40
personages, to speak to you out of their coaches, and come
home to your house? Were you ever so much as looked
upon by a lord, or a lady, before I married you, but on the

29 *instrument* formal legal agreement
36 *horse-meat* horse-fodder
39 *bands* collars
   *mar'l* marvel

---

21 *horsed.* Glancing at the sexual senses of *ride* and *mount.*
22 *Poetarum Pegasus.* The poets' Pegasus. Cf. Jonson's poem on the Apollo Inn,
   12–14: 'Wine it is the Milk of Venus,/And the Poets' Horse accounted./Ply it,
   and you all are mounted' (H&S, VIII, 657).
23–4 *Jupiter . . . bull.* When he seduced Europa.
32–3 *peremptory.* Self-willed (*OED*, a., 3), and glancing at the legal term *peremptory challenge*, 'an objection without showing any cause' (a., 1).
37–8 *three suits . . . worsted.* This associates Otter with domestic servants, who were
   allowed this number of suits and wore worsted stockings; cf. *King Lear*, II.ii,
   17, III.iv, 135–6.

Easter or Whitsun holidays, and then out at the Banqueting House window, when Ned Whiting or George Stone    45
were at the stake?

TRUEWIT

[*Aside*] For God's sake, let's go stave her off him.

MISTRESS OTTER

Answer me to that. And did not I take you up from thence
in an old greasy buff-doublet, with points, and green vellet
sleeves out at the elbows? You forget this.    50

TRUEWIT

[*Aside*] She'll worry him, if we help not in time.

[*They come forward*]

MISTRESS OTTER

Oh, here are some o' the gallants! Go to, behave yourself
distinctly, and with good morality, or I protest, I'll take
away your exhibition.


## Act III, Scene ii

TRUEWIT

By your leave, fair Mistress Otter, I'll be bold to enter
these gentlemen in your acquaintance.

MISTRESS OTTER

It shall not be obnoxious of difficil, sir.

TRUEWIT

How does my noble captain? Is the bull, bear, and horse in
*rerum natura* still?    5

---

49  *buff-doublet* leather jerkin, as worn by common soldiers
    *points* laces
    *vellet* velvet
54  *exhibition* allowance
4–5  *in rerum natura* i.e. in existence

---

44–5  *Banqueting House*. At Whitehall. Bear-baiting, outside in the courtyard, was
      among the entertainments.
45  *Ned Whiting . . . George Stone*. Champion bears, the second particularly famous;
      he died in 1606, being baited before the King of Denmark.
47, 51  *stave her off . . . worry*. As in bear-baiting.
53  *distinctly . . . with good morality*. Affected phrases for 'well'; *distinctly* is a
      nonce-usage (Latin *distincte*) and this is *OED*'s first example of
      *morality* = 'moral conduct'.
3  *obnoxious or difficil*. Offensive or troublesome; 'Mrs. Otter's affectation of what
      she thinks is courtly idiom' (Partridge). *OED* does not give this sense of
      *obnoxious* before 1675, and *difficil* keeps close to Latin *difficilis*.

OTTER

Sir, *sic visum superis.*

MISTRESS OTTER

I would you would but intimate 'em, do. Go your ways in,
and get toasts and butter made for the woodcocks. That's a
fit province for you.

[*Exit* OTTER]

CLERIMONT

[*Aside to* TRUEWIT *and* DAUPHINE] Alas, what a tyranny is    10
this poor fellow married to!

TRUEWIT

Oh, but the sport will be anon, when we get him loose.

DAUPHINE

Dares he ever speak?

TRUEWIT

No Anabaptist ever railed with the like license: but mark
her language in the meantime, I beseech you.                   15

MISTRESS OTTER

Gentlemen, you are very aptly come. My cousin, Sir
Amorous, will be here briefly.

TRUEWIT

In good time, lady. Was not Sir John Daw here, to ask for
him and the company?

MISTRESS OTTER

I cannot assure you, Master Truewit. Here was a very        20
melancholy knight in a ruff, that demanded my subject for
somebody, a gentleman, I think.

CLERIMONT

Ay, that was he, lady.

MISTRESS OTTER

But he departed straight, I can resolve you.

---

6 *sic visum superis* as those above decree
14 *Anabaptist* here loosely for 'Puritan'
17 *briefly* soon
21 *my subject* Otter

---

7 *intimate.* Become intimate with, go and join (your animals). Another of Mistress
  Otter's coinages.
8–9 *get ... you.* The right way to serve woodcock, and 'fit' because a *toast and
  butter* was a milksop (cf. *1 Henry IV*, IV.ii, 21) and a *woodcock* a fool.
14 *license.* (i) lack of restraint; (ii) license to preach (denied the 'silenced brethren').
21 *in a ruff.* Suggests that Daw is sporting one of the very large ruffs fashionable
  among gallants.
24 *I ... you.* Often singled out by Jonson as an affected phrase; see H&S, IX, 317.

DAUPHINE

What an excellent choice phrase this lady expresses in!    25

TRUEWIT

Oh, sir, she is the only authentical courtier that is not
naturally bred one, in the city.

MISTRESS OTTER

You have taken that report upon trust, gentlemen.

TRUEWIT

No, I assure you, the court governs it so, lady, in your
behalf.                                                    30

MISTRESS OTTER

I am the servant of the court and courtiers, sir.

TRUEWIT

They are rather your idolaters.

MISTRESS OTTER

Not so, sir.

[*Enter* CUTBEARD. DAUPHINE, TRUEWIT and CLERIMONT
*converse with him apart*]

DAUPHINE

How now, Cutbeard? Any cross?

CUTBEARD

Oh, no, sir, *omnia bene*. 'Twas never better o' the hinges,    35
all's sure. I have so pleased him with a curate that he's gone
to't almost with the delight he hopes for soon.

DAUPHINE

What is he for a vicar?

CUTBEARD

One that has catched a cold, sir, and can scarce be heard six
inches off, as if he spoke out of a bulrush that were not    40
picked, or his throat were full of pith; a fine quick fellow
and an excellent barber of prayers. I came to tell you, sir,
that you might *omnem movere lapidem*, as they say, be ready
with your vexation.

DAUPHINE

Gramercy, honest Cutbeard; be thereabouts with thy key    45
to let us in.

26 *authentical* genuine (*OED*'s only example of this sense)
29 *governs* determines      34 *cross* hindrance
35 *omnia bene* all's well
  *o' the hinges* on the hinges, running smoothly
38 *What ... vicar* what sort of a vicar is he
40–1 *as ... picked* i.e. he has a thin reedy voice
43 *omnem movere lapidem* leave no stone unturned
45 *Gramercy* thanks

CUTBEARD

I will not fail you, sir: *ad manum*.                    [*Exit*]

TRUEWIT

Well, I'll go watch my coaches.

CLERIMONT

Do, and we'll send Daw to you if you meet him not.

[*Exit* TRUEWIT]

MISTRESS OTTER

Is Master Truewit gone?                                    50

DAUPHINE

Yes, lady, there is some unfortunate business fallen out.

MISTRESS OTTER

So I judged by the physiognomy of the fellow that came in,
and I had a dream last night too of the new pageant and my
Lady Mayoress, which is always very ominous to me. I told
it my Lady Haughty t'other day, when her honour came      55
hither to see some China stuffs, and she expounded it out
of Artemidorus, and I have found it since very true. It has
done me many affronts.

CLERIMONT

Your dream, lady?

MISTRESS OTTER

Yes, sir, anything I do but dream o' the city. It stained me a  60
damask table-cloth, cost me eighteen pound at one time,
and burnt me a black satin gown as I stood by the fire at my
Lady Centaure's chamber in the college another time. A
third time, at the lord's masque, it dropped all my wire and
my ruff with wax candle, that I could not go up to the      65
banquet. A fourth time, as I was taking coach to go to Ware
to meet a friend, it dashed me a new suit all over—a

47 *ad manum* (I'm) at hand
64 *lord's* ed. (Lords F)
    *wire* see II.v, 78

---

53 *pageant*. Entertainment marking the installation of the new Lord Mayor.
57 *Artemidorus*. Second-century Greek author of a treatise on the interpretation of
    dreams.
57, 60 *it*. Mistress Otter's confused pronoun references reveal the confusion of her
    mind (Partridge).
66 *Ware*. 20 miles north of London, a favourite spot for assignations; cf. V.i, 58.
    *Friend* is a common euphemism for 'lover'.

crimson satin doublet and black velvet skirts—with a
brewer's horse, that I was fain to go in and shift me, and
kept my chamber a leash of days for the anguish of it.     70

DAUPHINE

These were dire mischances, lady.

CLERIMONT

I would not dwell in the city, and 'twere so fatal to me.

MISTRESS OTTER

Yes, sir, but I do take advice of my doctor, to dream of it as
little as I can.

DAUPHINE

You do well, Mistress Otter.                        75

*[Enter* DAW; CLERIMONT *takes him aside]*

MISTRESS OTTER

Will it please you to enter the house farther, gentlemen?

DAUPHINE

And your favour, lady; but we stay to speak with a knight,
Sir John Daw, who is here come. We shall follow you,
lady.

MISTRESS OTTER

At your own time, sir. It is my cousin Sir Amorous his     80
feast—

DAUPHINE

I know it, lady.

MISTRESS OTTER

And mine together. But it is for his honour, and therefore I
take no name of it, more than of the place.

DAUPHINE

You are a bounteous kinswoman.                    85

MISTRESS OTTER

`Your servant, sir.                            *[Exit]*

---

69 *shift me* change my clothes
70 *leash* in hunting, a set of three
72 *fatal* ominous
84 *name* credit
     *the place* i.e. its taking place in my house

---

68 *crimson satin.* Fashionable and very expensive. Both the colour and the cloth
     were usually associated with the nobility; see M. C. Linthicum, *Costume in the*
     *Drama of Shakespeare and his Contemporaries*, Oxford, 1936, pp. 123, 151 n.4,
     198.
     *doublet.* Normally a man's garment.
80–1 *Amorous his feast.* Jonson calls this form of the genitive 'monstrous Syntaxe' in
     his *English Grammar* (H&S, VIII, 511).

## Act III, Scene iii

[CLERIMONT *comes forward with* DAW]

CLERIMONT

Why, do not you know it, Sir John Daw?

DAW

No, I am a rook if I do.

CLERIMONT

I'll tell you then: she's married by this time! And whereas
you were put i' the head that she was gone with Sir
Dauphine, I assure you Sir Dauphine has been the nob-        5
lest, honestest friend to you that ever gentleman of your
quality could boast of. He has discovered the whole plot,
and made your mistress so acknowledging and indeed so
ashamed of her injury to you, that she desires you to
forgive her, and but grace her wedding with your presence   10
today—she is to be married to a very good fortune, she
says, his uncle, old Morose; and she willed me in private to
tell you that she shall be able to do you more favours, and
with more security now than before.

DAW

Did she say so, i' faith?                                   15

CLERIMONT

Why, what do you think of me, Sir John? Ask Sir
Dauphine.

DAW

Nay, I believe you. Good Sir Dauphine, did she desire me
to forgive her?

DAUPHINE

I assure you, Sir John, she did.                            20

DAW

Nay, then, I do with all my heart, and I'll be jovial.

CLERIMONT

Yes, for look you, sir, this was the injury to you. La Foole
intended this feast to honour her bridal day, and made you

4 *put i' the head* made to think
18 s.p. DAW ed. (DAVP. F)
20 s.p. DAUPHINE ed. (CLE. F)

---

6–7 *of your quality*. Ambiguously implying 'someone like you deserves far worse'.
21 *jovial*. Italicized throughout F, probably to indicate Daw's affected use of a word
   only recently coined into English. Partridge suggests that the gallants take it up
   in ironic awareness of its astrological sense (lit. 'pertaining to Jupiter'), since
   Daw is the helplessly susceptible victim of their 'influence'.

the property to invite the college ladies and promise to
bring her; and then at the time she should have appeared,      25
as his friend, to have given you the dor. Whereas now, Sir
Dauphine has brought her to a feeling of it, with this kind
of satisfaction, that you shall bring all the ladies to the place
where she is, and be very jovial; and there she will have a
dinner which shall be in your name, and so disappoint La      30
Foole, to make you good again and, as it were, a saver i' the
man.

DAW

As I am a knight, I honour her and forgive her heartily.

CLERIMONT

About it then presently. Truewit is gone before to confront
the coaches, and to acquaint you with so much if he meet      35
you. Join with him, and 'tis well.

[*Enter* LA FOOLE]

See, here comes your antagonist, but take you no notice,
but be very jovial.

LA FOOLE

Are the ladies come, Sir John Daw, and your mistress?

[*Exit* DAW]

Sir Dauphine! You are exceeding welcome, and honest      40
Master Clerimont. Where's my cousin? Did you see no
collegiates, gentlemen?

DAUPHINE

Collegiates! Do you not hear, Sir Amorous, how you are
abused?

LA FOOLE

How, sir!      45

CLERIMONT

Will you speak so kindly to Sir John Daw, that has done
you such an affront?

24 *property* tool, mere means
27 *feeling of* sensitivity to
44 *abused* deceived

26 *the dor*. A snub; cf. II.iii, 42. Methods of 'giving the dor' in situations of sexual
 rivalry are elaborated in *C.R.*, V.ii.
31–2 *i' the man*. i.e. of your manhood; with a pun on *main* = (i) the main or overall
 consideration; (ii) the fixed score in the dice game of hazard, which if thrown by
 one player enables the others to be 'savers' (recoup their losses). Most editors
 emend to *main*, but Clerimont's preliminary 'as it were' indicates, as it still does
 today, that he is about to make precisely this kind of verbal joke.

LA FOOLE

Wherein, gentlemen? Let me be a suitor to you to know, I
beseech you!

CLERIMONT

Why, sir, his mistress is married today to Sir Dauphine's    50
uncle, your cousin's neighbour, and he has diverted all the
ladies and all your company thither, to frustrate your
provision and stick a disgrace upon you. He was here now
to have enticed us away from you too, but we told him his
own, I think.                                                55

LA FOOLE

Has Sir John Daw wronged me so inhumanly?

DAUPHINE

He has done it, Sir Amorous, most maliciously, and
treacherously; but if you'll be ruled by us, you shall quit
him, i' faith.

LA FOOLE

Good gentlemen, I'll make one, believe it! How, I pray?     60

DAUPHINE

Marry, sir, get me your pheasants, and your godwits, and
your best meat, and dish it in silver dishes of your cousin's
presently, and say nothing, but clap me a clean towel about
you, like a sewer, and bare-headed march afore it with a
good confidence—'tis but over the way, hard by—and       65
we'll second you, where you shall set it o' the board, and
bid 'em welcome to't, which shall show 'tis yours and
disgrace his preparation utterly; and for your cousin,
whereas she should be troubled here at home with care of
making and giving welcome, she shall transfer all that      70
labour thither and be a principal guest herself, sit ranked
with the college-honours, and be honoured, and have her
health drunk as often, as bare, and as loud as the best of
'em.

LA FOOLE

I'll go tell her presently. It shall be done, that's resolved.  75
                                                    [*Exit*]

53 *provision* preparations
54–5 *his own* his true character
58 *quit* repay
60 *make one* join in
64 *sewer* chief servant at a meal who superintended the seating and serving of guests

56 *inhumanly* (in-humanely F). The two words did not become separate until the
eighteenth century.
73 *bare.* Bare-headed, as a sign of respect; with a pun, reinforced by *loud*, on
'shamelessly'.

CLERIMONT

I thought he would not hear it out, but 'twould take him.

DAUPHINE

Well, there be guests and meat now; how shall we do for music?

CLERIMONT

The smell of the venison going through the street will invite one noise of fiddlers or other. 80

DAUPHINE

I would it would call the trumpeters thither.

CLERIMONT

Faith, there is hope; they have intelligence of all feasts. There's good correspondence betwixt them and the London cooks. 'Tis twenty to one but we have 'em.

DAUPHINE

'Twill be a most solemn day for my uncle, and an excellent 85 fit of mirth for us.

CLERIMONT

Ay, if we can hold up the emulation betwixt Foole and Daw, and never bring them to expostulate.

DAUPHINE

Tut, flatter 'em both, as Truewit says, and you may take their understandings in a purse-net. They'll believe them- 90 selves to be just such men as we make 'em, neither more nor less. They have nothing, not the use of their senses, but by tradition.

[LA FOOLE] *enters like a sewer*

CLERIMONT

See! Sir Amorous has his towel on already. Have you persuaded your cousin? 95

LA FOOLE

Yes, 'tis very feasible: she'll do anything, she says, rather than the La Fooles shall be disgraced.

DAUPHINE

She is a noble kinswoman. It will be such a pestling device,

80 *noise* band
85 *solemn* (i) ceremonious; (ii) gloomy
87 *emulation* ambitious rivalry
88 *expostulate* set forth their grievances to one another
90 *purse-net* bag-shaped net, the mouth of which can be drawn together with cords; used especially for catching rabbits
93 *tradition* i.e. handing over (Latin *traditio*)
s.d. [LA FOOLE] ed. (*He* F)
98 *pestling* crushing, as with a pestle

Sir Amorous! It will pound all your enemy's practices to
powder and blow him up with his own mine, his own train.    100

LA FOOLE

Nay, we'll give fire, I warrant you.

CLERIMONT

But you must carry it privately, without any noise, and
take no notice by any means—

[*Enter* OTTER]

OTTER

Gentlemen, my princess says you shall have all her silver
dishes, *festinate*; and she's gone to alter her tire a little and    105
go with you—

CLERIMONT

And yourself too, Captain Otter.

DAUPHINE

By any means, sir.

OTTER

Yes, sir, I do mean it; but I would entreat my cousin Sir
Amorous, and you gentlemen, to be suitors to my princess,    110
that I may carry my bull and my bear, as well as my horse.

CLERIMONT

That you shall do, Captain Otter.

LA FOOLE

My cousin will never consent, gentlemen.

DAUPHINE

She must consent, Sir Amorous, to reason.

LA FOOLE

Why, she says they are no decorum among ladies.        115

OTTER

But they are *decora*, and that's better, sir.

CLERIMONT

Ay, she must hear argument. Did not Pasiphae, who was a
queen, love a bull? And was not Callisto, the mother of

99 *practices* plots
100 *train* (i) line of gunpowder conveying fire to a mine; (ii) snare, trick
102 *carry* manage
105 *festinate* with despatch
    *tire* head-dress

---

116 *decora*. Beautiful; and 'better' also because, if La Foole's 'decorum' is taken as
    Latin, *decora* is the grammatically correct form.
117–18 *Pasiphae . . . bull*. Their offspring was the Minotaur.
118 *Callisto*. Loved by Jupiter and changed by Juno into a bear, and after her death
    into a constellation, *Ursa Major*, the Great Bear, by Jupiter; recounted in
    *Metamorphoses*, II, 401–507.

Arcas, turned into a bear and made a star, Mistress Ursula,
i' the heavens?                                                    120

OTTER

Oh God, that I could ha' said as much! I will have these
stories painted i' the Bear Garden, *ex Ovidii Metamorphosi*.

DAUPHINE

Where is your princess, captain? Pray'be our leader.

OTTER

That I shall, sir.

CLERIMONT

Make haste, good Sir Amorous.                   [*Exeunt*]  125


### Act III, Scene iv

[*Enter*] MOROSE, EPICOENE, PARSON, CUTBEARD

MOROSE

Sir, there's an angel for yourself, and a brace of angels for
your cold. Muse not at this manage of my bounty. It is fit
we should thank fortune double to nature, for any benefit
she confers upon us; besides, it is your imperfection, but
my solace.                                                          5

PARSON

I thank your worship, so is it mine now.

*The* PARSON *speaks as having a cold*

MOROSE

What says he, Cutbeard?

CUTBEARD

He says *praesto*, sir: whensoever your worship needs him,
he can be ready with the like. He got this cold with sitting
up late and singing catches with cloth-workers.          10

MOROSE

No more. I thank him.

1 *angel* gold coin worth at this time about ten shillings
2 *manage* management
3 *double to* twice as much as we do
8 *praesto* Latin for 'at your service'
10 *catches* part-songs for three or four, in which the second singer begins the first
   line as the first begins the second line, and so on

---

122 *ex . . . Metamorphosi*. Out of Ovid's *Metamorphoses*. The story of Pasiphae, who
   loved a real bull (not Jupiter; cf. III.i, 23–4), and was not transformed, is in
   fact told in Ovid's *Ars Amatoria*, I, 295–326.
10 *cloth-workers*. Who sang while they sat at their work. Many were Puritans, much
   given to hymn-singing; cf. *1 Henry IV*, II.iv, 133–4: 'I would I were a weaver,
   I could sing psalms, or anything'.

PARSON

    God keep your worship and give you much joy with your
    fair spouse. Umh, umh.                    *He coughs*

MOROSE

    Oh, oh! Stay, Cutbeard! Let him give me five shillings of
    my money back. As it is bounty to reward benefits, so is it   15
    equity to mulct injuries. I will have it. What says he?

CUTBEARD

    He cannot change it, sir.

MOROSE

    It must be changed.

CUTBEARD

    [*Aside to* PARSON] Cough again.

MOROSE

    What says he?                                  20

CUTBEARD

    He will cough out the rest, sir.

PARSON

    Umh, umh, umh.                      *[Coughs] again*

MOROSE

    Away, away with him, stop his mouth, away, I forgive it—
                          *[Exit* CUTBEARD *with* PARSON]

EPICOENE

    Fie, Master Morose, that you will use this violence to a
    man of the church.                              25

MOROSE

    How!

EPICOENE

    It does not become your gravity or breeding—as you
    pretend in court—to have offered this outrage on a water-
    man, or any more boist'rous creature, much less on a man
    of his civil coat.                             30

MOROSE

    You can speak then!

EPICOENE

    Yes, sir.

MOROSE

    Speak out, I mean.

15 *benefits* acts of kindness (an archaic use at this date)
16 *mulct* punish by a fine
28 *pretend* profess to have
30 *civil coat* sober profession

---

28–9 *waterman*. The Thames boatmen were notorious for their loud cries to attract
passengers.

EPICOENE

Ay, sir. Why, did you think you had married a statue? or a
motion only? one of the French puppets with the eyes      35
turned with a wire? or some innocent out of the hospital,
that would stand with her hands thus, and a plaice-mouth,
and look upon you?

MOROSE

Oh immodesty! A manifest woman! What, Cutbeard!

EPICOENE

Nay, never quarrel with Cutbeard, sir, it is too late now. I      40
confess it doth bate somewhat of the modesty I had, when I
writ simply maid; but I hope I shall make it a stock still
competent to the estate and dignity of your wife.

MOROSE

She can talk!

EPICOENE

Yes, indeed, sir.                                                45

MOROSE

What sirrah! None of my knaves there?

[*Enter* MUTE]

Where is this impostor, Cutbeard?      [MUTE *makes signs*]

EPICOENE

Speak to him, fellow, speak to him. I'll have none of this
coacted, unnatural dumbness in my house, in a family
where I govern.                                                  50

[*Exit* MUTE]

---

35 *motion* puppet
36 *innocent* half-wit
37 *plaice-mouth* small, puckered mouth, like the fish's
41 *it* her speaking out
   *bate* lessen
43 *competent* appropriate, sufficient
   *estate* status, rank
46 *knaves* servants
49 *coacted* enforced
   *family* household

---

36 *hospital*. Bethlehem Hospital (Bedlam), rather than Christ's.
37 *hands thus*. Loosely placed one over the other and hanging down limply in front,
   to indicate placid obedience, or idiocy. Beaurline compares Durer's drawings of
   a rustic couple and a Turkish woman (E. Panofsky, *The Life and Art of Albrecht
   Durer*, Princeton, 1955, plates 43, 256).
39 *A manifest woman*. As one might say, 'a manifest villain'.

MOROSE

She is my regent already! I have married a Penthesilea, a
Semiramis, sold my liberty to a distaff!

### Act III, Scene v

*[Enter]* TRUEWIT

TRUEWIT

Where's Master Morose?

MOROSE

Is he come again? Lord have mercy upon me!

TRUEWIT

I wish you all joy, Mistress Epicoene, with your grave and
honourable match.

EPICOENE

I return you the thanks, Master Truewit, so friendly a wish          5
deserves.

MOROSE

She has acquaintance too!

TRUEWIT

God save you, sir, and give you all contentment in your fair
choice here. Before I was the bird of night to you, the owl,
but now I am the messenger of peace, a dove, and bring          10
you the glad wishes of many friends, to the celebration of
this good hour.

MOROSE

What hour, sir?

TRUEWIT

Your marriage hour, sir. I commend your resolution, that,
notwithstanding all the dangers I laid afore you, in the          15
voice of a night-crow, would yet go on, and be yourself. It
shows you are a man constant to your own ends, and

---

3 *grave* (i) worthy of respect, dignified; (ii) sombre

---

51 *Penthesilea.* Amazon queen who fought against the Greeks at Troy; cf. III.v, 39.
52 *Semiramis.* Warrior queen of the Assyrians who after her husband's death
   disguised herself in men's clothes, in order to govern.
   *distaff.* The insignia of the sexes were the sword and the distaff; see *OED*, sb.,
   3.b.
 5 *return . . . thanks.* Probably the second of two kisses is exchanged here; *friendly*
   glances tauntingly at *friend* = 'lover'.
 9, 16 *owl . . . night-crow.* Conventional bearers of evil omen, the latter not denoting
   a specific bird.

upright to your purposes, that would not be put off with left-handed cries.

MOROSE

How should you arrive at the knowledge of so much?          20

TRUEWIT

Why, did you ever hope, sir, committing the secrecy of it to a barber, that less than the whole town should know it? You might as well ha' told it the conduit, or the bakehouse, or the infantry that follow the court, and with more security. Could your gravity forget so old and noted a          25
remnant as *lippis et tonsoribus notum*? Well, sir, forgive it yourself now, the fault, and be communicable with your friends. Here will be three or four fashionable ladies from the college to visit you presently, and their train of minions and followers.          30

MOROSE

Bar my doors! Bar my doors! Where are all my eaters, my mouths now?

[*Enter* SERVANTS]

Bar up my doors, you varlets!

EPICOENE

He is a varlet that stirs to such an office. Let 'em stand open. I would see him that dares move his eyes toward it.          35
Shall I have a barricado made against my friends, to be barred of any pleasure they can bring in to me with honourable visitation?

[*Exit* SERVANTS]

MOROSE

Oh Amazonian impudence!

---

27 *communicable* communicative
39 *impudence* shamelessness

---

19 *left-handed*. Ill-omened, sinister (*OED*'s first example). In Latin literature birds of ill omen conventionally cry on one's left.
23 *conduit* ... *bakehouse*. Centres of gossip, since people gathered there each morning to get water and bread.
24 *infantry* ... *court*. The 'Blacke guard' of *M.V.*, 86, i.e. the army of lower domestic servants employed by the court. *Follow* means literally 'follow' as well as 'serve', since these servants would bring up the rear on royal progresses.
25 *your gravity*. Truewit's mocking variation of 'your honour'.
26 *remnant*. Scrap of quotation. Jonson's coinage, in *E.M.I.*, III.iv, 75 (Quarto version).
   *lippis* ... *notum*. 'Known to the bleary-eyed [i.e. frequenters of apothecary shops] and to barbers'; a compression of Horace, *Satires*, I.vii, 3.

TRUEWIT

Nay, faith, in this, sir, she speaks but reason, and methinks     40
is more continent than you. Would you go to bed so
presently, sir, afore noon? A man of your head and hair
should owe more to that reverend ceremony, and not
mount the marriage-bed like a town bull or a mountain
goat, but stay the due season, and ascend it then with     45
religion and fear. Those delights are to be steeped in the
humour and silence of the night; and give the day to other
open pleasures and jollities of feast, of music, of revels, of
discourse: we'll have all, sir, that may make your hymen
high and happy.     50

MOROSE

Oh, my torment, my torment!

TRUEWIT

Nay, if you endure the first half hour, sir, so tediously, and
with this irksomeness, what comfort or hope can this fair
gentlewoman make to herself hereafter, in the consideration of so many years as are to come—     55

MOROSE

Of my affliction. Good sir, depart and let her do it alone.

TRUEWIT

I have done, sir.

MOROSE

That cursed barber!

TRUEWIT

Yes, faith, a cursed wretch indeed, sir.

MOROSE

I have married his cittern, that's common to all men. Some     60
plague above the plague—

TRUEWIT

All Egypt's ten plagues—

MOROSE

Revenge me on him.

42 *head and hair* judgement and character, glancing ironically at Morose's appear-
     ance
45 *stay* await
47 *humour* (i) moisture (cf. 'steeped'); (ii) inclination, fancy
49 *hymen* wedding
52 *tediously* (i) irritatedly; (ii) tiresomely (cf. IV.ii, 135)

---

60 *cittern*. Instrument like a lute kept in barbers' shops for customers to amuse
     themselves with.
62 *ten plagues*. Sent by God to persuade Pharaoh to release the Israelites (Exodus,
     vii-xii).

TRUEWIT

'Tis very well, sir. If you laid on a curse or two more, I'll
assure you he'll bear 'em. As, that he may get the pox with        65
seeking to cure it, sir? Or, that while he is curling another
man's hair, his own may drop off? Or, for burning some
male bawd's lock, he may have his brain beat out with the
curling-iron?

MOROSE

No, let the wretch live wretched. May he get the itch, and          70
his shop so lousy as no man dare come at him, nor he come
at no man.

TRUEWIT

Ay, and if he would swallow all his balls for pills, let not
them purge him.

MOROSE

Let his warming-pan be ever cold.                                   75

TRUEWIT

A perpetual frost underneath it, sir.

MOROSE

Let him never hope to see fire again.

TRUEWIT

But in hell, sir.

MOROSE

His chairs be always empty, his scissors rust, and his
combs mould in their cases.                                         80

TRUEWIT

Very dreadful that! And may he lose the invention, sir, of
carving lanterns in paper.

MOROSE

Let there be no bawd carted that year to employ a basin of
his, but let him be glad to eat his sponge for bread.

70 *the itch* contagious skin disease, scabies
73 *balls* of soap

---

66 *cure it*. At this date barbers were also surgeons.
68 *lock*. Love-lock, often large and ribanded.
76 *perpetual frost*. A reference to the Great Frost of 1608, when the Thames froze
for six weeks.
82 *lanterns in paper*. 'oild Lanterne-paper . . . every Barber . . . has it' (*T.T.*, V.ii,
31–2).
83 *basin*. Metal basins, hired from barbers, were beaten before sexual offenders as
they were carted through the streets (H&S, who quote a contemporary
account).

TRUEWIT

And drink lotium to it, and much good do him.                    85

MOROSE

Or, for want of bread—

TRUEWIT

Eat ear-wax, sir. I'll help you. Or, draw his own teeth and add them to the lute-string.

MOROSE

No, beat the old ones to powder and make bread of them.

TRUEWIT

Yes, make meal o' the millstones.                                 90

MOROSE

May all the botches and burns that he has cured on others break out upon him.

TRUEWIT

And he now forget the cure of 'em in himself, sir; or, if he do remember it, let him ha' scraped all his linen into lint for't, and have not a rag left him to set up with.        95

MOROSE

Let him never set up again, but have the gout in his hands forever. Now no more, sir.

TRUEWIT

Oh, that last was too high set! You might go less with him, i' faith, and be revenged enough; as, that he be never able to new-paint his pole—                                        100

MOROSE

Good sir, no more. I forgot myself.

TRUEWIT

Or, want credit to take up with a comb-maker—

MOROSE

No more, sir.

TRUEWIT

Or, having broken his glass in a former despair, fall now into a much greater, of ever getting another—             105

85 *lotium* stale urine used by barbers as hair-lotion
   *to* with
91 *botches* boils
95–6 *set up ... set up* set up business ... set hair
98 *set ... go less* the metaphor is from gambling
102 *want ... with* not to be able to obtain supplies on credit from

87 *ear-wax ... teeth.* Barbers cleaned ears and pulled teeth, which they hung on strings as a form of advertising.

MOROSE

I beseech you, no more.

TRUEWIT

Or, that he never be trusted with trimming of any but
chimney-sweepers—

MOROSE

Sir—

TRUEWIT

Or, may he cut a collier's throat with his razor by chance-   110
medley, and yet hang for't.

MOROSE

I will forgive him, rather than hear any more. I beseech
you, sir.

### Act III, Scene vi

[*Enter*] DAW, HAUGHTY, CENTAURE, MAVIS, TRUSTY

DAW

This way, madam.

MOROSE

Oh, the sea breaks in upon me! Another flood! An inunda-
tion! I shall be o'erwhelmed with noise. It beats already at
my shores. I feel an earthquake in myself for't.

DAW

[*Kissing* EPICOENE] 'Give you joy, mistress.                          5

MOROSE

Has she servants too!

DAW

I have brought some ladies here to see and know you.
                    *She kisses them severally as he presents them*
My Lady Haughty, this my Lady Centaure, Mistress Dol
Mavis, Mistress Trusty, my Lady Haughty's woman.
Where's your husband? Let's see him: can he endure no    10
noise? Let me come to him.

110–11 *chance-medley* homicide by misadventure
7 s.d. *severally* each in turn

---

108 *chimney-sweepers*. With colliers, the least desirable customers, because likely to
  be the dirtiest.
110 *collier*. Colliers (coalmen) were proverbially dishonest.
  2 *Another flood*. Possibly *another* with regard to the flood of words released in the
  last two scenes, but Morose's tendency to dramatize his afflictions by means of
  classical and other references suggests that *another* may mean 'second', the first
  being the flood of Genesis, vii.

MOROSE

What nomenclator is this!

TRUEWIT

Sir John Daw, sir, your wife's servant, this.

MOROSE

A Daw, and her servant! Oh, 'tis decreed, 'tis decreed of
me, and she have such servants.                                    15

*[Makes to go out]*

TRUEWIT

Nay, sir, you must kiss the ladies, you must not go away
now; they come toward you to seek you out.

HAUGHTY

I' faith, Master Morose, would you steal a marriage thus,
in the midst of so many friends, and not acquaint us? Well,
I'll kiss you, notwithstanding the justice of my quarrel.      20
You shall give me leave, mistress, to use a becoming famil-
iarity with your husband.

EPICOENE

Your ladyship does me an honour in it, to let me know he is
so worthy your favour; as you have done both him and me
grace to visit so unprepared a pair to entertain you.          25

MOROSE

Compliment! Compliment!

EPICOENE

But I must lay the burden of that upon my servant here.

HAUGHTY

It shall not need, Mistress Morose; we will all bear, rather
than one shall be oppressed.

MOROSE

I know it, and you will teach her the faculty, if she be to    30
learn it.

*[The collegiates talk apart with* TRUEWIT]

HAUGHTY

Is this the silent woman?

---

12 *nomenclator* announcer of the names of guests (a sense coined by Jonson in *C.R.*,
    V.x, 5); punning here on 'clatter'. See note to I.ii, 73
14–15 *'tis decreed of me* judgement is passed on me, I am a condemned man (H&S,
    who compare Latin *actum est de me*)
15 *and* if
18 *steal a marriage* get married secretly (a stock phrase)
24 *Compliment* see I.i, 129 and note

---

30–1 *faculty ... it.* Ability (to bear [sexual] burdens) if she has not learned it
    already; taking up the sexual sense of *oppressed*, 'ravished' (Latin *opprimere*).

CENTAURE

Nay, she has found her tongue since she was married,
Master Truewit says.

HAUGHTY

Oh, Master Truewit! 'Save you. What kind of creature is    35
your bride here? She speaks, methinks!

TRUEWIT

Yes, madam, believe it, she is a gentlewoman of very
absolute behaviour and of a good race.

HAUGHTY

And Jack Daw told us she could not speak.

TRUEWIT

So it was carried in plot, madam, to put her upon this old    40
fellow, by Sir Dauphine, his nephew, and one or two more
of us; but she is a woman of an excellent assurance, and an
extraordinary happy wit and tongue. You shall see her
make rare sport with Daw ere night.

HAUGHTY

And he brought us to laugh at her!    45

TRUEWIT

That falls out often, madam, that he that thinks himself the
master-wit is the master-fool. I assure your ladyship, ye
cannot laugh at her.

HAUGHTY

No, we'll have her to the college: and she have wit, she
shall be one of us! Shall she not, Centaure? We'll make her    50
a collegiate.

CENTAURE

Yes, faith, madam, and Mavis and she will set up a side.

TRUEWIT

Believe it, madam, and Mistress Mavis, she will sustain her
part.

MAVIS

I'll tell you that when I have talked with her and tried her.    55

HAUGHTY

Use her very civilly, Mavis.

MAVIS

So I will, madam.    [MAVIS *walks apart with* EPICOENE]

38 *absolute* perfect
44 *with* of, at the expense of
52 *a side* a partnership in cards (perhaps metaphorical here)

46–7 *he . . . fool*. Adapting the proverb 'Who seem most crafty prove oft times most
fools' (Middleton, *A Trick to Catch the Old One*, V.ii, 193).

MOROSE

Blessed minute, that they would whisper thus ever.

TRUEWIT

In the meantime, madam, would but your ladyship help to
vex him a little: you know his disease, talk to him about the    60
wedding-ceremonies, or call for your gloves, or—

HAUGHTY

Let me alone. Centaure, help me. Master bridegroom,
where are you?

MOROSE

Oh, it was too miraculously good to last!

HAUGHTY

We see no ensigns of a wedding here, no character of a    65
bridal: where be our scarfs and our gloves? I pray you give
'em us. Let's know your bride's colours and yours at least.

CENTAURE

Alas, madam, he has provided none.

MOROSE

Had I known your ladyship's painter, I would.

HAUGHTY

He has given it you, Centaure, i' faith. But do you hear,    70
Master Morose, a jest will not absolve you in this manner.
You that have sucked the milk of the court, and from
thence have been brought up to the very strong meats and
wine of it, been a courtier from the biggin to the night-cap,
as we may say, and you to offend in such a high point of    75
ceremony as this, and let your nuptials want all marks of
solemnity! How much plate have you lost today—if you
had but regarded your profit—what gifts, what friends,
through your mere rusticity?

62 *Let me alone* i.e. you can trust me for that
65 *ensigns* tokens
69 *painter* cosmetician
70 *given it you* paid you out, given you what for
74 *biggin* baby-bonnet
77 *solemnity* observance of ceremony
79 *mere* absolute

---

61, 66 *gloves . . . scarfs.* Presented to guests at weddings.
67 *colours.* Bride and groom each had their colour, which was worn by their
respective friends.
73 *strong meats.* Greek στερεας τροφης, solid food, as opposed to easily digested
food such as milk; see *OED*, 'strong', a., 9.d; *wine* introduces a pun on a less
learned sense of 'strong'.

MOROSE

Madam—                                                                    80

HAUGHTY

Pardon me, sir, I must insinuate your errors to you. No
gloves? No garters? No scarfs? No epithalamium? No
masque?

DAW

Yes, madam, I'll make an epithalamium, I promised my
mistress, I have begun it already: will your ladyship hear   85
it?

HAUGHTY

Ay, good Jack Daw.

MOROSE

Will it please your ladyship command a chamber and be
private with your friend? You shall have your choice of
rooms to retire to after; my whole house is yours. I know it   90
hath been your ladyship's errand into the city at other
times, however now you have been unhappily diverted
upon me; but I shall be loath to break any honourable
custom of your ladyship's. And therefore, good madam—

EPICOENE

Come, you are a rude bridegroom, to entertain ladies of   95
honour in this fashion.

CENTAURE

He is a rude groom indeed.

TRUEWIT

By that light, you deserve to be grafted, and have your
horns reach from one side of the island to the other.—
[*Aside to* MOROSE] Do not mistake me, sir; I but speak this   100
to give the ladies some heart again, not for any malice to
you.

88 *chamber* bedchamber
89 *friend* lover (i.e. Daw)
91 *errand* purpose of going (i.e. an assignation)
97 *groom* (i) bridegroom; (ii) servant, lackey

---

81 *insinuate*. Latin *insinuare* means 'introduce, make known', but the English sense
'hint obliquely' is funnier, since this is the opposite of what Haughty proceeds to
do.
82 *garters*. After the ceremony the young men and bridesmaids would strive to
possess the bride's garters.
*epithalamium*. Nuptial song in honour of the bride and groom; glossed in detail
by Jonson in *Hym.*, 435–43.
98 *grafted*. Grafted with foreign stock, i.e. made a cuckold, with a consequent
'growth' of horns.

MOROSE

Is this your bravo, ladies?

TRUEWIT

As God help me, if you utter such another word, I'll take
mistress bride in and begin to you in a very sad cup, do you    105
see? Go to, know your friends and such as love you.

### Act III, Scene vii

*[Enter]* CLERIMONT *[with* MUSICIANS*]*

CLERIMONT

By your leave, ladies. Do you want any music? I have
brought you variety of noises. Play, sirs, all of you.

*Music of all sorts*

MOROSE

Oh, a plot, a plot, a plot, a plot upon me! This day I shall
be their anvil to work on, they will grate me asunder. 'Tis
worse than the noise of a saw.                                  5

CLERIMONT

No, they are hair, rosin, and guts. I can give you the
receipt.

TRUEWIT

Peace, boys.

CLERIMONT

Play, I say.

TRUEWIT

Peace, rascals.—You see who's your friend now, sir? Take    10
courage, put on a martyr's resolution. Mock down all their
attemptings with patience. 'Tis but a day, and I would
suffer heroically. Should an ass exceed me in fortitude?

---

103 *bravo* hired thug
105 *begin ... cup* drink your health in a very unpleasant manner
106 *Go to* common expression of reproof
  2 *noises* bands of musicians, and glancing at the normal sense (cf. II.vi, 36)
  4 *grate* (i) annoy, harass; (ii) grind; (iii) make grating noises
  7 *receipt* formula, recipe
 12 *with* by means of

---

  6 *hair ... guts.* Which produce the noise from a violin: strings of gut, a bow of
    horsehair, rosin to rub on the bow.
 13 *ass.* The type of patient endurance—but also of stupidity.

No. You betray your infirmity with your hanging dull ears,
and make them insult: bear up bravely and constantly.          15

LA FOOLE [*with* SERVANTS] *passes over sewing the meat,*
          [*followed by* MISTRESS OTTER]

Look you here, sir, what honour is done you unexpected
by your nephew: a wedding-dinner come, and a knight-
sewer before it, for the more reputation; and fine Mistress
Otter, your neighbour, in the rump or tail of it.
MOROSE
Is that Gorgon, that Medusa come? Hide me, hide me!          20
TRUEWIT
I warrant you, sir, she will not transform you. Look upon
her with a good courage. Pray you entertain her and con-
duct your guests in. No?—Mistress bride, will you entreat
in the ladies? Your bridegroom is so shamefaced here—
EPICOENE
Will it please your ladyship, madam?          25
HAUGHTY
With the benefit of your company, mistress.
EPICOENE
Servant, pray you perform your duties.
DAW
And glad to be commanded, mistress.
CENTAURE
How like you her wit, Mavis?
MAVIS
Very prettily absolutely well.          30
MISTRESS OTTER
[*Trying to take precedence*] 'Tis my place.
MAVIS
You shall pardon me, Mistress Otter.
MISTRESS OTTER
Why, I am a collegiate.

14 *infirmity* weakness
15 *insult* scornfully exult
   *constantly* steadfastly
   s.d. *sewing the meat* directing the serving of the food
22 *entertain* receive
24 *shamefaced* shy, bashful

---

20 *Medusa*. The most terrible of the three Gorgons.
21 *transform*. i.e. turn to stone; see note to II.iv, 14.
30 *Very ... well*. 'Prettily' modifies the rest of the phrase, giving an affected
   example of 'compliment'; cf. *B.F.*, III,iv, 80.

MAVIS
  But not in ordinary.
MISTRESS OTTER
  But I am.                                             35
MAVIS
  We'll dispute that within.          [*Exit* DAW *with ladies*]
CLERIMONT
  Would this had lasted a little longer.
TRUEWIT
  And that they had sent for the heralds.

              [*Enter* OTTER]

  Captain Otter, what news?
OTTER
  I have brought my bull, bear, and horse in private, and      40
  yonder are the trumpeters without, and the drum, gentle-
  men.
                  *The drum and trumpets sound*
MOROSE
  Oh, oh, oh!
OTTER
  And we will have a rouse in each of 'em anon, for bold
  Britons, i' faith.                     [*They sound again*]      45
MOROSE
  Oh, oh, oh!                                [*Exit* MOROSE]
ALL
  Follow, follow, follow!                        [*Exeunt*]

34 *in ordinary* see note II.iii, 89
47 *Follow* a hunting-cry

38 *heralds*. Since they determine questions of precedence, and *heralds* (of a rather
    different sort) blow trumpets.
44 *rouse*. Full draught of liquor; often marked by a fanfare, as in *Hamlet*, I.iv, 7–8,
    where there is '*A flourish of trumpets, and two pieces goes off*'.

### Act IV, Scene i

[*Enter*] TRUEWIT, CLERIMONT

TRUEWIT

Was there ever poor bridegroom so tormented? or man,
indeed?

CLERIMONT

I have not read of the like in the chronicles of the land.

TRUEWIT

Sure, he cannot but go to a place of rest after all this
purgatory.                                                          5

CLERIMONT

He may presume it, I think.

TRUEWIT

The spitting, the coughing, the laughter, the neezing, the
farting, dancing, noise of the music, and her masculine and
loud commanding and urging the whole family, makes him
think he has married a Fury.                                        10

CLERIMONT

And she carries it up bravely.

TRUEWIT

Ay, she takes any occasion to speak: that's the height on't.

CLERIMONT

And how soberly Dauphine labours to satisfy him that it
was none of his plot!

TRUEWIT

And has almost brought him to the faith i' the article.            15

[*Enter* DAUPHINE]

Here he comes.—Where is he now? What's become of
him, Dauphine?

---

7  *neezing* sneezing
9  *urging ... family* driving all the servants
11  *carries ... bravely* keeps it up splendidly

---

10  *Fury*. One of the ferocious female beings sent from Tartarus to avenge wrong or
punish crime; see above, p. xxxiii.
15  *faith ... article*. Referring to the Articles of Faith, the 39 statements to which
Church of England ministers must subscribe.

DAUPHINE

Oh, hold me up a little, I shall go away i' the jest else. He
has got on his whole nest of night-caps, and locked himself
up i' the top o' the house, as high as ever he can climb from          20
the noise. I peeped in at a cranny and saw him sitting over a
cross-beam o' the roof, like him o' the saddler's horse in
Fleet Street, upright; and he will sleep there.

CLERIMONT

But where are your collegiates?

DAUPHINE

Withdrawn with the bride in private.                                   25

TRUEWIT

Oh, they are instructing her i' the college grammar. If she
have grace with them, she knows all their secrets instantly.

CLERIMONT

Methinks the Lady Haughty looks well today, for all my
dispraise of her i' the morning. I think I shall come about to
thee again, Truewit.                                                   30

TRUEWIT

Believe it, I told you right. Women ought to repair the
losses time and years have made i' their features with
dressings. And an intelligent woman, if she know by herself the least defect, will be most curious to hide it; and it
becomes her. If she be short, let her sit much, lest when        35
she stands she be thought to sit. If she have an ill foot, let
her wear her gown the longer and her shoe the thinner. If a
fat hand and scald nails, let her carve the less, and act in
gloves. If a sour breath, let her never discourse fasting, and
always talk at her distance. If she have black and rugged           40

---

18 *go ... jest* die laughing
19 *nest* set of objects of diminishing sizes fitting one inside the other
29–30 *come ... thee* come round to your opinion (*OED*'s first example)
33 *by* about
34 *curious* careful (suggested by Ovid's *cura*)
38 *scald* scaly, scabbed (*scaber*, Ovid)

---

22 *him ... horse.* The model of a horse and rider outside a saddler's shop. Cf.
   *E.M I.*, V.v, 49–51, where Clement calls Bobadill and Matthew the 'signe o' the
   Souldier, and picture o' the *Poet* (but, both so false, I will not ha' you hang'd out
   at my dore till midnight)'.
33 *dressings.* Personal decorations. Jonson's coinage, translating Ovid's *munditiis*.
38–9 *let ... gloves. Act* at this date meant specifically 'gesture', as could *carve* (as
   well as 'carve the meat at table'). Cf. Hamlet's advice to the players: 'do not saw
   the air too much with your hand, thus' (III.ii, 4–5).
39 *fasting.* Ovid has *jejuna*, i.e. while her stomach is empty (when the breath is
   sourest).

teeth, let her offer the less at laughter, especially if she
laugh wide and open.

CLERIMONT

Oh, you shall have some women, when they laugh, you
would think they brayed, it is so rude, and—

TRUEWIT

Ay, and others that will stalk i' their gait like an ostrich, and          45
take huge strides. I cannot endure such a sight. I love
measure i' the feet and number i' the voice: they are
gentlenesses that oft-times draw no less than the face.

DAUPHINE

How cam'st thou to study these creatures so exactly? I
would thou wouldst make me a proficient.          50

TRUEWIT

Yes, but you must leave to live i' your chamber, then, a
month together upon *Amadis de Gaule* or *Don Quixote*, as
you are wont, and come abroad where the matter is frequent, to court, to tiltings, public shows and feasts, to
plays, and church sometimes: thither they come to show          55
their new tires too, to see and to be seen. In these places a
man shall find whom to love, whom to play with, whom to
touch once, whom to hold ever. The variety arrests his
judgement. A wench to please a man comes not down
dropping from the ceiling, as he lies on his back droning a          60
tobacco-pipe. He must go where she is.

DAUPHINE

Yes, and be never the near.

47 *measure* due proportion in moving
   *number* harmonious rhythm
48 *gentlenesses* graces
   *draw* attract
50 *proficient* learner (as opposed to one who is perfect)
51 *leave* cease
53–4 *abroad ... frequent* away from home where the subject-matter is plentiful
54 *tiltings* jousts (at this date mock-combats for courtly entertainment)
60 *droning* sucking, as though playing a bagpipe (*OED*); glancing at *drone* = act
   indolently, idle away the time
62 *near* nearer, comparative of *nigh*

52 *Amadis ... Quixote.* Romances which Jonson regarded as frivolous enter-
   tainments, 'publique Nothings;/Abortives of the fabulous, darke cloyster,/Sent
   out to poison courts, and infest manners' (*N.I.*, I.vi, 126–8).
58 *arrests.* In law, to *arrest a judgement* is to stay proceedings after a verdict, on the
   ground of error (*OED*, v., 5.d, earliest example 1768); translating Ovid's
   *judicium morata est.*

TRUEWIT

Out, heretic! That diffidence makes thee worthy it should
be so.

CLERIMONT

He says true to you, Dauphine.                              65

DAUPHINE

Why?

TRUEWIT

A man should not doubt to overcome any woman. Think
he can vanquish 'em, and he shall; for though they deny,
their desire is to be tempted. Penelope herself cannot hold
out long. Ostend, you saw, was taken at last. You must     70
persévér and hold to your purpose. They would solicit us,
but that they are afraid. Howsoever, they wish in their
hearts we should solicit them. Praise 'em, flatter 'em, you
shall never want eloquence or trust; even the chastest
delight to feel themselves that way rubbed. With praises    75
you must mix kisses too. If they take them, they'll take
more. Though they strive, they would be overcome.

CLERIMONT

Oh, but a man must beware of force.

TRUEWIT

It is to them an acceptable violence, and has oft-times the
place of the greatest courtesy. She that might have been    80
forced, and you let her go free without touching, though
she then seem to thank you, will ever hate you after; and
glad i' the face, is assuredly sad at the heart.

CLERIMONT

But all women are not to be taken all ways.

TRUEWIT

'Tis true. No more than all birds or all fishes. If you appear   85
learned to an ignorant wench, or jocund to a sad, or witty to
a foolish, why, she presently begins to mistrust herself.

67 *doubt to* doubt that he may
77 *strive ... would be* struggle ... wish to be
81 *and* if
84 *all ways* ed. (alwaies F)
87 *presently* at once

---

68 *deny*. Say no. 'Maids say nay and take it' (Tilley, M34).
69–70 *Penelope ... Ostend*. Ancient and modern examples of steadfast resistance.
The wife of Odysseus put off her suitors for twenty years until her husband
returned from Troy; the Belgian port fell to the Spanish in September 1604 after
a three-year siege.
73–4 *you ... trust*. Lack eloquence in yourself, or trust from your audience.

You must approach them i' their own height, their own
line; for the contrary makes many that fear to commit
themselves to noble and worthy fellows run into the 90
embraces of a rascal. If she love wit, give verses, though
you borrow 'em of a friend, or buy 'em, to have good. If
valour, talk of your sword, and be frequent in the mention
of quarrels, though you be staunch in fighting. If activity,
be seen o' your barbary often, or leaping over stools, for the 95
credit of your back. If she love good clothes or dressing,
have your learned council about you every morning, your
French tailor, barber, linener, *et cetera*. Let your powder,
your glass, and your comb be your dearest acquaintance.
Take more care for the ornament of your head than the 100
safety, and wish the commonwealth rather troubled than a
hair about you. That will take her. Then if she be covetous
and craving, do you promise anything, and perform spar-
ingly; so shall you keep her in appetite still. Seem as you
would give, but be like a barren field that yields little, or 105
unlucky dice to foolish and hoping gamesters. Let your
gifts be slight and dainty, rather than precious. Let cunning be above cost. Give cherries at time of year, or
apricots; and say they were sent you out o' the country,
though you bought 'em in Cheapside. Admire her tires, 110
like her in all fashions, compare her in every habit to some
deity, invent excellent dreams to flatter her, and riddles;
or, if she be a great one, perform always the second parts to
her: like what she likes, praise whom she praises, and fail
not to make the household and servants yours, yea, the 115
whole family, and salute 'em by their names—'tis but light
cost if you can purchase 'em so—and make her physician
your pensioner, and her chief woman. Nor will it be out of
your gain to make love to her too, so she follow, not usher,

94 *staunch* restrained
   *activity* physical exercise
95 *barbary* horse, of high quality Arab stock
107–8 *Let ... cost* let your ingenuity be greater than your expense
108 *at time of year* in season
113 *great one* person of rank
   *perform ... parts* act a subordinate role (Latin *agere secundae partes*)
117–18 *make ... pensioner* i.e. buy his support
118 *woman* maidservant
118–19 *out ... her* irrelevant to your interests to behave amorously towards

88–9 *height ... line.* The metaphor is, appropriately, from fencing (referring to the
   'high' and 'low' ward, and the angle of the sword).
96 *back.* A 'good back' implies sexual prowess; cf. IV.v, 190.

her lady's pleasure. All blabbing is taken away when she 120
comes to be a part of the crime.

DAUPHINE

On what courtly lap hast thou late slept, to come forth so
sudden and absolute a courtling?

TRUEWIT

Good faith, I should rather question you, that are so
heark'ning after these mysteries. I begin to suspect your 125
diligence, Dauphine. Speak, art thou in love in earnest?

DAUPHINE

Yes, by my troth, am I; 'twere ill dissembling before thee.

TRUEWIT

With which of 'em, I pray thee?

DAUPHINE

With all the collegiates.

CLERIMONT

Out on thee! We'll keep you at home, believe it, i' the 130
stable, and you be such a stallion.

TRUEWIT

No; I like him well. Men should love wisely, and all
women: some one for the face, and let her please the eye;
another for the skin, and let her please the touch; and third
for the voice, and let her please the ear; and where the 135
objects mix, let the senses so too. Thou wouldst think it
strange if I should make 'em all in love with thee afore
night!

DAUPHINE

I would say thou hadst the best philtre i' the world, and
couldst do more than Madam Medea or Doctor Forman. 140

TRUEWIT

If I do not, let me play the mountebank for my meat while I
live, and the bawd for my drink.

DAUPHINE

So be it, I say.

---

123  *courtling* courtier (Jonson's coinage in *C.R.*, V.iv, 33)
133  *some one* a certain one

---

140  *Medea*. The classical enchantress who helped Jason win the Golden Fleece, and
restored his father Aeson's youth.
*Forman*. Simon Forman (1552–1611), well-known London astrologer, quack,
and supplier of love-philtres to the court; see A. L. Rowse's biography (1974).

### Act IV, Scene ii

[*Enter*] OTTER [*carrying his cups*], DAW, LA FOOLE

OTTER

Oh lord, gentlemen, how my knights and I have missed
you here!

CLERIMONT

Why, captain, what service, what service?

OTTER

To see me bring up my bull, bear, and horse to fight.

DAW

Yes, faith, the captain says we shall be his dogs to bait 'em.     5

DAUPHINE

A good employment.

TRUEWIT

Come on, let's see a course then.

LA FOOLE

I am afraid my cousin will be offended if she come.

OTTER

Be afraid of nothing. Gentlemen, I have placed the drum
and the trumpets and one to give 'em the sign when you are    10
ready. Here's my bull for myself, and my bear for Sir John
Daw, and my horse for Sir Amorous. Now, set your foot to
mine, and yours to his, and—

LA FOOLE

Pray God my cousin come not.

OTTER

Saint George and Saint Andrew, fear no cousins. Come,    15
sound, sound! *Et rauco strepuerunt cornua cantu.*
                  [*Drum and trumpets sound. They drink*]

TRUEWIT

Well said, captain, i' faith; well fought at the bull.

CLERIMONT

Well held at the bear.

3 *service* in the military sense: operation
17 *Well said* well done

---

4 *to fight.* The animal-baiting metaphors continue to l. 70.
7 *course.* (i) (drinking-) round; (ii) in bull- and bear-baiting, a bout between the
   baited animal and the dogs; cf. *Macbeth*, V.vii, 1–2.
12–13 *set . . . mine.* The stance in drinking-bouts; cf. the ballad 'Uptails All': 'set
   your foote to my foote, & up tails all' (H&S).
15 *fear no cousins.* Adapting the proverb 'Fear no colours' (Tilley, C520).
16 *Et . . . cantu.* 'The horns blared out with hoarse note' (Virgil, *Aeneid*, VIII, 2).

TRUEWIT
'Loo, 'loo, captain!
DAUPHINE
Oh, the horse has kicked off his dog already.                          20
LA FOOLE
I cannot drink it, as I am a knight.
TRUEWIT
Gods so! Off with his spurs, somebody.
LA FOOLE
It goes again my conscience. My cousin will be angry with
it.
DAW
I ha' done mine.                                                       25
TRUEWIT
You fought high and fair, Sir John.
CLERIMONT
At the head.
DAUPHINE
Like an excellent bear-dog.
CLERIMONT
[*Aside to* DAW] You take no notice of the business, I hope.
DAW
[*Aside to* CLERIMONT] Not a word, sir; you see we are jovial.        30
OTTER
Sir Amorous, you must not equivocate. It must be pulled
down, for all my cousin.
CLERIMONT
[*Aside to* LA FOOLE] 'Sfoot, if you take not your drink,
they'll think you are discontented with something; you'll
betray all if you take the least notice.                              35
LA FOOLE
[*Aside to* CLERIMONT] Not I, I'll both drink and talk then.
OTTER
You must pull the horse on his knees, Sir Amorous. Fear
no cousins: *jacta est alea.*
TRUEWIT
[*Aside to* DAUPHINE *and* CLERIMONT] Oh, now he's in his
vein, and bold. The least hint given him of his wife now              40
will make him rail desperately.

22 *Off ... spurs* i.e. deprive him of his knighthood
41 *desperately* recklessly

---

19 *'Loo* (Low F). A cry to urge on dogs; cf. *Troilus and Cressida*, V. vii, 10 (here the
    early tests have 'lowe').
38 *jacta est alea.* 'The die is cast': Caesar's remark on crossing the Rubicon.

CLERIMONT

Speak to him of her.

TRUEWIT

Do you, and I'll fetch her to the hearing of it.    [*Exit*]

DAUPHINE

Captain he-Otter, your she-Otter is coming, your wife.

OTTER

Wife! Buz! *Titivilitium*. There's no such thing in nature. I   45
confess, gentlemen, I have a cook, a laundress, a house-
drudge, that serves my necessary turns and goes under that
title; but he's an ass that will be so uxorious to tie his
affections to one circle. Come, the name dulls appetite.
Here, replenish again: another bout. Wives are nasty,   50
sluttish animals.

                                          [*Fills the cups*]

DAUPHINE

Oh captain!

OTTER

As ever the earth bare, *tribus verbis*. Where's Master
Truewit?

DAW

He's slipped aside, sir.   55

CLERIMONT

But you must drink and be jovial.

DAW

Yes, give it me.

LA FOOLE

And me too.

DAW

Let's be jovial.

LA FOOLE

As jovial as you will.   60

OTTER

Agreed. Now you shall ha' the bear, cousin, and Sir John
Daw the horse, and I'll ha' the bull still. Sound, Tritons o'

---

45 *Buz* exclamation of impatience or contempt
53 *tribus verbis* in three (i.e. few) words
62 *Tritons* classical sea-gods, commonly depicted blowing shell-trumpets

---

45 *Titivilitium*. A worthless trifle, bagatelle. Coined by Plautus, *Casina*, 347.
48–9 *to . . . circle*. Like a donkey driving a rotary mill.
51 *animals* (*animalls* F). F usually italicizes only proper, foreign, or technical
    words; possibly a mistake for Latin *animalia*; cf. 1. 70.
55 *slipped*. Used of dogs in hunting and coursing.

the Thames. *Nunc est bibendum, nunc pede libero*—
                                        [*They drink.*]
           MOROSE *speaks from above, the trumpets sounding*
MOROSE

Villains, murderers, sons of the earth, and traitors, what
do you there?                                              65

CLERIMONT

Oh, now the trumpets have waked him we shall have his
company.

OTTER

A wife is a scurvy clogdogdo, an unlucky thing, a very
foresaid bear-whelp, without any good fashion or breeding: *mala bestia*.                                        70

   *His wife is brought out to hear him* [*by* TRUEWIT]

DAUPHINE

Why did you marry one then, captain?

OTTER

A pox—I married with six thousand pound, I. I was in
love with that. I ha' not kissed my Fury these forty weeks.

CLERIMONT

The more to blame you, captain.

TRUEWIT

Nay, Mistress Otter, hear him a little first.             75

OTTER

She has a breath worse than my grandmother's, *profecto*.

MISTRESS OTTER

Oh treacherous liar! Kiss me, sweet Master Truewit, and
prove him a slandering knave.

TRUEWIT

I'll rather believe you, lady.

OTTER

And she has a peruke that's like a pound of hemp made up   80
in shoe-threads.

---

64 *sons ... earth* bastards, i.e. low-born knaves (Latin *terrae filii*)
70 *mala bestia* evil beast
76 *profecto* truly

---

63 *Nunc ... libero.* 'Now is the time for drinking, now with free foot ...'. The first
   line of Horace's ode (I.xxxvii) on the downfall of Cleopatra, the type of the
   man-destroying female.
68 *clogdogdo.* Baffling. Perhaps, if *foresaid* = 'aforesaid', Bear Garden slang for
   'bear-whelp without "fashion or breeding".' Other editors suggest 'clog fit for a
   dog', i.e. the weight or *trash* placed round a dog's neck when training it, and gloss
   *foresaid* as either 'predictable, i.e. certain to be bad', or = *forsaid*, 'forbidden'.

MISTRESS OTTER

Oh viper, mandrake!

OTTER

A most vile face! And yet she spends me forty pound a year
in mercury and hogs' bones. All her teeth were made i' the
Blackfriars, both her eyebrows i' the Strand, and her hair          85
in Silver Street. Every part o' the town owns a piece of her.

MISTRESS OTTER

I cannot hold.

OTTER

She takes herself asunder still when she goes to bed, into
some twenty boxes, and about next day noon is put
together again, like a great German clock; and so comes           90
forth and rings a tedious larum to the whole house, and
then is quiet again for an hour, but for her quarters.—Ha'
you done me right, gentlemen?

MISTRESS OTTER

No, sir, I'll do you right with my quarters, with my quarters.                                                               95

*She falls upon him and beats him*

OTTER

Oh hold, good princess!

TRUEWIT

Sound, sound.                    [*Drum and trumpets sound*]

CLERIMONT

A battle, a battle.

---

82 *mandrake* poisonous plant, the root of which was thought to resemble a human
   figure, hence a common term of abuse
91 *larum* chime, alarm (of a clock)
92 *quarters* (i) quarter-hours; (ii) living-quarters
93 *done me right* matched me drink for drink (a set phrase)
94 *quarters* strokes, blows (in fencing and fighting with staves)

---

84 *mercury . . . hogs' bones*. 'crude mercurie . . . with the jaw-bones of a sow' are the
   ingredients of the Perfumer's fucus in *C.R.*, V.iv, 403–4.
84–90 The most elaborate and imaginative of Jonson's imitations of a passage in
   Martial (see Appendix II), imitated previously in *C.R.*, IV.i, 145–9, and *Sej.*, I,
   307–10; the places are chosen as amusingly the right ones to remedy black teeth,
   coarse eyebrows, and grey hair. For a brilliantly savage later treatment, cf.
   Swift's 'A Beautiful Young Nymph Going to Bed'.
86 *Silver Street*. Where Shakespeare once lodged, in Cheapside.
90 *like . . . clock*. A frequent comparison in Jacobean drama, deriving from *Love's
   Labour's Lost*, III.i, 190–2: 'A woman, that is like a German clock,/Still
   a-repairing, ever out of frame,/And never going aright'. Tilley, W658, gives
   examples from Dekker, Middleton, and Fletcher.

MISTRESS OTTER

You notorious stinkardly bearward, doe

OTTER

Under correction, dear princess. Look
horse, gentlemen.

MISTRESS OTTER

Do I want teeth and eyebrows, thou

TRUEWIT

Sound, sound still.                         [*They sound again.*]

OTTER

No, I protest, under correction—

MISTRESS OTTER

Ay, now you are under correction, you protest; but you did    105
not protest before correction, sir. Thou Judas, to offer to
betray thy princess! I'll make thee an example—

MOROSE *descends with a long sword*

MOROSE

I will have no such examples in my house, Lady Otter.

MISTRESS OTTER

Ah!            [*She runs off, followed by* DAW *and* LA FOOLE]

MOROSE

Mistress Mary Ambree, your examples are dangerous.—    110
Rogues, hell-hounds, Stentors, out of my doors, you sons
of noise and tumult, begot on an ill May-day, or when the
galley-foist is afloat to Westminster! [*Drives out the
MUSICIANS*] A trumpeter could not be conceived but then!

DAUPHINE

What ails you, sir?                                           115

MOROSE

They have rent my roof, walls, and all my windows asunder, with their brazen throats.                        [*Exit*]

100 *Under correction* cf. III.i, 10
104 *protest* avow

---

110 *Mary Ambree*. A modern Amazon; according to a popular ballad, she dressed
up and fought as a soldier at the siege of Ghent in 1584.
111 *Stentors*. Stentor was a Greek herald at Troy whose 'iron voice' was as loud as
the shout of fifty men (*Iliad*, V, 785–6).
112 *ill May-day*. The immediate reference is to the 'Ill' or 'Evil' May-day of 1517,
when the London apprentices attacked wealthy foreign merchants; but as
Partridge notes, any 1 May, with its maypole dancing and merrymaking, would
be an ill day to a man who hated noise.
113 *galley-foist*. State barge which once a year brought the new Lord Mayor to be
sworn in at Westminster. A contemporary account quoted by H&S mentions
'drumming, and piping, and trumpetting' accompanying the celebrations.

‸T

st follow him, Dauphine.

**‸PHINE**

So I will.                                        [*Exit*]

**CLERIMONT**

Where's Daw and La Foole?                          120

**OTTER**

They are both run away, sir. Good gentlemen, help to
pacify my princess, and speak to the great ladies for me.
Now must I go lie with the bears this fortnight, and keep
out o' the way till my peace be made, for this scandal she
has taken. Did you not see my bull-head, gentlemen?    125

**CLERIMONT**

Is't not on, captain?

**TRUEWIT**

No: — [*Aside to* CLERIMONT] but he may make a new one,
by that is on.

**OTTER**

Oh, here 'tis. And you come over, gentlemen, and ask for
Tom Otter, we'll go down to Ratcliffe, and have a course i'  130
faith, for all these disasters. There's *bona spes* left.

**TRUEWIT**

Away, captain, get off while you are well.

                                      [*Exit* OTTER]

**CLERIMONT**

I am glad we are rid of him.

**TRUEWIT**

You had never been, unless we had put his wife upon him.
His humour is as tedious at last, as it was ridiculous at first.   135

---

124 *scandal* offence
126 *on* (i) on the cup; (ii) on your shoulders (suggesting, because of the bull's
  horns, that Otter is a cuckold)
128 *by that* by copying the one that
129 *And … over* if you come across the Thames (to the Bankside)
130 *course* cf. l. 7

---

130 *Ratcliffe*. A sea-faring area down-river in Stepney, where Dol and Subtle plan
  to escape to in *Alch*.
131 *bona spes*. From Cicero, *In Catilinam*, II.25: 'Good hope fights against despair
  of all things' (Beaurline).

## Act IV, Scene iii

[*Enter*] HAUGHTY, MISTRESS OTTER, MAVIS, DAW, LA FOOLE, CENTAURE, EPICOENE. [TRUEWIT *and* CLERIMONT *move aside and observe*]

HAUGHTY
We wondered why you shrieked so, Mistress Otter.
MISTRESS OTTER
Oh God, madam, he came down with a huge long naked weapon in both his hands, and looked so dreadfully! Sure, he's beside himself.
MAVIS
Why, what made you there, Mistress Otter?                    5
MISTRESS OTTER
Alas, Mistress Mavis, I was chastising my subject, and thought nothing of him.
DAW
[*To* EPICOENE] Faith, mistress, you must do so too. Learn to chastise. Mistress Otter corrects her husband so, he dares not speak but under correction.                    10
LA FOOLE
And with his hat off to her: 'twould do you good to see.
HAUGHTY
In sadness, 'tis good and mature counsel: practise it, Morose. I'll call you Morose still now, as I call Centaure and Mavis: we four will be all one.
CENTAURE
And you'll come to the college and live with us?                    15
HAUGHTY
Make him give milk and honey.
MAVIS
Look how you manage him at first, you shall have him ever after.
CENTAURE
Let him allow you your coach and four horses, your woman, your chambermaid, your page, your gentleman-    20
usher, your French cook, and four grooms.

---

5 *made you* were you doing
12 *In sadness* seriously
17 *manage* train, handle (said of horses)

---

13 *Morose*. The masculine form of address.

HAUGHTY

And go with us to Bedlam, to the china-houses, and to the
Exchange.

CENTAURE

It will open the gate to your fame.

HAUGHTY

Here's Centaure has immortalized herself with taming of     25
her wild male.

MAVIS

Ay, she has done the miracle of the kingdom.

EPICOENE

But ladies, do you count it lawful to have such plurality of
servants, and do 'em all graces?

HAUGHTY

Why not? Why should women deny their favours to men?     30
Are they the poorer, or the worse?

DAW

Is the Thames the less for the dyer's water, mistress?

LA FOOLE

Or a torch for lighting many torches?

TRUEWIT

[*Aside*] Well said, La Foole; what a new one he has
got!                                                                                        35

CENTAURE

They are empty losses women fear in this kind.

HAUGHTY

Besides, ladies should be mindful of the approach of age,
and let no time want his due use. The best of our days pass
first.

MAVIS

We are rivers that cannot be called back, madam: she that     40
now excludes her lovers may live to lie a forsaken beldame
in a frozen bed.

34 *new one* i.e. new expression
41 *beldame* crone

---

22 *Bedlam*. See note to II.ii, 33.
22–3 *china-houses … Exchange*. Cf. I.iii, 35–6.
24 *open … fame*. Cf. Centaure's similarly unfortunate ambiguity at ll. 45–6.
32–3 *Is … torches*. Daw and La Foole's arguments are mechanical clichés, as
Truewit ironically indicates; cf. 'To cast water into the Thames' and 'One candle
can light many more' (Tilley, W106, C45). They also introduce, unwittingly,
ideas of (sexual) pollution; in sexual slang *water* meant semen, *torch* penis, and
*burn* infect with venereal disease.

CENTAURE

'Tis true, Mavis; and who will wait on us to coach then? or write, or tell us the news then? make anagrams of our names, and invite us to the cockpit, and kiss our hands all 45 the play-time, and draw their weapons for our honours?

HAUGHTY

Not one.

DAW

Nay, my mistress is not altogether unintelligent of these things; here be in presence have tasted of her favours.

CLERIMONT

[*Aside*] What a neighing hobby-horse is this! 50

EPICOENE

But not with intent to boast 'em again, servant. And have you those excellent receipts, madam, to keep yourselves from bearing of children?

HAUGHTY

Oh yes, Morose. How should we maintain our youth and beauty else? Many births of a woman make her old, as 55 many crops make the earth barren.

## Act IV, Scene iv

[*Enter*] MOROSE, DAUPHINE; [*they speak apart*]

MOROSE

Oh my cursed angel, that instructed me to this fate!

DAUPHINE

Why, sir?

MOROSE

That I should be seduced by so foolish a devil as a barber will make!

DAUPHINE

I would I had been worthy, sir, to have partaken your 5 counsel; you should never have trusted it to such a minister.

---

43 *wait on* escort
52 *receipts* preparations, mixtures
 1 *instructed* directed

---

45 *cockpit*. Probably the Cockpit in Whitehall, where plays as well as cock-fighting (a sport made fashionable by the King's enthusiasm for it) took place. An inadvertent sexual innuendo (cf. 'An Epigram on the Court Pucelle', 3–4) is brought out by *weapons*.

MOROSE

Would I could redeem it with the loss of an eye, nephew, a
hand, or any other member.

DAUPHINE

Marry, God forbid, sir, that you should geld yourself to      10
anger your wife.

MOROSE

So it would rid me of her! And that I did supererogatory
penance, in a belfry, at Westminster Hall, i' the cockpit, at
the fall of a stag, the Tower Wharf—what place is there
else?—London Bridge, Paris Garden, Belinsgate, when      15
the noises are at their height and loudest. Nay, I would sit
out a play that were nothing but fights at sea, drum,
trumpet, and target!

DAUPHINE

I hope there shall be no such need, sir. Take patience, good
uncle. This is but a day, and 'tis well worn too now.        20

MOROSE

Oh, 'twill be so forever, nephew, I foresee it, forever.
Strife and tumult are the dowry that comes with a wife.

TRUEWIT

I told you so, sir, and you would not believe me.

MOROSE

Alas, do not rub those wounds, Master Truewit, to blood
again; 'twas my negligence. Add not affliction to affliction.   25
I have perceived the effect of it, too late, in Madam Otter.

EPICOENE

[*Coming forward*] How do you, sir?


18 *target* shield
26 *effect* fulfilment, embodiment

---

13 *Westminster Hall*. Its shops and law-courts drew noisy crowds.
   *i' the cockpit* F corr. (in a Cock-pit F uncorr.). See notes to I.i, 177,
   IV.iii, 45.
14 *fall ... stag*. Accompanied by the clamour of hounds and huntsmen's
   horns.
15 *London Bridge*. The bridge-piers obstructing the stream made the water roar
   loudly; cf. Middleton and Rowley's *A Fair Quarrel*, IV.iv, 46.
   *Paris Garden*. Centre for bear-baiting and other noisy sports; cf. III.i, 15.
   *Belinsgate*. Billingsgate, wharf east of London Bridge specializing in fish and
   fruit, supposedly built by King Belin; its fishwives made it a byword for coarse
   and raucous language.
17 *play ... sea*. Such as Heywood and Rowley's *Fortune by Land and Sea* (1607), an
   episodic romance drama of the sort Jonson despised.

MOROSE

Did you ever hear a more unnecessary question? As if she did not see! Why, I do as you see, empress, empress.

EPICOENE

You are not well, sir! You look very ill! Something has    30
distempered you.

MOROSE

Oh horrible, monstrous impertinencies! Would not one of these have served? Do you think, sir? Would not one of these have served?

TRUEWIT

Yes, sir, but these are but notes of female kindness, sir;    35
certain tokens that she has a voice, sir.

MOROSE

Oh, is't so? Come, and't be no otherwise—what say you?

EPICOENE

How do you feel yourself, sir?

MOROSE

Again that!

TRUEWIT

Nay, look you, sir: you would be friends with your wife    40
upon unconscionable terms, her silence—

EPICOENE

They say you are run mad, sir.

MOROSE

Not for love, I assure you, of you; do you see?

EPICOENE

Oh lord, gentlemen! Lay hold on him for God's sake. What shall I do? Who's his physician—can you tell—that knows    45
the state of his body best, that I might send for him? Good sir, speak. I'll send for one of my doctors else.

MOROSE

What, to poison me, that I might die intestate and leave you possessed of all?

EPICOENE

Lord, how idly he talks, and how his eyes sparkle! He looks    50
green about the temples! Do you see what blue spots he has?

---

32 *impertinencies* irrelevances
35 *notes* marks
   *kindness* punning on the sense 'natural tendency, behaviour according to kind'
41 *unconscionable* unreasonably demanding

CLERIMONT
Ay, it's melancholy.

EPICOENE
Gentlemen, for heaven's sake counsel me. Ladies! Servant, you have read Pliny and Paracelsus: ne'er a word now    55
to comfort a poor gentlewoman? Ay me! What fortune had
I to marry a distracted man?

DAW
I'll tell you, mistress—

TRUEWIT
[*Aside*] How rarely she holds it up!
[TRUEWIT *and* CLERIMONT *prevent* MOROSE *from leaving*]

MOROSE
What mean you, gentlemen?    60

EPICOENE
What will you tell me, servant?

DAW
The disease in Greek is called μανία, in Latin *insania,
furor, vel ecstasis melancholica*, that is, *egressio*, when a man
*ex melancholico evadit fanaticus*.

MOROSE
Shall I have a lecture read upon me alive?    65

DAW
But he may be but *phreneticus* yet, mistress, and *phrenetis* is
only *delirium* or so—

EPICOENE
Ay, that is for the disease, servant; but what is this to the
cure? We are sure enough of the disease.

MOROSE
Let me go!    70

TRUEWIT
Why, we'll entreat her to hold her peace, sir.

66 *mistress* ed. (mistris? F)
68 *is this to* has this got to do with

---

53 *melancholy*. Perhaps in the original Greek sense, 'frenzy, madness' (H&S). In
Elizabethan psychology the term indicated an excess of bile in the mixture of the
four humours, causing irascibility and broodiness.
55 *Pliny*. 1st-century Roman author of the encyclopedic *Historia Naturalis*.
*Paracelsus*. Famous Swiss scientist (1493–1541); the first to introduce chemistry
to the study of medicine.
62 μανία ... *fanaticus*. Emptily repetitive: 'madness ... insanity, frenzy, or
melancholic ecstasy ... a going out of one's mind, when a man from being
melancholy becomes mad'. Daw's next speech only extends the tautology.
65 *have ... alive*. i.e. be treated as a specimen in an anatomy class.

MOROSE

Oh no, labour not to stop her. She is like a conduit-pipe
that will gush out with more force when she opens again.

HAUGHTY

I'll tell you, Morose, you must talk divinity to him
altogether, or moral philosophy.                                    75

LA FOOLE

Ay, and there's an excellent book of moral philosophy,
madam, of Reynard the Fox and all the beasts, called
*Doni's Philosophy*.

CENTAURE

There is indeed, Sir Amorous La Foole.

MOROSE

Oh misery!                                                          80

LA FOOLE

I have read it, my Lady Centaure, all over to my cousin
here.

MISTRESS OTTER

Ay, and 'tis a very good book as any is of the moderns.

DAW

Tut, he must have Seneca read to him, and Plutarch and
the ancients; the moderns are not for this disease.                85

CLERIMONT

Why, you discommended them too today, Sir John.

DAW

Ay, in some cases; but in these they are best, and Aristotle's *Ethics*.

MAVIS

Say you so, Sir John? I think you are deceived: you took it
upon trust.                                                         90

HAUGHTY

Where's Trusty, my woman? I'll end this difference. I
prithee, Otter, call her. Her father and mother were both
mad when they put her to me.

[*Exit* MISTRESS OTTER]

MOROSE

I think so.—Nay, gentlemen, I am tame. This is but an

---

93 *put ... me* placed her in my charge

---

78 *Doni's Philosophy*. A collection of oriental beast fables translated into Italian by
Doni and into English by Thomas North, with the title *The Moral Philosophy of
Doni* (1570): La Foole is clearly as mesmerized by titles as Daw. The fable of
Reynard is not included.

exercise, I know, a marriage ceremony, which I must    95
endure.

HAUGHTY

And one of 'em—I know not which—was cured with *The Sick Man's Salve*, and the other with Greene's *Groat's-worth of Wit*.

TRUEWIT

A very cheap cure, madam.    100

HAUGHTY

Ay, it's very feasible.

[*Enter* MISTRESS OTTER *with* TRUSTY]

MISTRESS OTTER

My lady called for you, Mistress Trusty; you must decide a controversy.

HAUGHTY

Oh, Trusty, which was it you said, your father or your mother, that was cured with *The Sick Man's Salve*?    105

TRUSTY

My mother, madam, with the *Salve*.

TRUEWIT

Then it was *The Sick Woman's Salve*.

TRUSTY

And my father with the *Groat's-worth of Wit*. But there was other means used: we had a preacher that would preach folk asleep still; and so they were prescribed to go to    110
church by an old woman that was their physician, thrice a week—

EPICOENE

To sleep?

TRUSTY

Yes, forsooth; and every night they read themselves asleep on those books.    115

---

101 *feasible* practicable
110 *still* always

---

95 *exercise*. Several senses are involved: (i) performance of a ceremony; (ii) training, as of an animal (cf. *tame*); (iii) disciplinary suffering, trial. Sense (iii) was often used of saints and martyrs, and thus fits Morose's view of his plight; cf. I.i, 165, III.vii, 11–13.

97–8 *The . . . Salve*. Religious tract by Thomas Becon urging patience and humility in time of illness; seventeen editions appeared between 1561 and 1632.

98–9 *Greene's . . . Wit*. Robert Greene's popular admonitory and confessional pamphlet (1592), written on his death-bed.

EPICOENE

Good faith, it stands with great reason. I would I knew
where to procure those books.

MOROSE

Oh!

LA FOOLE

I can help you with one of 'em, Mistress Morose, the
*Groat's-worth of Wit.*                                              120

EPICOENE

But I shall disfurnish you, Sir Amorous. Can you spare it?

LA FOOLE

Oh, yes, for a week or so; I'll read it myself to him.

EPICOENE

No, I must do that, sir; that must be my office.

MOROSE

Oh, oh!

EPICOENE

Sure, he would do well enough, if he could sleep.            125

MOROSE

No, I should do well enough if you could sleep. Have I no
friend that will make her drunk? or give her a little
ladanum, or opium?

TRUEWIT

Why, sir, she talks ten times worse in her sleep.

MOROSE

How!                                                         130

CLERIMONT

Do you not know that, sir? Never ceases all night.

TRUEWIT

And snores like a porcpisce.

MOROSE

Oh, redeem me, fate, redeem me, fate! For how many
causes may a man be divorced, nephew?

DAUPHINE

I know not truly, sir.                                       135

TRUEWIT

Some divine must resolve you in that, sir, or canon lawyer.

MOROSE

I will not rest, I will not think of any other hope or comfort,
till I know.                    [*Exeunt* MOROSE *and* DAUPHINE]

121 *disfurnish you* deprive you (of the little wit you have)
128 *ladanum* laudanum (Jonson characteristically reverts to the classical, as
   opposed to the medieval, Latin form)
132 *porcpisce* porpoise (Latin *porcus piscis*, pig fish)
136 *canon lawyer* lawyer specializing in ecclesiastical law

CLERIMONT

Alas, poor man.

TRUEWIT

You'll make him mad indeed, ladies, if you pursue this.    140

HAUGHTY

No, we'll let him breathe now a quarter of an hour or so.

CLERIMONT

By my faith, a large truce.

HAUGHTY

Is that his keeper that is gone with him?

DAW

It is his nephew, madam.

LA FOOLE

Sir Dauphine Eugenie.    145

CENTAURE

He looks like a very pitiful knight—

DAW

As can be. This marriage has put him out of all.

LA FOOLE

He has not a penny in his purse, madam—

DAW

He is ready to cry all this day.

LA FOOLE

A very shark, he set me i' the nick t'other night at primero.    150

TRUEWIT

[*Aside*] How these swabbers talk!

CLERIMONT

[*Aside*] Ay, Otter's wine has swelled their humours above a spring-tide.

HAUGHTY

Good Morose, let's go in again. I like your couches exceeding well: we'll go lie and talk there.    155

EPICOENE

I wait on you, madam.

[*Exeunt* HAUGHTY, CENTAURE, MAVIS, TRUSTY, LA FOOLE
*and* DAW]

TRUEWIT

'Slight, I will have 'em as silent as signs, and their posts

143 *keeper* i.e. as though Morose were a lunatic
150 *shark* predatory cheat, sharper (Jonson's coinage)
151 *swabbers* louts (*OED*'s first example of this sense)

---

150 *set ... nick.* Implying 'cleaned me out'; to *set* is to bet against, and the *nick*, in
the dice game of hazard, the predetermined winning score. *Primero* is a card
game: La Foole is muddling his terms.

too, ere I ha' done. Do you hear, lady bride? I pray thee
now, as thou art a noble wench, continue this discourse of
Dauphine within; but praise him exceedingly. Magnify    160
him with all the height of affection thou canst—I have
some purpose in't—and but beat off these two rooks, Jack
Daw and his fellow, with any discontentment hither, and
I'll honour thee forever.

EPICOENE
I was about it here. It angered me to the soul to hear 'em    165
begin to talk so malapert.

TRUEWIT
Pray thee perform it, and thou winn'st me an idolater to
thee everlasting.

EPICOENE
Will you go in and hear me do it?

TRUEWIT
No, I'll stay here. Drive 'em out of your company, 'tis all I    170
ask; which cannot be any way better done than by extolling
Dauphine, whom they have so slighted.

EPICOENE
I warrant you; you shall expect one of 'em presently.
                                                          [*Exit*]

CLERIMONT
What a cast of kastrils are these, to hawk after ladies thus?

TRUEWIT
Ay, and strike at such an eagle as Dauphine.                    175

CLERIMONT
He will be mad when we tell him. Here he comes.


### Act IV, Scene v

[*Enter*] DAUPHINE

CLERIMONT
Oh sir, you are welcome.

TRUEWIT
Where's thine uncle?


163 *discontentment* annoyance, vexation
165 *about it* setting about it
166 *malapert* impudently

---

174 *cast of kastrils*. Pair of kestrels (which were cast off in pairs). *Kestrel*, like the
cognate *coistrel*, 'base fellow', was a term of contempt; cf. I.iv, 74 and note.

**DAUPHINE**

Run out o' doors in's night-caps to talk with a casuist about
his divorce. It works admirably.

**TRUEWIT**

Thou wouldst ha' said so and thou hadst been here! The          5
ladies have laughed at thee most comically since thou
went'st, Dauphine.

**CLERIMONT**

And asked if thou wert thine uncle's keeper?

**TRUEWIT**

And the brace of baboons answered yes, and said thou wert
a pitiful poor fellow and didst live upon posts, and hadst      10
nothing but three suits of apparel and some few benevol-
ences that lords ga' thee to fool to 'em and swagger.

**DAUPHINE**

Let me not live, I'll beat 'em. I'll bind 'em both to grand
madam's bed-posts and have 'em baited with monkeys.

**TRUEWIT**

Thou shalt not need, they shall be beaten to thy hand,         15
Dauphine. I have an execution to serve upon 'em I warrant
thee shall serve; trust my plot.

**DAUPHINE**

Ay, you have many plots! So you had one to make all the
wenches in love with me.

**TRUEWIT**

Why, if I do not yet afore night, as near as 'tis, and that they   20
do not every one invite thee and be ready to scratch for
thee, take the mortgage of my wit.

**CLERIMONT**

'Fore God, I'll be his witness; thou shalt have it,
Dauphine; thou shalt be his fool forever if thou dost not.

---

3 *casuist* theologian or other person who resolves cases of conscience or doubtful
   questions regarding duty or conduct (*OED*'s first example of the word)
10 *upon posts* by running errands
11 *three suits* like a servant; cf. III.i,37
16 *execution* legal writ enforcing a judgement
20 *night* evening
21 *scratch for* struggle fiercely to obtain (*OED*, v., 6.b); also literally: scratch each
   other

---

6 *comically.* (i) satirically, derisively (as though Dauphine were a comic character); (ii) in a comical manner. *OED*'s first example of the word.
8 *if ... keeper.* Cf. 'Am I my brothers keper?' (Genesis, iv.9, Geneva Bible).
15 *to thy hand.* For you, without exertion on your part; cf. *Antony and Cleopatra*,
   IV.xiv, 28–9: 'What thou wouldst do/Is done unto thy hand'.
24 *thou ... fool.* Truewit will be Dauphine's jester and butt.

TRUEWIT

Agreed. Perhaps 'twill be the better estate. Do you observe    25
this gallery, or rather lobby, indeed? Here are a couple of
studies, at each end one: here will I act such a tragicomedy
between the Guelphs and the Ghibellines, Daw and La
Foole. Which of 'em comes out first will I seize on. You
two shall be the chorus behind the arras, and whip out        30
between the acts and speak. If I do not make 'em keep the
peace for this remnant of the day, if not of the year, I have
failed once—I hear Daw coming. Hide, and do not laugh,
for God's sake.

[DAUPHINE *and* CLERIMONT *hide*]

[*Enter* DAW]

DAW

Which is the way into the garden, trow?                        35

TRUEWIT

Oh, Jack Daw! I am glad I have met with you. In good
faith, I must have this matter go no further between you. I
must ha' it taken up.

DAW

What matter, sir? Between whom?

TRUEWIT

Come, you disguise it: Sir Amorous and you. If you love      40
me, Jack, you shall make use of your philosophy now, for
this once, and deliver me your sword. This is not the
wedding the Centaurs were at, though there be a she-one

---

35 *trow* do you think
37 *matter* dispute (cf. *Hamlet*, II.ii,193–4)
38 *taken up* made up

---

25 *better estate.* Picking up *mortgage*: better for Dauphine to receive Truewit as his
  fool than the ladies as his lovers.
27 *tragicomedy.* A new type of drama introduced by Beaumont and Fletcher about
  the time *Epicoene* was written. The suggestion is that Daw and La Foole lack the
  dignity requisite to tragedy, and that such a hybrid unclassical form deserves
  such idiotic protagonists, as well as they it.
28 *Guelphs ... Ghibellines.* Papal and imperial factions which fought for power in
  medieval Italy. H&S note a reference to a lost play of this title, a 'tearing
  Tragaedy full of fights and skirmishes'.
30 *arras.* Thick tapestry hung across a recess at the back of the stage; handy for
  hiding behind, as Polonius found in *Hamlet*.
42–3 *This ... at.* At the marriage of Pirithous, King of the Lapiths, and Hip-
  podamia a bloody fight broke out when a Centaur tried to rape the bride
  (*Metamorphoses*, XII, 210ff.).

here. The bride has entreated me I will see no blood shed at
her bridal; you saw her whisper me erewhile.                    45

*[Takes his sword]*

DAW

As I hope to finish Tacitus, I intend no murder.

TRUEWIT

Do you not wait for Sir Amorous?

DAW

Not I, by my knighthood.

TRUEWIT

And your scholarship too?

DAW

And my scholarship too.                                         50

TRUEWIT

Go to, then I return you your sword, and ask you mercy;
but put it not up, for you will be assaulted. I understood
that you had apprehended it, and walked here to brave
him, and that you had held your life contemptible in regard
of your honour.                                                 55

DAW

No, no, no such thing, I assure you. He and I parted now
as good friends as could be.

TRUEWIT

Trust not you to that visor. I saw him since dinner with
another face: I have known many men in my time vexed
with losses, with deaths, and with abuses, but so offended    60
a wight as Sir Amorous did I never see, or read of. For
taking away his guests, sir, today, that's the cause, and he
declares it behind your back with such threat'nings and
contempts. He said to Dauphine you were the arrant'st
ass—                                                           65

DAW

Ay, he may say his pleasure.

TRUEWIT

And swears you are so protested a coward that he knows

---

52 *put ... up* do not sheathe it
53 *brave* defy
58 *visor* mask
62 *cause* subject of dispute, as at l. 165
67 *protested* declared

---

46 *Tacitus.* The Roman historian was a prolific author.
61 *wight.* Person. Truewit uses the archaic word to help evoke an atmosphere of
romantic chivalry (cf. 'read of').

you will never do him any manly or single right, and
therefore he will take his course.

DAW

I'll give him any satisfaction, sir—but fighting.                    70

TRUEWIT

Ay, sir, but who knows what satisfaction he'll take? Blood
he thirsts for, and blood he will have; and whereabouts on
you he will have it, who knows but himself?

DAW

I pray you, Master Truewit, be you a mediator.

TRUEWIT

Well, sir, conceal yourself then in this study till I return.    75
                                        *He puts him up*
Nay, you must be content to be locked in; for, for mine
own reputation, I would not have you seen to receive a
public disgrace, while I have the matter in managing.
Gods so, here he comes! Keep your breath close, that he do
not hear you sigh.—In good faith, Sir Amorous, he is not    80
this way; I pray you be merciful, do not murder him; he is
a Christian as good as you; you are armed as if you sought a
revenge on all his race. Good Dauphine, get him away
from this place. I never knew a man's choler so high but he
would speak to his friends, he would hear reason.—Jack    85
Daw. Jack Daw! Asleep?

DAW

Is he gone, Master Truewit?

TRUEWIT

Ay, did you hear him?

DAW

Oh God, yes.

TRUEWIT

[*Aside*] What a quick ear fear has!                    90

DAW

But is he so armed, as you say?

TRUEWIT

Armed? Did you ever see a fellow set out to take possession?

DAW

Ay, sir.

---

68 *do . . . right* grant him the right to meet you man-to-man in an honourable duel

---

90 *What . . . has.* Proverbial: 'Fear has a quick ear' (Tilley, F134).
92–3 *take possession.* i.e. of his property, a mission which often required force, or the
    threat of it.

TRUEWIT

That may give you some light to conceive of him; but 'tis    95
nothing to the principal. Some false brother i' the house
has furnished him strangely. Or, if it were out o' the house,
it was Tom Otter.

DAW

Indeed, he's a captain, and his wife is his kinswoman.

TRUEWIT

He has got somebody's old two-hand sword, to mow you    100
off at the knees. And that sword hath spawned such a
dagger!—But then he is so hung with pikes, halberds,
petronels, calivers, and muskets, that he looks like a justice
of peace's hall; a man of two thousand a year is not sessed at
so many weapons as he has on. There was never fencer    105
challenged at so many several foils. You would think he
meant to murder all Saint Pulchre's parish. If he could but
victual himself for half a year in his breeches, he is sufficiently armed to overrun a country.

DAW

Good lord, what means he, sir! I pray you, Master    110
Truewit, be you a mediator.

TRUEWIT

Well, I'll try if he will be appeased with a leg or an arm; if
not, you must die once.

DAW

I would be loath to lose my right arm, for writing madrigals.

TRUEWIT

Why, if he will be satisfied with a thumb or a little finger,    115
all's one to me. You must think I'll do my best.

  96 *principal* original, La Foole himself
     *false brother* treacherous associate
  97 *strangely* exceptionally, i.e. with many kinds of weapons
 103 *petronels* large pistols or carbines used by cavalry
     *calivers* light muskets
 113 *once* a common intensive: once for all, in short

───────────────────────────────

 100 *two-hand sword*. A large, fearsome, antiquated weapon, swung from side to side
     rather like a scythe. Clement comes close to mowing Brainworm off at the knees
     with one in *E.M.I.*, V.iii, 36.
 103–4 *justice . . . hall*. Commonly hung with weapons ancient and modern.
 104 *sessed*. Assessed; i.e. to be able to provide so many when required by the
     monarch.
 106 *at . . . foils*. To fence with so many different types of sword.
 107 *Pulchre's*. Or Sepulchre's, a large and crowded parish in north-west London.
 108 *breeches*. Daw is wearing the fashionable continental breeches with enormous
     stuffed legs, known as 'slops'.

DAW

Good sir, do.

*He puts him up again, and then* [DAUPHINE *and* CLERIMONT]
*come forth*

CLERIMONT

What hast thou done?

TRUEWIT

He will let me do nothing, man, he does all afore me; he
offers his left arm.      120

CLERIMONT

His left wing, for a Jack Daw.

DAUPHINE

Take it by all means.

TRUEWIT

How! Maim a man forever for a jest? What a conscience
hast thou?

DAUPHINE

'Tis no loss to him: he has no employment for his arms but    125
to eat spoon-meat. Beside, as good maim his body as his
reputation.

TRUEWIT

He is a scholar and a Wit, and yet he does not think so. But
he loses no reputation with us, for we all resolved him an
ass before. To your places again.      130

CLERIMONT

I pray thee let me be in at the other a little.

TRUEWIT

Look, you'll spoil all: these be ever your tricks.

CLERIMONT

No, but I could hit of some things that thou wilt miss, and
thou wilt say are good ones.

TRUEWIT

I warrant you. I pray forbear, I'll leave it off else.      135

DAUPHINE

Come away, Clerimont.            [*They hide*]

117 s.d. *come* ed. (*came* F)
126 *spoon-meat* baby-food
129 *resolved him* decided he was
133 *hit of* light upon

---

128 *so.* That his body might as well be maimed.
131 *in at.* Involved in (the fooling of). *OED* does not cite this expression before
     1814, when it gives 'in at the kill' (Supplement, 'kill', sb., 2.b). In view of the
     play's hunting and baiting imagery, this association would be highly appro-
     priate.

[*Enter* LA FOOLE]

TRUEWIT
Sir Amorous!
LA FOOLE
Master Truewit.
TRUEWIT
Whither were you going?
LA FOOLE
Down into the court to make water.                              140
TRUEWIT
By no means, sir; you shall rather tempt your breeches.
LA FOOLE
Why, sir?
TRUEWIT
[*Opening the other door*] Enter here if you love your life.
LA FOOLE
Why? Why?
TRUEWIT
Question till your throat be cut, do; dally till the enraged   145
soul find you.
LA FOOLE
Who's that?
TRUEWIT
Daw it is; will you in?
LA FOOLE
Ay, ay, I'll in; what's the matter?
TRUEWIT
Nay, if he had been cool enough to tell us that, there had    150
been some hope to atone you, but he seems so implacably
enraged.
LA FOOLE
'Slight, let him rage. I'll hide myself.
TRUEWIT
Do, good sir. But what have you done to him within that
should provoke him thus? You have broke some jest upon      155
him afore the ladies—
LA FOOLE
Not I, never in my life broke jest upon any man. The bride

141  *tempt* make trial of
151  *atone* set 'at one', reconcile
155  *broke ... him* cracked some joke at his expense

157  *never*. The colloquial omission of 'I' is paralleled in *E.M.I.*, IV.vii, 97.

was praising Sir Dauphine, and he went away in snuff, and
I followed him, unless he took offence at me in his drink
erewhile, that I would not pledge all the horse-full.          160

TRUEWIT

By my faith, and that may be, you remember well; but he
walks the round up and down, through every room o' the
house, with a towel in his hand, crying, 'Where's La Foole?
Who saw La Foole?' And when Dauphine and I demanded
the cause, we can force no answer from him but 'Oh          165
revenge, how sweet art thou! I will strangle him in this
towel'—which leads us to conjecture that the main cause of
his fury is for bringing your meat today, with a towel about
you, to his discredit.

LA FOOLE

Like enough. Why, and he be angry for that, I'll stay here   170
till his anger be blown over.

TRUEWIT

A good becoming resolution, sir. If you can put it on o' the
sudden.

LA FOOLE

Yes, I can put it on. Or I'll away into the country presently.

TRUEWIT

How will you get out o' the house, sir? He knows you are i'  175
the house, and he'll watch you this se'en-night but he'll
have you. He'll outwait a sergeant for you.

LA FOOLE

Why then I'll stay here.

TRUEWIT

You must think how to victual yourself in time then.

LA FOOLE

Why, sweet Master Truewit, will you entreat my cousin      180
Otter to send me a cold venison pasty, a bottle or two of
wine, and a chamber-pot?

158 *in snuff* in a huff
159 *unless* lest, in case
172 *put ... on* (i) adopt; (ii) feign
174 *presently* at once
176 *watch* keep watch for

---

162 *walks the round*. A military metaphor from the patrol which goes round a camp
    or fortress to check that the sentries are vigilant (H&S).
177 *sergeant*. Sheriff's officer. 'All the vacation hee lies imboagde behinde the
    lattice of some ... Ale-house, and if he spy his prey out he leaps' (Overbury, 'A
    Sargeant', *Characters*, 1618, sig. N6ᵛ).

TRUEWIT

A stool were better, sir, of Sir A-jax his invention.

LA FOOLE

Ay, that will be better indeed; and a pallet to lie on.

TRUEWIT

Oh, I would not advise you to sleep by any means.                    185

LA FOOLE

Would you not, sir? Why then I will not.

TRUEWIT

Yet there's another fear—

LA FOOLE

Is there, sir? What is't?

TRUEWIT

No, he cannot break open this door with his foot, sure.

LA FOOLE

I'll set my back against it, sir. I have a good back.                190

TRUEWIT

But then if he should batter.

LA FOOLE

Batter! If he dare, I'll have an action of batt'ry against him.

TRUEWIT

Cast you the worst. He has sent for powder already, and
what he will do with it, no man knows; perhaps blow up
the corner o' the house where he suspects you are. Here he  195
comes! In, quickly.

*He feigns as if one were present, to fright the other, who*
*is run in to hide himself*

I protest, Sir John Daw, he is not this way. What will you
do? Before God, you shall hang no petard here. I'll die
rather. Will you not take my word? I never knew one but
would be satisfied.—Sir Amorous, there's no standing        200
out. He has made a petard of an old brass pot, to force your
door. Think upon some satisfaction or terms to offer him.

LA FOOLE

[*Within*] Sir, I'll give him any satisfaction. I dare give any
terms.

TRUEWIT

You'll leave it to me then?                                         205

184 *pallet* straw mattress
193 *Cast* forecast, anticipate
198 *petard* bomb used to breach walls and blow down gates
200–1 *standing out* resisting

---

183 *A-jax.* Referring to Sir John Harington's treatise on the flushing toilet, *The*
*Metamorphosis of Ajax* (1596), with its pun on 'a jakes'.

LA FOOLE

Ay, sir. I'll stand to any conditions.

[TRUEWIT] *calls forth* CLERIMONT *and* DAUPHINE

TRUEWIT

How now, what think you, sirs? Were't not a difficult thing
to determine which of these two feared most?

CLERIMONT

Yes, but this fears the bravest; the other a whiniling das-
tard, Jack Daw. But La Foole, a brave heroic coward! And    210
is afraid in a great look and a stout accent. I like him rarely.

TRUEWIT

Had it not been pity these two should ha' been concealed?

CLERIMONT

Shall I make a motion?

TRUEWIT

Briefly. For I must strike while 'tis hot.

CLERIMONT

Shall I go fetch the ladies to the catastrophe?             215

TRUEWIT

Umh? Ay, by my troth.

DAUPHINE

By no mortal means. Let them continue in the state of
ignorance, and err still; think 'em wits and fine fellows as
they have done. 'Twere sin to reform them.

TRUEWIT

Well, I will have 'em fetched, now I think on't, for a private    220
purpose of mine; do, Clerimont, fetch 'em, and discourse
to 'em all that's past, and bring 'em into the gallery here.

DAUPHINE

This is thy extreme vanity now; thou think'st thou wert
undone if every jest thou mak'st were not published.

TRUEWIT

Thou shalt see how unjust thou art presently. Clerimont,    225
say it was Dauphine's plot. [*Exit* CLERIMONT] Trust me not
if the whole drift be not for thy good. There's a carpet i' the
next room; put it on, with this scarf over thy face and a
cushion o' thy head, and be ready when I call Amorous.
Away. [*Exit* DAUPHINE]—John Daw! [*Brings* DAW *out of his*    230
*study*]

206 s.d. TRUEWIT ed. (*He* F)
209 *whiniling* whimpering
213 *motion* proposal
215 *catastrophe* dénouement (as in a play; cf. ll. 6, 17–18, 27–31)
224 *published* made generally known, as at l. 300
227 *carpet* tablecloth of thick wool

DAW

What good news, sir?

TRUEWIT

Faith, I have followed and argued with him hard for you. I
told him you were a knight and a scholar, and that you
knew fortitude did consist *magis patiendo quam faciendo,
magis ferendo quam feriendo.* 235

DAW

It doth so indeed, sir.

TRUEWIT

And that you would suffer, I told him: so at first he
demanded, by my troth, in my conceit too much.

DAW

What was it, sir?

TRUEWIT

Your upper lip, and six o' your fore-teeth. 240

DAW

'Twas unreasonable.

TRUEWIT

Nay, I told him plainly, you could not spare 'em all. So
after long argument—*pro et con*, as you know—I brought
him down to your two butter-teeth, and them he would
have. 245

DAW

Oh, did you so? Why, he shall have 'em.

[*Enter above* HAUGHTY, CENTAURE, MAVIS, MISTRESS
OTTER, EPICOENE, TRUSTY, *and* CLERIMONT]

TRUEWIT

But he shall not, sir, by your leave. The conclusion is this,
sir: because you shall be very good friends hereafter, and
this never to be remembered or upbraided, besides that he
may not boast he has done any such thing to you in his own 250
person, he is to come here in disguise, give you five kicks in
private, sir, take your sword from you, and lock you up in
that study, during pleasure. Which will be but a little
while, we'll get it released presently.

238 *conceit* opinion
244 *butter-teeth* front teeth
248–51 *sir: ... person,* ed. (sir, ... person: F)
249 *upbraided* brought up as a ground for reproach
253 *during pleasure* for as long as he pleases

234–5 *magis ... feriendo.* 'More in suffering than in doing, more in enduring than in
striking'. Quoted elsewhere (see H&S), but the source is unknown.

**DAW**

Five kicks? He shall have six, sir, to be friends. 255

**TRUEWIT**

Believe me, you shall not overshoot yourself to send him
that word by me.

**DAW**

Deliver it, sir. He shall have it with all my heart, to be
friends.

**TRUEWIT**

Friends? Nay, and he should not be so, and heartily too, 260
upon these terms, he shall have me to enemy while I live.
Come, sir, bear it bravely.

**DAW**

Oh God, sir, 'tis nothing.

**TRUEWIT**

True. What's six kicks to a man that reads Seneca?

**DAW**

I have had a hundred, sir. 265

**TRUEWIT**

Sir Amorous! No speaking one to another, or rehearsing
old matters.

DAUPHINE *comes forth and kicks him*

**DAW**

One, two, three, four, five. I protest, Sir Amorous, you
shall have six.

**TRUEWIT**

Nay, I told you, you should not talk. Come, give him six, 270
and he will needs. [DAUPHINE *kicks him again*] Your sword.
[DAW *gives* TRUEWIT *his sword*] Now return to your safe
custody: you shall presently meet afore the ladies, and be
the dearest friends one to another. [DAW *goes into his study*]
—Give me the scarf; now thou shalt beat the other 275
barefaced. Stand by. [*Exit* DAUPHINE]—Sir Amorous!
[*Brings out* LA FOOLE]

**LA FOOLE**

What's here? A sword!

---

256 *overshoot yourself to* overreach yourself if you
267 *old matters* former quarrels
270 *you, you* ed. (you F)
276 *by.* ed. (by F) to one side

---

264 *Seneca.* The stoic philosopher. Cf. I.i, 59, 63 and note.

TRUEWIT

I cannot help it, without I should take the quarrel upon
myself; here he has sent you his sword—

LA FOOLE

I'll receive none on't. 280

TRUEWIT

And he wills you to fasten it against a wall, and break your
head in some few several places against the hilts.

LA FOOLE

I will not: tell him roundly. I cannot endure to shed my
own blood.

TRUEWIT

Will you not? 285

LA FOOLE

No. I'll beat it against a fair flat wall, if that will satisfy
him; if not, he shall beat it himself for Amorous.

TRUEWIT

Why, this is strange starting off when a man undertakes for
you! I offered him another condition: will you stand to
that? 290

LA FOOLE

Ay, what is't?

TRUEWIT

That you will be beaten in private.

LA FOOLE

Yes. I am content, at the blunt.

TRUEWIT

Then you must submit yourself to be hoodwinked in this
scarf, and be led to him, where he will take your sword 295

---

278 *without* unless
282 *several* different
283 *roundly* plainly
288 *starting off* swerving aside, shying away (said of horses)
    *undertakes* makes himself answerable
294 *hoodwinked* (i) blindfolded; (ii) duped

---

282 *hilts*. Because the hilt comprises several parts, pommel, handle, and shell, it
was often spoken of as plural.
287 *for Amorous*. 'For all Amorous cares' is preferable to 'on Amorous's behalf'; cf.
V.i, 87.
293 *at the blunt*. i.e. with the flat of the sword; strictly the phrase means to fence
with capped sword-points.

from you, and make you bear a blow over the mouth, gules,
and tweaks by the nose *sans nombre*.

LA FOOLE

I am content. But why must I be blinded?

TRUEWIT

That's for your good, sir: because if he should grow insolent upon this and publish it hereafter to your disgrace—      300
which I hope he will not do—you might swear safely and
protest he never beat you, to your knowledge.

LA FOOLE

Oh, I conceive.

TRUEWIT

I do not doubt but you'll be perfect good friends upon't,
and not dare to utter an ill thought one of another in future.   305

LA FOOLE

Not I, as God help me, of him.

TRUEWIT

Nor he of you, sir. If he should—Come, sir. [*Blindfolds
him*]—All hid, Sir John.

DAUPHINE *enters to tweak him*

LA FOOLE

Oh, Sir John, Sir John! Oh, o-o-o-o-o-Oh—[DAUPHINE
*takes his sword*]

TRUEWIT

Good Sir John, leave tweaking, you'll blow his nose off.     310
[*Exit* DAUPHINE *with the two swords*] 'Tis Sir John's
pleasure you should retire into the study. [*Unbinds* LA
FOOLE's *eyes and shuts him in*]Why, now you are friends. All
bitterness between you, I hope, is buried; you shall come
forth by and by Damon and Pythias upon't, and embrace     315
with all the rankness of friendship that can be.

296 *bear* (i) endure; (ii) in heraldry, carry, display
297 *nombre* ed. (*numbre* F)
299–300 *insolent* arrogant, overbearing, as at V.ii, 64
316 *rankness* (i) abundance; (ii) foulness

---

296–7 *a blow . . . nombre*. In ironic correspondence to I.iv, 39–42. La Foole's new
coat-of-arms will be a bloody mouth surrounded by numberless tweaked noses.
Cf. *Hamlet*, III.i, 571–4: 'Am I a coward?/Who . . ./Tweaks me by the nose?'
308 *All hid*. The cry in hide-and-seek; '[he] cryes all-hidde as boyes do' (Dekker,
*Satiromastix*, V.ii, 154).
315 *Damon and Pythias*. A type of loyal friendship. Pythias, sentenced to death by
the King of Syracuse, returned to save his friend Damon, who had gone bail for
him, and was reprieved for his fidelity.

[*Enter* DAUPHINE]

I trust we shall have 'em tamer i' their language hereafter.
Dauphine, I worship thee.—God's will, the ladies have
surprised us!

### Act IV, Scene vi

[*Enter from above*] HAUGHTY, CENTAURE, MAVIS, MISTRESS
OTTER, EPICOENE, TRUSTY, [*and* CLERIMONT,] *having
discovered part of the past scene above*

HAUGHTY
Centaure, how our judgements were imposed on by these
adulterate knights!
CENTAURE
Nay, madam, Mavis was more deceived than we; 'twas her
commendation uttered 'em in the college.
MAVIS
I commended but their wits, madam, and their braveries. I          5
never looked toward their valours.
HAUGHTY
Sir Dauphine is valiant, and a wit too, it seems.
MAVIS
And a Bravery too.
HAUGHTY
Was this his project?
MISTRESS OTTER
So Master Clerimont intimates, madam.          10
HAUGHTY
Good Morose, when you come to the college, will you
bring him with you? He seems a very perfect gentleman.
EPICOENE
He is so, madam, believe it.
CENTAURE
But when will you come, Morose?
EPICOENE
Three of four days hence, madam, when I have got me a          15
coach and horses.

---

319 *surprised* caught unawares (spoken for the ladies' benefit)
  2 *adulterate* counterfeit
  4 *uttered 'em* made them known
  5 *braveries* fine clothes
  8 *Bravery* cf. I.i,74

HAUGHTY

No, tomorrow, good Morose; Centaure shall send you her
coach.

MAVIS

Yes, faith, do, and bring Sir Dauphine with you.

HAUGHTY

She has promised that, Mavis.    20

MAVIS

He is a very worthy gentleman in his exteriors, madam.

HAUGHTY

Ay, he shows he is judicial in his clothes.

CENTAURE

And yet not so superlatively neat as some, madam, that
have their faces set in a brake!

HAUGHTY

Ay, and have every hair in form!    25

MAVIS

That wear purer linen than ourselves, and profess more
neatness than the French hermaphrodite!

EPICOENE

Ay, ladies, they, what they tell one of us, have told a
thousand, and are the only thieves of our fame, that think
to take us with that perfume or with that lace, and laugh at    30
us unconscionably when they have done.

HAUGHTY

But Sir Dauphine's carelessness becomes him.

CENTAURE

I could love a man for such a nose!

MAVIS

Or such a leg!

CENTAURE

He has an exceeding good eye, madam!    35

22 *judicial* a ludicrous mistake: not 'like a judge' but 'judicious'
23 *superlatively* exaggeratedly
26 *profess* practice
29 *fame* reputation

---

24 *in a brake*. In an immovable expression of countenance; cf. V.iii, 20. Another
image from horses: a *brake* was a frame for the horse's hoof while being shod.

27 *French hermaphrodite*. Mavis may only be indicating a type (the English tended
to envy the French for being ahead of them in fashion while despising them for
being effeminate), but she may also be making a historical reference: possibly to
the hermaphrodite said to be on show in London in Beaumont's *The Knight of the
Burning Pestle* (*c.* 1607–10), III, 276; or perhaps, as Beaurline suggests, to
Henry III of France (d. 1589), a notorious transvestite satirized in Thomas
Arthus's *Isle des Hermaphrodites* (1605).

MAVIS
And a very good lock!

CENTAURE
Good Morose, bring him to my chamber first.

MISTRESS OTTER
Please your honours to meet at my house, madam?

TRUEWIT
[*Aside to* DAUPHINE] See how they eye thee, man! They are
taken, I warrant thee.                                                    40

HAUGHTY
[*Approaching* TRUEWIT *and* DAUPHINE] You have unbraced
our brace of knights here, Master Truewit.

TRUEWIT
Not I, madam, it was Sir Dauphine's engine; who, if he
have disfurnished your ladyship of any guard or service by
it, is able to make the place good again in himself.                      45

HAUGHTY
There's no suspicion of that, sir.

CENTAURE
God so, Mavis, Haughty is kissing.

MAVIS
Let us go too and take part.

HAUGHTY
But I am glad of the fortune—beside the discovery of two
such empty caskets—to gain the knowledge of so rich a           50
mine of virtue as Sir Dauphine.

CENTAURE
We would be all glad to style him of our friendship, and see
him at the college.

MAVIS
He cannot mix with a sweeter society, I'll prophesy, and I
hope he himself will think so.                                            55

DAUPHINE
I should be rude to imagine otherwise, lady.

TRUEWIT
[*Aside to* DAUPHINE] Did not I tell thee, Dauphine? Why,
all their actions are governed by crude opinion, without
reason or cause; they know not why they do anything; but

36 *lock* see note to III.v, 68
41 *unbraced* disarmed, implying 'exposed, disgraced'
43 *engine* device
44 *service* glancing at the amatory sense; cf. *servant* = lover
46 *suspicion* affectedly for 'doubt'
49 *discovery* uncovery, exposure
52 *style ... friendship* affectedly for 'call him one of our friends'

as they are informed, believe, judge, praise, condemn,          60
love, hate, and in emulation one of another, do all these
things alike. Only, they have a natural inclination sways
'em generally to the worst, when they are left to themselves. But pursue it, now thou hast 'em.

HAUGHTY
Shall we go in again, Morose?                                   65

EPICOENE
Yes, madam.

CENTAURE
We'll entreat Sir Dauphine's company.

TRUEWIT
Stay, good madam, the interview of the two friends,
Pylades and Orestes: I'll fetch 'em out to you straight.

HAUGHTY
Will you, Master Truewit?                                       70

DAUPHINE
Ay, but, noble ladies, do not confess in your countenance
or outward bearing to 'em any discovery of their follies,
that we may see how they will bear up again, with what
assurance and erection.

HAUGHTY
We will not, Sir Dauphine.                                      75

CENTAURE [and] MAVIS
Upon our honours, Sir Dauphine.

TRUEWIT
Sir Amorous, Sir Amorous! The ladies are here.

LA FOOLE
[Within] Are they?

TRUEWIT
Yes, but slip out by and by as their backs are turned and
meet Sir John here, as by chance, when I call you.—Jack        80
Daw!

DAW
[Within] What say you, sir?

TRUEWIT
Whip out behind me suddenly, and no anger i' your looks
to your adversary.—Now, now!

68 *Stay* remain for

---

69 *Pylades and Orestes*. In the tragedies of Aeschylus and Euripides, Pylades is the
loyal friend who helps Orestes revenge the murder of his father, Agamemnon.

74 *erection*. Uprightness, confidence of bearing. The sexual pun is appropriate after
the ritual castration (Beaurline).

[LA FOOLE *and* DAW *come out of their studies and
salute each other*]

LA FOOLE

Noble Sir John Daw! Where ha' you been?                85

DAW

To seek you, Sir Amorous.

LA FOOLE

Me! I honour you.

DAW

I prevent you, sir.

CLERIMONT

They have forgot their rapiers!

TRUEWIT

Oh, they meet in peace, man.                90

DAUPHINE

Where's your sword, Sir John?

CLERIMONT

And yours, Sir Amorous?

DAW

Mine? My boy had it forth to mend the handle, e'en now.

LA FOOLE

And my gold handle was broke too, and my boy had it
forth.                95

DAUPHINE

Indeed, sir? How their excuses meet!

CLERIMONT

What a consent there is i' the handles!

TRUEWIT

Nay, there is so i' the points too, I warrant you.

MISTRESS OTTER

Oh me! Madam, he comes again, the madman! Away!
[*Exeunt hastily* HAUGHTY, CENTAURE, EPICOENE, MAVIS,
MISTRESS OTTER, TRUSTY, DAW *and* LA FOOLE]


### Act IV, Scene vii

[*Enter*] MOROSE [*with a sword in each hand*;] *he had found
the two swords drawn within*

MOROSE

What make these naked weapons here, gentlemen?

88  *prevent* anticipate, forestall
93  *had it forth* took it away from here
98  *points* (i) sword-points, which both have been afraid to use; (ii) various points of
their excuses

TRUEWIT

Oh, sir! Here hath like to been murder since you went! A
couple of knights fallen out about the bride's favours. We
were fain to take away their weapons, your house had been
begged by this time else—　　　　　　　　　　　　　　5

MOROSE

For what?

CLERIMONT

For manslaughter, sir, as being accessary.

MOROSE

And for her favours?

TRUEWIT

Ay, sir, heretofore, not present. Clerimont, carry 'em their
swords now. They have done all the hurt they will do.　10

[*Exit* CLERIMONT *with the swords*]

DAUPHINE

Ha' you spoke with a lawyer, sir?

MOROSE

Oh no! There is such a noise i' the court that they have
frighted me home with more violence than I went! Such
speaking and counter-speaking, with their several voices of
citations, appellations, allegations, certificates, attach-　15
ments, intergatories, references, convictions, and afflictions indeed among the doctors and proctors, that the noise
here is silence to't! A kind of calm midnight!

TRUEWIT

Why, sir, if you would be resolved indeed, I can bring you
hither a very sufficient lawyer and a learned divine, that　20
shall enquire into every least scruple for you.

MOROSE

Can you, Master Truewit?

TRUEWIT

Yes, and are very sober grave persons, that will dispatch it
in a chamber, with a whisper or two.

4 *fain* obliged
5 *begged* begged for by some courtier in anticipation of the confiscation of
Morose's property as that of a criminal
9 *heretofore* i.e. past ones
15–16 *attachments* writs of arrest
16 *intergatories* interrogatories
*references* submissions
17 *doctors ... proctors* barristers ... attorneys
21 *scruple* uncertainty, doubt

MOROSE

Good sir, shall I hope this benefit from you, and trust    25
myself into your hands?

TRUEWIT

Alas, sir! Your nephew and I have been ashamed, and
oft-times mad, since you went, to think how you are
abused. Go in, good sir, and lock yourself up till we call
you; we'll tell you more anon, sir.                  30

MOROSE

Do your pleasure with me, gentlemen; I believe in you,
and that deserves no delusion—

TRUEWIT

You shall find none, sir  [*Exit* MOROSE]—but heaped,
heaped plenty of vexation.

DAUPHINE

What wilt thou do now, Wit?                         35

TRUEWIT

Recover me hither Otter and the barber if you can, by any
means, presently.

DAUPHINE

Why? To what purpose?

TRUEWIT

Oh, I'll make the deepest divine and gravest lawyer out o'
them two for him—                            40

DAUPHINE

Thou canst not, man; these are waking dreams.

TRUEWIT

Do not fear me. Clap but a civil gown with a welt o' the one,
and a canonical cloak with sleeves o' the other, and give 'em
a few terms i' their mouths; if there come not forth as able a
doctor and complete a parson for this turn as may be    45
wished, trust not my election. And I hope, without wrong-
ing the dignity of either profession, since they are but
persons put on, and for mirth's sake, to torment him. The
barber smatters Latin, I remember.

---

28  *mad* furious
42  *fear* doubt
    *welt* border (here, of fur)
46  *election* ability to make choices, judgement

---

46–8  *without . . . sake.* Jonson is referring to, and guarding against a recurrence of,
    the trouble caused by his satire on lawyers in *Poet.*, I.ii, 117ff; cf. the Apolo-
    getical Dialogue, 81–2, and *Satiromastix*, IV.iii, 184–8.
49, 51  *smatters Latin . . . wrangle out.* *OED*'s first examples of these usages.

DAUPHINE
   Yes, and Otter too.                         50

TRUEWIT
   Well then, if I make 'em not wrangle out this case to his no
   comfort, let me be thought a Jack Daw, or La Foole, or
   anything worse. Go you to your ladies, but first send for
   them.

DAUPHINE
   I will.                              [*Exeunt*]    55

### Act V, Scene i

[*Enter*] LA FOOLE, CLERIMONT, DAW

LA FOOLE
Where had you our swords, Master Clerimont?
CLERIMONT
Why, Dauphine took 'em from the madman.
LA FOOLE
And he took 'em from our boys, I warrant you.
CLERIMONT
Very like, sir.
LA FOOLE
Thank you, good Master Clerimont. Sir John Daw and I          5
are both beholden to you.
CLERIMONT
Would I knew how to make you so, gentlemen.
DAW
Sir Amorous and I are your servants, sir.

[*Enter* MAVIS]

MAVIS
Gentlemen, have any of you a pen and ink? I would fain
write out a riddle in Italian for Sir Dauphine to translate.          10
CLERIMONT
Not I, in troth, lady, I am no scrivener.
DAW
I can furnish you, I think, lady.

[*Exeunt* DAW *and* MAVIS]

CLERIMONT
He has it in the haft of a knife, I believe!
LA FOOLE
No, he has his box of instruments.
CLERIMONT
Like a surgeon!                                                      15
LA FOOLE
For the mathematics: his squire, his compasses, his brass
pens, and black lead, to draw maps of every place and
person where he comes.
CLERIMONT
How, maps of persons!

16 *squire* square

LA FOOLE

    Yes, sir, of Nomentack, when he was here, and of the   20
    Prince of Moldavia, and of his mistress, Mistress
    Epicoene.

CLERIMONT

    Away! He has not found out her latitude, I hope.

LA FOOLE

    You are a pleasant gentleman, sir.

*[Enter DAW]*

CLERIMONT

    Faith, now we are in private, let's wanton it a little and talk   25
    waggishly. Sir John, I am telling Sir Amorous here that
    you two govern the ladies; where'er you come, you carry
    the feminine gender afore you.

DAW

    They shall rather carry us afore them, if they will, sir.

CLERIMONT

    Nay, I believe that they do, withal; but that you are the   30
    prime men in their affections, and direct all their actions—

DAW

    Not I; Sir Amorous is.

LA FOOLE

    I protest Sir John is.

DAW

    As I hope to rise i' the state, Sir Amorous, you ha' the
    person.   35

LA FOOLE

    Sir John, you ha' the person, and the discourse too.

DAW

    Not I, sir. I have no discourse—and then you have activity
    beside.

---

24 *pleasant* humorous, jocular
27 *ladies;* ed. (ladies, F)
37 *activity* gymnastic skill

---

20 *Nomentack*. Red Indian brought from Virginia to England in 1608 and sent back
    in May 1609.
21 *Prince of Moldavia*. See Introduction, p. xvii.
27–8 *you . . . afore you*. A punning jibe at the knights' effeminacy.
29 *They . . . them*. Waggishly referring to the male's superincumbency during
    coition.
30 *Nay . . . withal*. Glancing at the collegiates' masculinity.
35 *person*. Daw is apparently saying, affectedly, 'it is you who are'. La Foole
    understands him to mean, or puns weakly on, 'presence, attractiveness'.

LA FOOLE

I protest, Sir John, you come as high from Tripoli as I do every whit, and lift as many joined stools and leap over 'em, 40 if you would use it—

CLERIMONT

Well, agree on't together, knights, for between you you divide the kingdom or commonwealth of ladies' affections: I see it and can perceive a little how they observe you, and fear you, indeed. You could tell strange stories, my mas-  45 ters, if you would, I know.

DAW

Faith, we have seen somewhat, sir.

LA FOOLE

That we have: vellet petticoats and wrought smocks or so.

DAW

Ay, and—

CLERIMONT

Nay, out with it, Sir John; do not envy your friend the   50 pleasure of hearing, when you have had the delight of tasting.

DAW

Why—a—do you speak, Sir Amorous.

LA FOOLE

No, do you, Sir John Daw.

DAW

I' faith, you shall.    55

LA FOOLE

I' faith, you shall.

DAW

Why, we have been—

LA FOOLE

In the great bed at Ware together in our time. On, Sir John.

---

41 *use* practise

---

39 *come ... Tripoli*. 'To vault and tumble with activity. It was, I believe, first applied to the tricks of an ape or monkey, which might be supposed to come from that part of the world' (Nares). A more obvious explanation of the phrase, which Jonson uses elsewhere (cf. Epigram CXV), is a pun on *trip*.

43 *commonwealth*. Implying that Daw and La Foole's women are shared by everyone.

48 *vellet ... smocks*. Worn by high-class prostitutes; cf. *B.F.*, IV.vi, 19–20.

58 *great ... Ware*. Famous bed at the Saracen's Head, Ware, made about 1580, 7½ feet high and nearly 11 feet square, sleeping twelve people; mentioned in *Twelfth Night*, III.ii, 47–8. Now in the Victoria and Albert Museum.

DAW

Nay, do you, Sir Amorous.                                    60

CLERIMONT

And these ladies with you, knights?

LA FOOLE

No, excuse us, sir.

DAW

We must not wound reputation.

LA FOOLE

No matter; they were these, or others. Our bath cost us
fifteen pound, when we came home.                           65

CLERIMONT

Do you hear, Sir John, you shall tell me but one thing
truly, as you love me.

DAW

If I can, I will, sir.

CLERIMONT

You lay in the same house with the bride here?

DAW

Yes, and conversed with her hourly, sir.                    70

CLERIMONT

And what humour is she of? Is she coming and open, free?

DAW

Oh, exceeding open, sir. I was her servant, and Sir Amorous was to be.

CLERIMONT

Come, you have both had favours from her? I know and
have heard so much.                                         75

DAW

Oh no, sir.

LA FOOLE

You shall excuse us, sir: we must not wound reputation.

CLERIMONT

Tut, she is married now, and you cannot hurt her with any
report, and therefore speak plainly: how many times, i'
faith? Which of you led first? Ha?                          80

LA FOOLE

Sir John had her maidenhead, indeed.

---

72 *servant* cf. The Persons of the Play, l. 6

---

64 *bath.* La Foole seems to mean a medicinal bath for treating lice or venereal
disease, and absurdly offers this as a boast.

71 *coming and open.* For the innuendoes cf. *E.M.I.*, IV.x, 74, where Cob asks his
wife, 'doe you let [your doors] lie open for all commers?'

DAW

Oh, it pleases him to say so, sir, but Sir Amorous knows
what's what as well.

CLERIMONT

Dost thou i' faith, Amorous?

LA FOOLE

In a manner, sir.       85

CLERIMONT

Why, I commend you, lads. Little knows Don Bridegroom
of this. Nor shall he, for me.

DAW

Hang him, mad ox.

CLERIMONT

Speak softly: here comes his nephew, with the Lady
Haughty. He'll get the ladies from you, sirs, if you look not    90
to him in time.

LA FOOLE

Why, if he do, we'll fetch 'em home again, I warrant you.

                               [*Exeunt*]

## Act V, Scene ii

### [*Enter*] HAUGHTY, DAUPHINE

HAUGHTY

I assure you, Sir Dauphine, it is the price and estimation of
your virtue only that hath embarked me to this adventure,
and I could not but make out to tell you so; nor can I repent
me of the act, since it is always an argument of some virtue
in ourselves that we love and affect it so in others.       5

DAUPHINE

Your ladyship sets too high a price on my weakness.

HAUGHTY

Sir, I can distinguish gems from pebbles—

---

3  *make out* make shift, contrive (*OED* has no other example before 1776)
4  *argument* proof, token
5  *affect* love

---

86  *Don.* The Spanish title for 'Master' was often used contemptuously or jocularly,
    somewhat the way we now use 'Comrade' (Partridge).
88  *mad ox.* Crazy fool, and suggesting 'maddened cuckold', because of the ox's
    horns.
 1  *price.* Value, worth. The near synonimity with 'estimation' is symptomatic of
    Haughty's extravagant language; cf. the similarly redundant couplings at ll. 5,
    10, 16, and Dauphine's ironic play on 'price' at l. 6.

DAUPHINE

Are you so skilful in stones?

HAUGHTY

And howsoever I may suffer in such a judgement as yours,
by admitting equality of rank or society with Centaure or          10
Mavis—

DAUPHINE

You do not, madam; I perceive they are your mere foils.

HAUGHTY

Then are you a friend to truth, sir. It makes me love you
the more. It is not the outward but the inward man that I
affect. They are not apprehensive of an eminent perfec-          15
tion, but love flat and dully.

CENTAURE

[*Within*] Where are you, my Lady Haughty?

HAUGHTY

I come presently, Centaure. — My chamber, sir, my page
shall show you; and Trusty, my woman, shall be ever
awake for you; you need not fear to communicate anything          20
with her, for she is a Fidelia. I pray you wear this jewel for
my sake, Sir Dauphine.

[*Enter* CENTAURE]

Where's Mavis, Centaure?

CENTAURE

Within, madam, a-writing. I'll follow you presently. I'll
but speak a word with Sir Dauphine.          25

[*Exit* HAUGHTY]

DAUPHINE

With me, madam?

CENTAURE

Good Sir Dauphine, do not trust Haughty, nor make any
credit to her, whatever you do besides. Sir Dauphine, I
give you this caution, she is a perfect courtier and loves
nobody but for her uses, and for her uses she loves all.          30
Besides, her physicians give her out to be none o' the
clearest—whether she pay 'em or no, heav'n knows; and

---

8 *stones* (i) gemstones; (ii) testicles
12 *foils* (i) settings for a jewel; (ii) contrasts which show one off to advantage

---

21 *Fidelia*. Latin for 'trusty'; also a common name for a heroine in popular
romances.
27–8 *make ... to*. Put any faith in (Latin *fidem facere*). More loose tautological
language.

she's above fifty too, and pargets! See her in a forenoon. Here comes Mavis, a worse face than she! You would not like this by candlelight. If you'll come to my chamber one     35 o' these mornings early, or late in an evening, I'll tell you more.

[*Enter* MAVIS]

Where's Haughty, Mavis?

MAVIS
Within, Centaure.

CENTAURE
What ha' you there?     40

MAVIS
An Italian riddle for Sir Dauphine.—You shall not see it i' faith, Centaure.—Good Sir Dauphine, solve it for me. I'll call for it anon.

[*Exeunt* MAVIS *and* CENTAURE]
[*Enter* CLERIMONT]

CLERIMONT
How now, Dauphine? How dost thou quit thyself of these females?     45

DAUPHINE
'Slight, they haunt me like fairies, and give me jewels here; I cannot be rid of 'em.

CLERIMONT
Oh, you must not tell though.

DAUPHINE
Mass, I forgot that; I was never so assaulted. One loves for virtue, and bribes me with this. Another loves me with     50

44 *quit ... of* (i) acquit yourself with; (ii) rid yourself of
50 *this* this jewel

---

33 *pargets*. Plasters (herself with make-up); more usually used of roughcasting walls than face-painting.
35 *by candlelight*. Even by candlelight, by which all women are said to look attractive; cf. Tilley, W682, and 'An Epigram on the Court Pucelle', 32: 'Her face there's none can like by Candle light'.
41–2 *You ... Centaure*. Bracketed in F, which may indicate that Mavis says this to herself, or as a tart aside to Centaure, or merely that this is a temporary diversion in the main flow of the speech.
48 *you ... tell*. 'Fairies treasure ... reveal'd, brings on the blabbers, ruine' (Massinger, *The Fatal Dowry*, IV.i, 191–2; *Plays and Poems*, ed. P. Edwards and C. Gibson, Oxford, 1976).

caution, and so would possess me. A third brings me a
riddle here, and all are jealous and rail each at other.

CLERIMONT

A riddle? Pray' le' me see't?        *He reads the paper*
'Sir Dauphine, I chose this way of intimation for privacy.
The ladies here, I know, have both hope and purpose to        55
make a collegiate and servant of you. If I might be so
honoured as to appear at any end of so noble a work, I
would enter into a fame of taking physic tomorrow and
continue it four or five days or longer, for your visitation.
Mavis.'—By my faith, a subtle one! Call you this a riddle?    60
What's their plain dealing, trow?

DAUPHINE

We lack Truewit to tell us that.

CLERIMONT

We lack him for somewhat else too: his knights *reformados*
are wound up as high and insolent as ever they were.

DAUPHINE

You jest.                                                      65

CLERIMONT

No drunkards, either with wine or vanity, ever confessed
such stories of themselves. I would not give a fly's leg in
balance against all the women's reputations here, if they
could be but thought to speak truth; and for the bride, they
have made their affidavit against her directly—                70

DAUPHINE

What, that they have lien with her?

CLERIMONT

Yes, and tell times and circumstances, with the cause why
and the place where. I had almost brought 'em to affirm
that they had done it today.

DAUPHINE

Not both of 'em.                                               75

51 *caution* warning advice
58 *enter ... fame* affectedly for 'begin a rumour'
71 *lien* lain

59 *visitation*. A smart quibble: 'the action or practice of visiting sick or distressed
persons as a work of charity or pastoral care' (*OED*, sb., 3).
63 *reformados*. Officers of disbanded companies who retained their rank; hence
'hollow, spurious'. Punning also on *reformed*.

CLERIMONT
Yes, faith; with a sooth or two more I had effected it. They
would ha' set it down under their hands.
DAUPHINE
Why, they will be our sport, I see, still! whether we will or
no.


## Act V, Scene iii

[*Enter*] TRUEWIT

TRUEWIT
Oh, are you here? Come, Dauphine. Go call your uncle
presently. I have fitted my divine and my canonist, dyed
their beards and all; the knaves do not know themselves,
they are so exalted and altered. Preferment changes any
man. Thou shalt keep one door and I another, and then          5
Clerimont in the midst, that he may have no means of
escape from their cavilling when they grow hot once. And
then the women—as I have given the bride her instructions—to break in upon him i' the *l'envoy*. Oh, 'twill be full
and twanging! Away, fetch him.          10

[*Exit* DAUPHINE]

[*Enter* CUTBEARD *disguised as a canon lawyer,* OTTER
*as a divine*]

Come, master doctor and master parson, look to your parts
now and discharge 'em bravely; you are well set forth,
perform it as well. If you chance to be out, do not confess it
with standing still or humming or gaping one at another,
but go on and talk aloud and eagerly, use vehement action,          15
and only remember your terms, and you are safe. Let the

5 *keep* guard
12 *bravely* worthily, finely
13 *be out* forget your words
15 *action* rhetorical gestures as an accompaniment to speech
16 *terms* i.e. technical Latin terms

---

76 *sooth . . . it*. Probably 'with one or two more exclamations of "sooth" (= really,
indeed)'. *OED*'s gloss, 'flattery, blandishment' (sb., 8), seems mistaken.
Neither of its other two examples is precisely parallel, and one may be the verb
*soothe* oddly spelled.
9 *l'envoy*. Conclusion. Literally, concluding stanza of a poem or ballad, hence 'full
and twanging'.

matter go where it will: you have many will do so. But at
first be very solemn and grave like your garments, though
you loose yourselves after and skip out like a brace of
jugglers on a table. Here he comes! Set your faces, and look    20
superciliously while I present you.

[*Enter* DAUPHINE *and* MOROSE]

MOROSE
Are these the two learned men?

TRUEWIT
Yes, sir; please you salute 'em?

MOROSE
Salute 'em? I had rather do anything than wear out time so
unfruitfully, sir. I wonder how these common forms, as      25
'God save you' and 'You are welcome', are come to be a
habit in our lives! Or 'I am glad to see you'! when I cannot
see what the profit can be of these words, so long as it is no
whit better with him whose affairs are sad and grievous
that he hears this salutation.                              30

TRUEWIT
'Tis true, sir; we'll go to the matter then. Gentlemen,
master doctor and master parson, I have acquainted you
sufficiently with the business for which you are come
hither. And you are not now to inform yourselves in the
state of the question, I know. This is the gentleman who    35
expects your resolution, and therefore, when you please,
begin.

OTTER
Please you, master doctor.

CUTBEARD
Please you, good master parson.

OTTER
I would hear the canon law speak first.                     40

CUTBEARD
It must give place to positive divinity, sir.

MOROSE
Nay, good gentlemen, do not throw me into circumstances. Let your comforts arrive quickly at me, those that are.

---

17 *matter* substance, content (of your discussion)
34 *are not now* do not need
41 *positive* practical, as opposed to theoretical or speculative (*OED*)

---

42–3 *circumstances*. Circumstantialities; suggested by *ne me in longae orationis
ambages coniiciatis* in the Latin translation of Libanius.

Be swift in affording me my peace, if so I shall hope any. I
love not your disputations or your court tumults. And that 45
it be not strange to you, I will tell you. My father, in my
education, was wont to advise me that I should always
collect and contain my mind, not suff'ring it to flow
loosely; that I should look to what things were necessary to
the carriage of my life, and what not, embracing the one 50
and eschewing the other. In short, that I should endear
myself to rest and avoid turmoil, which now is grown to be
another nature to me. So that I come not to your public
pleadings or your places of noise; not that I neglect those
things that make for the dignity of the commonwealth, but 55
for the mere avoiding of clamours and impertinencies of
orators, that know not how to be silent. And for the cause
of noise am I now a suitor to you. You do not know in what
a misery I have been exercised this day, what a torrent of
evil! My very house turns round with the tumult! I dwell 60
in a windmill! The perpetual motion is here, and not at
Eltham.

TRUEWIT

Well, good master doctor, will you break the ice? Master
parson will wade after.

CUTBEARD

Sir, though unworthy, and the weaker, I will presume. 65

OTTER

'Tis no presumption, *domine* doctor.

MOROSE

Yet again!

CUTBEARD

Your question is, for how many causes a man may have
*divortium legitimum*, a lawful divorce. First, you must
understand the nature of the word divorce, *a divertendo*— 70

---

54 *neglect* do not care about (Latin *negligo*)
56 *impertinencies* F corr. (pertinencies F uncorr.) irrelevances
66 *domine* master
70 *a divertendo* (it is derived) from 'separating'

---

59 *exercised*. 'Harassed, afflicted', but *in* rather than *with* suggests additional
senses: trained; disciplined in suffering, like a martyr; cf. IV.iv, 95 and note.
61 *perpetual motion*. Famous perpetual motion machine invented by a Dutch scientist, Cornelius Drebbel, on display at Eltham Palace, where Drebbel, who
had come to live in London about 1609/10, was probably staying; described and
illustrated in W. B. Rye, *England as Seen by Foreigners in the Days of . . . James I*,
1885, pp. 232–42.

MOROSE

No excursions upon words, good doctor; to the question briefly.

CUTBEARD

I answer then, the canon law affords divorce but in few cases, and the principal is in the common case, the adulterous case. But there are *duodecim impedimenta*, twelve 75 impediments—as we call 'em—all which do not *dirimere contractum*, but *irritum reddere matrimonium*, as we say in the canon law, not take away the bond, but cause a nullity therein.

MOROSE

I understood you before; good sir, avoid your imper- 80 tinency of translation.

OTTER

He cannot open this too much, sir, by your favour.

MOROSE

Yet more!

TRUEWIT

Oh, you must give the learned men leave, sir. To your impediments, master doctor. 85

CUTBEARD

The first is *impedimentum erroris*.

OTTER

Of which there are several species.

CUTBEARD

Ay, as *error personae*.

OTTER

If you contract yourself to one person, thinking her another. 90

CUTBEARD

Then, *error fortunae*.

OTTER

If she be a beggar, and you thought her rich.

CUTBEARD

Then, *error qualitatis*.

OTTER

If she prove stubborn or headstrong, that you thought obedient. 95

72 *briefly* at once
82 *open* expound

---

86 ff. See Introduction, p. xxviii.
87 *species*. Italicized in F, so possibly the three-syllable Latin word.

MOROSE

How? Is that, sir, a lawful impediment? One at once, I
pray you, gentlemen.

OTTER

Ay, *ante copulam*, but not *post copulam*, sir.

CUTBEARD

Master parson says right. *Nec post nuptiarum benedic-*
*tionem.* It doth indeed but *irrita reddere sponsalia*, annul the     100
contract; after marriage it is of no obstancy.

TRUEWIT

Alas, sir, what a hope are we fall'n from, by this time!

CUTBEARD

The next is *conditio*: if you thought her free-born, and she
prove a bondwoman, there is impediment of estate and
condition.                                                            105

OTTER

Ay, but master doctor, those servitudes are *sublatae* now,
among us Christians.

CUTBEARD

By your favour, master parson—

OTTER

You shall give me leave, master doctor.

MOROSE

Nay, gentlemen, quarrel not in that question; it concerns     110
not my case: pass to the third.

CUTBEARD

Well then, the third is *votum*. If either party have made a
vow of chastity. But that practice, as master parson said of
the other, is taken away among us, thanks be to discipline.
The fourth is *cognatio*: if the persons be of kin within the     115
degrees.

OTTER

Ay. Do you know what the degrees are, sir?

MOROSE

No, nor I care not, sir; they offer me no comfort in the
question, I am sure.

99–100 *Nec ... benedictionem* and not after the blessing of the marriage
101 *obstancy* oppositional force (Latin *obstantia*). *OED*'s only example
102 *time* i.e. timing               106 *sublatae* abolished
114 *discipline* the Church's rules for conduct
116 *degrees* degrees of consanguinity within which marriage is not allowed

96 *One at once.* Speak one at a time, as in *Alch.*, V.v, 21–2.
106 *servitudes.* Otter flings his law-terms about wildly: this one strictly refers to
   landed property (H&S).

CUTBEARD

But there is a branch of this impediment may, which is    120
*cognatio spiritualis*. If you were her godfather, sir, then the
marriage is incestuous.

OTTER

That comment is absurd and superstitious, master doctor.
I cannot endure it. Are we not all brothers and sisters, and
as much akin in that as godfathers and god-daughters?    125

MOROSE

Oh me! To end the controversy, I never was a godfather, I
never was a godfather in my life, sir. Pass to the next.

CUTBEARD

The fifth is *crimen adulterii*: the known case. The sixth,
*cultus disparitas*, difference of religion: have you ever
examined her what religion she is of?    130

MOROSE

No, I would rather she were of none, than be put to the
trouble of it!

OTTER

You may have it done for you, sir.

MOROSE

By no means, good sir; on to the rest. Shall you ever come
to an end, think you?    135

TRUEWIT

Yes, he has done half, sir.—On to the rest.—Be patient
and expect, sir.

CUTBEARD

The seventh is *vis:* if it were upon compulsion or force.

MOROSE

Oh no, it was too voluntary, mine; too voluntary.

CUTBEARD

The eighth is *ordo*: if ever she have taken holy orders.    140

OTTER

That's superstitious too.

MOROSE

No matter, master parson: would she would go into a
nunnery yet.

CUTBEARD

The ninth is *ligamen*: if you were bound, sir, to any other
before.    145

MOROSE

I thrust myself too soon into these fetters.

---

128 *crimen adulterii* the crime of adultery
     *case* (i) instance; (ii) vagina (a common pun)

CUTBEARD

The tenth is *publica honestas*, which is *inchoata quaedam affinitas*.

OTTER

Ay, or *affinitas orta ex sponsalibus*, and is but *leve impedimentum*.                                                      150

MOROSE

I feel no air of comfort blowing to me in all this.

CUTBEARD

The eleventh is *affinitas ex fornicatione*.

OTTER

Which is no less *vera affinitas* than the other, master doctor.

CUTBEARD

True, *quae oritur ex legitimo matrimonio*.

OTTER

You say right, venerable doctor. And *nascitur ex eo, quod*   155
*per conjugium duae personae efficiuntur una caro*—

MOROSE

Heyday, now they begin!

CUTBEARD

I conceive you, master parson. *Ita per fornicationem aeque est verus pater, qui sic generat*—

OTTER

*Et vere filius qui sic generatur*—                            160

MOROSE

What's all this to me?

CLERIMONT

[*Aside*] Now it grows warm.

CUTBEARD

The twelfth and last is *si forte coire nequibis*.

OTTER

Ay, that is *impedimentum gravissimum*. It doth utterly

147 *publica honestas* public reputation
147–8 *inchoata ... affinitas* some (previous) uncompleted relationship by marriage
149 *affinitas ... sponsalibus* relationship arising from a betrothal
     *leve* slight
152 *affinitas ex fornicatione* relationship arising from fornication
153 *vera* true
154 *quae ... matrimonio* (than that) which arises from legal marriage
155–6 *nascitur ... caro* it springs from this, that through physical union two people
     are made one flesh
158–9 *Ita ... generat* Thus he is equally a true father who begets through for-
     nication
160 *Et ... generatur* and he truly a son who is thus begotten
163 *si ... nequibis* if it chances that you are unable to copulate
164 *gravissimum* very weighty

annul and annihilate, that. If you have *manifestam* 165
*frigiditatem*, you are well, sir.
TRUEWIT
Why, there is comfort come at length, sir. Confess yourself
but a man unable, and she will sue to be divorced first.
OTTER
Ay, or if there be *morbus perpetuus et insanabilis*, as para-
lysis, elephantiasis, or so—                                  170
DAUPHINE
Oh, but *frigiditas* is the fairer way, gentlemen.
OTTER
You say troth, sir, and as it is in the canon, master doctor.
CUTBEARD
I conceive you, sir.
CLERIMONT
[*Aside*] Before he speaks.
OTTER
That 'a boy or child under years is not fit for marriage 175
because he cannot *reddere debitum*'. So your *omnipotentes*—
TRUEWIT
[*Aside to* OTTER] Your *impotentes*, you whoreson lobster.
OTTER
Your *impotentes*, I should say, are *minime apti ad con-
trahenda matrimonium*.
TRUEWIT
[*Aside to* OTTER] *Matrimonium*? We shall have most unmat- 180
rimonial Latin with you: *matrimonia*, and be hanged.
DAUPHINE
[*Aside to* TRUEWIT] You put 'em out, man.
CUTBEARD
But then there will arise a doubt, master parson, in our
case, *post matrimonium*: that *frigiditate praeditus*—do you
conceive me, sir?                                             185

165–6 *manifestam frigiditatem* evident frigidity
169 *morbus ... insanabilis* a continuous and incurable disease
176 *reddere debitum* render what is required
178–9 *minime ... matrimonium* least suited to contracting marriages
184 *frigiditate praeditus* one who is frigid (lit. 'equipped with')

---

177 *lobster*. 'An opprobrious name (?for a red-faced man)' (*OED*, which cites three
other examples, all close in date).
180–1 *unmatrimonial*. Because the grammatical inflexions are not correctly
'married'.
182 *put 'em out*. Specifically at this date, 'make them forget their words'; cf. *As You
Like It*, IV.i, 76.

OTTER

Very well, sir.

CUTBEARD

Who cannot *uti uxore pro uxore*, may *habere eam pro sorore*.

OTTER

Absurd, absurd, absurd, and merely apostatical.

CUTBEARD

You shall pardon me, master parson, I can prove it.

OTTER

You can prove a will, master doctor, you can prove nothing    190
else. Does not the verse of your own canon say, *Haec
socianda vetant conubia, facta retractant—*

CUTBEARD

I grant you, but how do they *retractare*, master parson?

MOROSE

Oh, this was it I feared.

OTTER

*In aeternum*, sir.    195

CUTBEARD

That's false in divinity, by your favour.

OTTER

'Tis false in humanity to say so. Is he not *prorsus inutilis ad
thorum*? Can he *praestare fidem datam*? I would fain know.

CUTBEARD

Yes: how if he do *convalere*?

OTTER

He cannot *convalere*, it is impossible.    200

TRUEWIT

[*To* MOROSE] Nay, good sir, attend the learned men; they'll
think you neglect 'em else.

CUTBEARD

Or if he do *simulare* himself *frigidum, odio uxoris*, or so?

OTTER

I say he is *adulter manifestus* then.

DAUPHINE

They dispute it very learnedly, i' faith.    205

---

187 *uti ... sorore* use a wife as a wife, may keep her as a sister
188 *merely apostatical* absolutely heretical
191–2 *Haec ... retractant* these things forbid joinings together in marriage, and
    after marriages have been made annul them
195 *In aeternum* forever
197–8 *prorsus ... thorum* utterly useless for marriage (Otter's blunder for *torum*)
198 *praestare ... datam* fulfil the promise given    199 *convalere* recover
203 *simulare ... uxoris* pretend to be frigid, out of hatred for his wife
204 *adulter manifestus* a manifest adulterer

OTTER
And *prostitutor uxoris*, and this is positive.

MOROSE
Good sir, let me escape.

TRUEWIT
You will not do me that wrong, sir?

OTTER
And therefore, if he be *manifeste frigidus*, sir—

CUTBEARD
Ay, if he be *manifeste frigidus*, I grant you—  210

OTTER
Why, that was my conclusion.

CUTBEARD
And mine too.

TRUEWIT
Nay, hear the conclusion, sir.

OTTER
Then *frigiditatis causa*—

CUTBEARD
Yes, *causa frigiditatis*—  215

MOROSE
Oh, mine ears!

OTTER
She may have *libellum divortii* against you.

CUTBEARD
Ay, *divortii libellum* she will sure have.

MOROSE
Good echoes, forbear.

OTTER
If you confess it.  220

CUTBEARD
Which I would do, sir—

MOROSE
I will do anything—

OTTER
And clear myself *in foro conscientiae*—

CUTBEARD
Because you want indeed—

---

206 *prostitutor uxoris* the prostitutor of his wife
209 *manifeste* manifestly
214 *causa* on the ground of
217 *libellum divortii* a petition of divorce
223 *in foro conscientiae* at the bar of conscience; a law proverb (H&S)
224 *want* lack

MOROSE

Yet more?                  225

OTTER

*Exercendi potestate.*

## Act V, Scene iv

[*Enter*] EPICOENE, HAUGHTY, CENTAURE, MAVIS,
MISTRESS OTTER, DAW, LA FOOLE

EPICOENE

I will not endure it any longer! Ladies, I beseech you help
me. This is such a wrong as never was offered to poor bride
before. Upon her marriage-day, to have her husband conspire against her, and a couple of mercenary companions to
be brought in for form's sake, to persuade a separation! If    5
you had blood or virtue in you, gentlemen, you would not
suffer such earwigs about a husband, or scorpions to creep
between man and wife—

MOROSE

Oh the variety and changes of my torment!

HAUGHTY

Let 'em be cudgelled out of doors by our grooms.    10

CENTAURE

I'll lend you my footman.

MAVIS

We'll have our men blanket 'em i' the hall.

MISTRESS OTTER

As there was one at our house, madam, for peeping in at
the door.

DAW

Content, i' faith.    15

TRUEWIT

Stay, ladies and gentlemen, you'll hear before you pro-
ceed?

MAVIS

I'd ha' the bridegroom blanketed too.

CENTAURE

Begin with him first.

---

226 *Exercendi potestate* the power of putting into effect
  4 *companions* fellows (contemptuous), as at l. 142
  7 *earwigs* ear whisperers, parasites
 12 *blanket* toss in a blanket (*OED*'s first example)

HAUGHTY

Yes, by my troth.                                                    20.

MOROSE

Oh mankind generation!

DAUPHINE

Ladies, for my sake forbear.

HAUGHTY

Yes, for Sir Dauphine's sake.

CENTAURE

He shall command us.

LA FOOLE

He is as fine a gentleman of his inches, madam, as any is    25
about the town, and wears as good colours when he list.

TRUEWIT

[*Aside to* MOROSE] Be brief, sir, and confess your infirmity,
she'll be afire to be quit of you; if she but hear that named
once, you shall not entreat her to stay. She'll fly you like
one that had the marks upon him.                                   30

MOROSE

Ladies, I must crave all your pardons—

TRUEWIT

Silence, ladies.

MOROSE

For a wrong I have done to your whole sex in marrying this
fair and virtuous gentlewoman—

CLERIMONT

Hear him, good ladies.                                             35

MOROSE

Being guilty of an infirmity which, before I conferred with
these learned men, I thought I might have concealed—

TRUEWIT

But now being better informed in his conscience by them,

---

28 *you;* ed. (you, F)

---

21 *mankind.* Unnaturally masculine, virago-like, as in H. Smith, *A Preparative to
   Marriage*, 1591, pp. 61–2: 'A mankind woman is a monster, that is, halfe a
   woman and halfe a man'. The sense is related to *mankeen* or *mankind* = furious,
   savage (used of animals inclined to attack men).
25 *of his inches.* Valiant; cf. 'a tall fellow of thy hands' in *The Winter's Tale*, V.ii, 64.
   Probably with a (unconscious) bawdy quibble: 'according to thy inches' in *B.F.*,
   I.iii, 77, refers punningly to the length of the penis.
26 *colours.* Heraldic colours, insignia of a knight. La Foole is thinking of, or (if he
   has them on) drawing the attention of the ladies to, his own gaudy colours; cf.
   I.iv, 39–42.
30 *marks.* Surely 'marks of impotency'. Other editors gloss 'plague-marks'.

he is to declare it and give satisfaction by asking your
public forgiveness.      40

MOROSE

I am no man, ladies.

ALL

How!

MOROSE

Utterly unabled in nature, by reason of frigidity, to perform the duties or any the least office of a husband.

MAVIS

Now out upon him, prodigious creature!      45

CENTAURE

Bridegroom uncarnate.

HAUGHTY

And would you offer it, to a young gentlewoman?

MISTRESS OTTER

A lady of her longings?

EPICOENE

Tut, a device, a device, this, it smells rankly, ladies. A
mere comment of his own.      50

TRUEWIT

Why, if you suspect that, ladies, you may have him
searched.

DAW

As the custom is, by a jury of physicians.

LA FOOLE

Yes, faith, 'twill be brave.

MOROSE

Oh me, must I undergo that!      55

MISTRESS OTTER

No, let women search him, madam: we can do it ourselves.

MOROSE

Out on me, worse!

EPICOENE

No, ladies, you shall not need, I'll take him with all his
faults.

MOROSE

Worst of all!      60

47 *offer it* attempt to do such a thing
50 *comment* invention, fiction (Latin *commentum*)
52 *searched* examined

---

46 *uncarnate*. i.e. without flesh and blood. Centaure's coinage, from *incarnate*.
48 *longings*. (i) belongings, wealth, as in the phrase 'a man of his havings'; (ii)
(sexual) longings.

CLERIMONT

Why, then 'tis no divorce, doctor, if she consent not?

CUTBEARD

No, if the man be *frigidus*, it is *de parte uxoris* that we grant
*libellum divortii*, in the law.

OTTER

Ay, it is the same in theology.

MOROSE

Worse, worse than worst!                                         65

TRUEWIT

Nay, sir, be not utterly disheartened, we have yet a small
relic of hope left, as near as our comfort is blown out.
[*Aside to* CLERIMONT] Clerimont, produce your brace of
knights.—What was that, master parson, you told me *in
errore qualitatis*, e'en now? [*Aside to* DAUPHINE] Dauphine,   70
whisper the bride that she carry it as if she were guilty and
ashamed.

OTTER

Marry, sir, *in errore qualitatis* — which master doctor did
forbear to urge—if she be found *corrupta*, that is, vitiated
or broken up, that was *pro virgine desponsa*, espoused for a   75
maid—

MOROSE

What then, sir?

OTTER

It doth *dirimere contractum* and *irritum reddere* too.

TRUEWIT

If this be true, we are happy again, sir, once more. Here are
an honourable brace of knights that shall affirm so much.      80

DAW

Pardon us, good Master Clerimont.

LA FOOLE

You shall excuse us, Master Clerimont.

CLERIMONT

Nay, you must make it good now, knights, there is no
remedy; I'll eat no words for you nor no men: you know
you spoke it to me?                                            85

---

74 *vitiated* deflowered
78 *dirimere ... reddere* dissolve the contract and render it null and void

---

67 *as near ... out*. Cf. V.iii, 151.
68–9 *produce ... knights*. Clerimont must in V.iii or earlier in this scene have
  whispered to Truewit Daw and La Foole's claim to have slept with Epicoene,
  and arranged this piece of business with him; cf. V.iv, 211, 'unexpected'.

DAW

Is this gentleman-like, sir?

TRUEWIT

[*Aside to* DAW] Jack Daw, he's worse than Sir Amorous,
fiercer a great deal. [*Aside to* LA FOOLE] Sir Amorous,
beware, there be ten Daws in this Clerimont.

LA FOOLE

I'll confess it, sir.                                            90

DAW

Will you, Sir Amorous? Will you wound reputation?

LA FOOLE

I am resolved.

TRUEWIT

So should you be too, Jack Daw: what should keep you off?
She is but a woman, and in disgrace. He'll be glad on't.

DAW

Will he? I thought he would ha' been angry.                      95

CLERIMONT

You will dispatch, knights; it must be done, i' faith.

TRUEWIT

Why, an' it must, it shall, sir, they say. They'll ne'er go
back. [*Aside to* DAW *and* LA FOOLE] Do not tempt his
patience.

DAW

It is true indeed, sir.                                         100

LA FOOLE

Yes, I assure you, sir.

MOROSE

What is true, gentlemen? What do you assure me?

DAW

That we have known your bride, sir—

LA FOOLE

In good fashion. She was our mistress, or so—

CLERIMONT

Nay, you must be plain, knights, as you were to me.             105

OTTER

Ay, the question is, if you have *carnaliter* or no.

LA FOOLE

*Carnaliter*? What else, sir?

OTTER

It is enough: a plain nullity.

EPICOENE

I am undone, I am undone!

106 *carnaliter* carnally

MOROSE
    Oh, let me worship and adore you, gentlemen!                    110
EPICOENE
    I am undone!
MOROSE
    Yes, to my hand, I thank these knights. Master parson, let
    me thank you otherwise. [*Gives* OTTER *money*]
CENTAURE
    And ha' they confessed?
MAVIS
    Now out upon 'em, informers!                    115
TRUEWIT
    You see what creatures you may bestow your favours on,
    madams.
HAUGHTY
    I would except against 'em as beaten knights, wench, and
    not good witnesses in law.
MISTRESS OTTER
    Poor gentlewoman, how she takes it!                    120
HAUGHTY
    Be comforted, Morose, I love you the better for't.
CENTAURE
    So do I, I protest.
CUTBEARD
    But, gentlemen, you have not known her since *mat-
    rimonium*?
DAW
    Not today, master doctor.                    125
LA FOOLE
    No, sir, not today.
CUTBEARD
    Why, then I say, for any act before, the *matrimonium* is
    good and perfect, unless the worshipful bridegroom did
    precisely, before witness, demand if she were *virgo ante
    nuptias*.                    130

112 *to my hand* see note IV.v,15
118 *except against* object to
129 *precisely* expressly
129–30 *virgo ... nuptias* a virgin before the wedding

---

119 *not good witnesses.* Until the mid-sixteenth century a recreant knight 'was no
    longer accounted *liber et legalis homo*; and being by the event supposed to be
    forsworn, he was never put upon a jury, or admitted as a witness in any cause'
    (Gifford).

EPICOENE

No, that he did not, I assure you, master doctor.

CUTBEARD

If he cannot prove that, it is *ratum conjugium*, notwithstanding the premises. And they do no way *impedire*. And
this is my sentence, this I pronounce.

OTTER

I am of master doctor's resolution too, sir, if you made not    135
that demand *ante nuptias*.

MOROSE

Oh my heart! Wilt thou break? Wilt thou break? This is
worst of all worst worsts! that hell could have devised!
Marry a whore! and so much noise!

DAUPHINE

Come, I see now plain confederacy in this doctor and this    140
parson, to abuse a gentleman. You study his affliction. I
pray be gone, companions. And gentlemen, I begin to
suspect you for having parts with 'em. Sir, will it please
you hear me?

MOROSE

Oh, do not talk to me, take not from me the pleasure of    145
dying in silence, nephew.

DAUPHINE

Sir, I must speak to you. I have been long your poor
despised kinsman, and many a hard thought has streng-
thened you against me; but now it shall appear if either I
love you or your peace, and prefer them to all the world    150
beside. I will not be long or grievous to you, sir. If I free
you of this unhappy match absolutely and instantly after all
this trouble, and almost in your despair now—

MOROSE

It cannot be.

DAUPHINE

Sir, that you be never troubled with a murmur of it more,    155
what shall I hope for or deserve of you?

MOROSE

Oh, what thou wilt, nephew! Thou shalt deserve me and
have me.

DAUPHINE

Shall I have your favour perfect to me, and love hereafter?

132 *ratum conjugium* a valid marriage
141 *study* seek, aim at; punning on scholarly study

---

137–8 *This . . . worsts.* Echoing St John Chrysostom's 'Ω κακὸν κακῶν κάκιϐτον,
     'O this is worst, of all worsts worst' (Upton).

MOROSE

That and anything beside. Make thine own conditions. My      160
whole estate is thine. Manage it, I will become thy ward.

DAUPHINE

Nay, sir, I will not be so unreasonable.

EPICOENE

Will Sir Dauphine be mine enemy too?

DAUPHINE

You know I have been long a suitor to you, uncle, that out
of your estate, which is fifteen hundred a year, you would      165
allow me but five hundred during life, and assure the rest
upon me after, to which I have often by myself and friends
tendered you a writing to sign, which you would never
consent or incline to. If you please but to effect it now—

MOROSE

Thou shalt have it, nephew. I will do it, and more.           170

DAUPHINE

If I quit you not presently and forever of this cumber, you
shall have power instantly, afore all these, to revoke your
act, and I will become whose slave you will give me to
forever.

MOROSE

Where is the writing? I will seal to it, that, or to a blank,   175
and write thine own conditions.

EPICOENE

Oh me, most unfortunate wretched gentlewoman!

HAUGHTY

Will Sir Dauphine do this?

EPICOENE

Good sir, have some compassion on me.          [*Weeps*]

MOROSE

Oh, my nephew knows you belike; away, crocodile!            180

CENTAURE

He does it not, sure, without good ground.

DAUPHINE

Here, sir.                              [*Gives him papers*]

MOROSE

Come, nephew, give me the pen. I will subscribe to any-

---

171 *presently* ed. (presently? F) at once
     *cumber* encumbrance, load of care
180 *belike* very likely

---

180 *crocodile*. Thought to weep as it took its prey; hence applied to someone who
     uses a show of grief to hide a malicious purpose.

thing, and seal to what thou wilt, for my deliverance. Thou
art my restorer. Here, I deliver it thee as my deed. If there     185
be a word in it lacking or writ with false orthography, I
protest before—I will not take the advantage.

*[Returns papers]*

DAUPHINE

Then here is your release, sir:

*He takes off* EPICOENE's *peruke*
you have married a boy: a gentleman's son that I have
brought up this half year at my great charges, and for this     190
composition which I have now made with you.—What say
you, master doctor? This is *justum impedimentum*, I hope,
*error personae?*

OTTER

Yes, sir, *in primo gradu.*

CUTBEARD

*In primo gradu.*                                                 195

DAUPHINE

I thank you, good Doctor Cutbeard and Parson Otter.

*He pulls off their beards and disguise*
You are beholden to 'em, sir, that have taken this pains for
you; and my friend, Master Truewit, who enabled 'em for
the business. Now you may go in and rest, be as private as
you will, sir. I'll not trouble you till you trouble me with     200
your funeral, which I care not how soon it come. [*Exit*
MOROSE] Cutbeard, I'll make your lease good. Thank me
not but with your leg, Cutbeard. And Tom Otter, your
princess shall be reconciled to you.—How now, gentle-
men! Do you look at me?                                           205

CLERIMONT

A boy.

---

191 *composition* contract, settlement, particularly of a financial kind
194 *in primo gradu* in the first or highest degree

---

187 *protest before—*. Declare in advance. Gifford and all later editors take F's dash
    to represent the omission of an oath, and substitute 'heaven' or 'God'. This
    seems unlikely. F makes good sense (leading to 'will not'), the use of the dash
    within speeches is common in the text, blasphemies are frequent (e.g. 'Before
    God', IV.v,198), and the Act against Abuses of Players (1606), which is cited
    to explain the omission, was not concerned with printed plays.
202 *make . . . good.* i.e. honour Morose's promise at II.v, 86.

DAUPHINE

Yes, Mistress Epicoene.

TRUEWIT

Well, Dauphine, you have lurched your friends of the
better half of the garland, by concealing this part of the
plot! But much good do it thee, thou deserv'st it, lad. And   210
Clerimont, for thy unexpected bringing in these two to
confession, wear my part of it freely. Nay, Sir Daw and Sir
La Foole, you see the gentlewoman that has done you the
favours! We are all thankful to you, and so should the
womankind here, specially for lying on her, though not   215
with her! You meant so, I am sure? But that we have stuck
it upon you today in your own imagined persons, and so
lately, this Amazon, the champion of the sex, should beat
you now thriftily for the common slanders which ladies
receive from such cuckoos as you are. You are they that,   220
when no merit or fortune can make you hope to enjoy their
bodies, will yet lie with their reputations and make their
fame suffer. Away, you common moths of these and all
ladies' honours. Go, travel to make legs and faces, and
come home with some new matter to be laughed at: you   225
deserve to live in an air as corrupted as that wherewith you
feed rumour. [*Exeunt* DAW *and* LA FOOLE] Madams, you are
mute upon this new metamorphosis! But here stands she

---

215  *on* i.e. about
216  *But* were it not
216–17  *stuck it* fastened the lie
218  *this Amazon* Mistress Otter
219  *thriftily* soundly
225  *matter* (i) subject; (ii) pus (cf. *corrupted*)

---

208  *lurched.* Cheated, robbed; as often at this date, though Jonson (or Truewit)
      may be consciously echoing *Coriolanus* (*c.* 1608), II.ii, 101: 'He lurch'd all
      swords of the garland'. Shakespeare scholars tend to regard the parallel as
      'another of [Jonson's] gibes at Shakespeare' (*Riverside Shakespeare*, p. 1392).
220  *cuckoos.* Fools, and referring to the cuckoo's laying its eggs in other birds' nests.
223–4  *moths . . . honours.* Cf. *The Revenger's Tragedy*, I.iv, 32, 'that moth to honour'
      (said of the violator of another man's wife).
224  *travel* (trauaile F). Both 'travel' and 'travail'. F's form represents the con-
      temporary pronunciation of both words.
      *make . . . faces.* i.e. learn new styles of facial expression and making bows; cf.
      Overbury's 'An Affected Traveller': '[He] is a speaking fashion; he hath taken
      paines to be ridiculous, and hath seen more then he hath perceived. His attire
      speakes *French* or *Italian*, and his *gate* cryes *Behold mee* . . . He chooseth rather
      to tell lyes then not wonders' (*Characters*, 1614, sig. E1ᵛ).

that has vindicated your fames. Take heed of such *insectae*
hereafter. And let it not trouble you that you have disco-    230
vered any mysteries to this young gentleman. He is,
a'most, of years, and will make a good visitant within this
twelvemonth. In the meantime we'll all undertake for his
secrecy, that can speak so well of his silence. [*Coming
forward*] Spectators, if you like this comedy, rise cheer-    235
fully, and now Morose is gone in, clap your hands. It may
be that noise will cure him, at least please him.

                                            [*Exeunt*]

THE END

---

237 *that noise* i.e. *that* noise, of applause

---

229 *insectae*. The substitution of the incorrect feminine form of the plural, in place
of neuter *insecta*, is probably not a blunder (H&S), but a jibe at the knights'
effeminacy.

This comedy was first
acted in the year
1609

By the Children of her Majesty's
Revels

The principal comedians were

| Nathan Field | William Barksted |
|---|---|
| Giles Carey | William Penn |
| Hugh Attawell | Richard Allin |
| John Smith | John Blaney |

With the allowance of the Master of Revels

*The principal comedians.* The columns are headed by the two most senior
members of the troupe. Field (1587–1633), one of the most famous players of
the time, was Jonson's 'Schollar & he had read to him the Satyres of Horace &
some Epigrames of Martiall' (*Conversations with Drummond*, H&S, I, 317). He
acted in at least three other plays by Jonson, *C.R.* (1600), *Poet.* (1601), and
*B.F.* (1614). In V.iii of this last play Cokes speaks of 'Your best *Actor*. Your
*Field*'. Barksted is not known as an actor before 1609. In 1607 he published a
narrative poem, *Mirrha*, and about 1610 he probably completed Marston's last
play, *The Insatiate Countess*. Nothing is heard of Carey, Penn, Attawell or
Blaney prior to 1609. Carey joined an adult company in 1611, the other three
probably some years later; see E. Nunzeger, *A Dictionary of Actors ... before
1642*, New Haven and London, 1929. Nothing is known about Allin or Smith.
Contemporary ascriptions give the part of Morose to Barksted and La Foole to
Attawell: see J. A. Riddell, 'Some Actors in Ben Jonson's Plays', *Shakespeare
Studies*, V (1969), 285–98.
*Master of Revels.* Who licensed plays for performance. Sir George Buc had held
the post since 1608.

# APPENDIX I

## AN EARLY SETTING OF 'STILL TO BE NEAT'
by F. W. Sternfeld and C. R. Wilson

Source: New York Public Library Drexel MSS 4041 and 4257 (John Gamble's commonplace book).

Music: Only the tune and bass occur in the MSS. The harmony has been supplied by us. The bass has been altered in bar 11, 2nd note, from C to G; in bar 18 it is conflated out of both MSS. The original is double-barred.

Text: In bar 11, the extra word 'and' has been retained from the sources. If preferred, it may be omitted, and the word 'still' sung to two notes. Where one syllable is to be sung to two or more notes, a slur has been added.

This setting of Clerimont's song is attributed in the MSS to William Lawes (1602–45), a musician in the court of Charles I. Murray Lefkowitz, *William Lawes*, 1960, p. 197, suggests that it was used in 1636 either at the revival at the Court of St James, or at the Cockpit-in-Court, or both, and this is supported by the fact that Lawes supplied a setting for Jonson's *Entertainment at Welbeck* in 1633. A different setting of the song appears in John Playford's *Select Ayres and Dialogues*, II, 1669, p. 51; this was probably composed for a Restoration revival.

No earlier setting is known, although the words of the song appear in several early seventeenth-century MSS, one of which almost certainly pre-dates the 1616 folio. This is Bodleian MS Rawl. poet. 31, a book of poems compiled by Sir John Harington (d. 1612). The version here (f. 9ᵛ) is the same as the folio, except for the last line, which has 'please' instead of 'strike'. Since this variant occurs elsewhere in MS versions of the song, it probably represents Jonson's own first decision. The lack of any earlier music for the song might imply that none was specially composed, and that for the 1609/10 production a pre-existing tune was employed, probably of popular origin.

Lawes preserves a popular idiom in his setting, which incorporates an isochronistic beat marked by regular barring, syncopated at two cadential points (bars 6–7, 21–2) by a *hemiola* pattern, characteristic both of Lawes' style and of early seventeenth-century composed 'ballad' songs.

1. Still to be neat, still to be dressed, As you were go-ing to a feast; Still to be pow-dered, and still per-

2. Give me a look, give me a face, That makes sim-pli-ci-ty a grace; Robes loose-ly flow-ing, hair as

-fumed: La - dy it is to be pre-
free: Such sweet neg - lect more ta - keth

-sumed, Though art's hid cau - ses are not found.
me Than all th'a - dul - te - ries of art:

All is not sweet, all is not sound.
They strike mine eyes, but not my heart.

# APPENDIX II

## JONSON'S CLASSICAL SOURCES

The following is a heavily abridged selection of the passages from classical literature to which Jonson is directly indebted in *Epicoene*. They can be read in the original Greek or Latin in the commentary of Herford and Simpson (X, 2–46). The translations are based on those in the Loeb series of classical texts, or, in the case of Libanius and the source of the song 'Still to be neat', on translations made for me by my colleague Dr D. M. Bain, but I depart from them frequently, either to make the English a more literal rendering of the original, or to suggest more clearly how Jonson may have arrived at his own wording. Occasionally I add in square brackets the original word or phrase for comparison with Jonson, or offer a comment when Jonson is in some special way close to, or remote from, his source. References are to the Loeb editions except for the Libanius declamation, for which two sets of references are provided: the first to the standard edition of R. Foerster (*Libanii Opera*, 8 vols., Leipzig, 1903–15, vol. VI), where the declamation is numbered XXVI and divided into sections; the second, which follows in brackets, to the page numbers in the Greek text in the edition of Frederic Morel (Paris, 1597), to which Morel prefixed a Latin translation. It is Morel's Greek text that is translated below, and divergences from Foerster's are not noted.

I.i, 87–98: anonymous lyric, 'Semper munditias, semper, Basilissa, decores', in the *Anthologia Latina*, first published in 1572

Always to see neatness, always, Basilissa, ornament, always hair artfully and newly arranged, and always an elegant style of dress and always cosmetics, everything ordered by careful hand, for this I do not care. Let a girl give herself to me who dresses carelessly and who conquers by the simplicity [*simplicitate*] of her attire. Do not worry over headbands that have come loose, nor about wax for the face: your face has its own honey. Always to be adorning oneself is to distrust love: besides, is not often ornament there when it is forbidden?

I.i, 108–31: Ovid, *Ars Amatoria*, III, 209–10, 215–21, 225–34, 243–7

Yet let no lover find the boxes set out upon the table; concealed art should aid your looks. . . . Nor should I approve your openly

taking the mixed marrow of a hind, or cleaning your teeth for all
to see; such things will give beauty, but they will be unseemly to
look on: many things, ugly in the doing, please when done; the
statues of industrious Myron that now are famous were once a
hard mass and lifeless weight; gold is first crushed that it may
become a ring. . . . So while you are at your toilet let us think that
you are asleep; it is more fitting you should be seen when the last
touch has been given. Why must I know the cause of the white-
ness of your cheek? Shut your chamber door: why show the
unfinished work? There is much that it befits men not to know;
most of your doings would offend, if you did not hide them
within. Those images that shine all golden in the decorated
theatre, see how thin is the gold leaf that conceals the wood; but
the people may not come near them until complete, and no more
save when men are absent should beauty be contrived. . . . Let
her who has poor hair set a guard at her door, or always be
dressed in the temple of the Good Goddess [i.e. where no man
may come; cf. Jonson's 'sacred']. My arrival was announced
suddenly to a woman once: thrown into confusion she put her
hair on all awry. Let my foes endure a cause of shame so fearful!

I.i, 144–54: Libanius, Declamation XXVI, 8, 36 (pp. 4, 16)

And indeed I avoid such workshops as have anvil and hammer
and din, silversmiths, workers in bronze, and many others. I
welcome those trades which are carried on in silence. And yet I
have seen painters singing while they painted. So sweet a thing it
is for most people to babble, and they cannot contain themselves. . . . Those sellers of goods who shout the praises of their
wares louder than heralds . . . drive me from [the market] more
than if they were pelting me with stones.

II.ii, 16–39: Juvenal, *Satires*, VI, 28, 30–2, 43, 60–3, 1–2, 14–15,
45–6, 53–6

Certainly you were once in your senses: are you taking a wife,
Postumus? . . . Can you submit to any mistress when there is so
much rope to be had, so many high and dizzying windows
standing open, and when the Aemilian bridge offers itself to you
nearby? . . . Latinus puts his silly head into the connubial
noose. . . . Is a woman shown to you in the arcades worthy of
your vows? Do all the tiers in our theatres hold one whom you
may love without misgiving, and pick out there? . . . In the reign
of Saturn [i.e. the golden age of innocence], I believe, Chastity
lingered on the earth, and was to be seen for a time. . . . Even
under Jupiter, perhaps, many, or some, traces of ancient Chastity existed. . . . And what think you of [Ursidius']searching for a
wife of the good old virtuous sort? . . . Does one man satisfy
Hiberina? Sooner will you compel her to be satisfied with one

eye! You tell me of the high repute of a certain girl, who lives on her father's farm?

II.ii, 106–34: Juvenal, *Satires*, VI, 362–7, 398–9, 402–3, 407–12, 434–46, 565–8, 572–5, 461–73

An extravagant woman does not feel her wealth going away; but as if the money sprouted up renewed from her exhausted coffer, and were always taken from a full heap, she never reckons what her pleasures cost her. There are women whom meek eunuchs and their soft kisses and despair of a beard [*desperatio barbae*] always delight, and because there is no need of an abortion.... But let [your wife] rather sing than that she should be rushing about the entire city, attending men's meetings.... This same woman knows what is going on all over the world: what the Chinese, what the Thracians are doing.... She is the first to notice the comet threatening the kings of Armenia and Parthia; she picks up the news and latest rumours at the city gates; some she invents: how the river Niphates has burst out upon the nations, and is overwhelming whole regions with a great flood, how cities are tottering and lands sinking, she tells to everyone she meets [Jonson's humorous equivalent is 'what [was done] at the Bath'].... Yet more intolerable is the woman who, as soon as she has sat down at table, commends Virgil, pardons the dying Dido, matches the poets and compares them, putting in the scales on the one side Virgil, on the other Homer. The grammarians give way, the rhetoricians are overcome, the whole crowd is silenced; neither lawyer nor auctioneer may speak, nor any other woman; such a torrent of words falls from her you would think that so many pots and bells were being clashed together. Let no one any longer weary out the trumpets or the cymbals: one woman will be able to bring succour to the labouring moon! She lays down definitions, and discourses on morals, like a philosopher. She who desires to be thought in the highest degree learned and eloquent ought to tuck up her skirts knee-high [i.e. wear the short tunic of a man].... Your Tanaquil consults [the astrologers] about the long-delayed death of her jaundiced mother, but first about your own; when she will bury her sister and her uncles; whether her lover will outlive herself—for what greater favour could the gods bestow? ... Remember also to avoid her ... who consults no one, and is herself consulted [Jonson's 'she'll study the art'].... Meanwhile the face [of the rich woman] is swollen with quantities of dough, and is hideous and ridiculous to see, or it smells of greasy Poppaean unguents, and these besmear the lips of her wretched husband. She will come to her lover with a clean-washed skin: when does she wish to appear beautiful at home? It is for her lovers she prepares the spikenard, for them she buys whatever the slender Indians send us. At length she lays bare her face: she removes the first layers of plaster [Juvenal's *tectoria* is satirical, since it denotes the stuccoing of walls: cf. V.ii, 33], and begins to be recognizable; she then is cherished [*fovetur*: lit. 'is warmed'] with that milk for which she would take she-asses with her as her companions, if she were to be sent off as an exile to the North Pole. But that which has been coated and treated with all those layers of medicaments, and had lumps of moist dough applied to it, shall it be called a face or a sore?

IV.i, 103–21: Ovid, *Ars Amatoria*, I, 443–5, 447–52; II, 261–8, 296–8, 303–4, 327–30, 198–200, 251–6, 259–60; I, 351–3, 357–8, 375, 385–6, 389–90

See that you promise: for what harm is there in promising? In promises anyone can be rich. Hope, if once it is trusted, endures for long.... If you have given something, you may be abandoned with reason: it will have gone, and she will have lost nothing. But what you have not given you may always seem about to give: in this way a barren field has often deceived its owner; in this way the gambler, lest he shall have lost, does not cease losing, and the dice often recall his eager hands.... Nor do I order you to give your mistress costly [*pretioso*] gifts: let them be small, but small ones chosen cunningly and well. While fields are in full abundance, while your branches droop with their burden, let a servant bring rural gifts in a basket. You can say they were sent to you from your country estate, though you bought them in the Via Sacra. Let him bring either grapes or nuts.... If she be in Tyrian clothes praise her Tyrian gown; if she is in Coan, find the Coan style becoming. ... Has she arranged her parting? praise it. Has she curled her hair with irons? curled tress, find favour [cf. Jonson's 'tires' (head-dresses), which was probably also influenced by Ovid's *Tyriis*, 'Tyrian']. ... Whenever you wish, have joyful dreams to tell her. And let an old woman come to purify her bed and chamber, and to bring sulphur and eggs with trembling hand [this perhaps suggested Jonson's 'riddles']. ... Do only this, play the parts she bids you play. Blame if she blames; approve whatever she approves; affirm what she affirms; deny what she denies. ... Do not be ashamed to win over the maidservants, as each stands first in rank, nor be ashamed to win over slaves. Salute each one by name: you lose nothing thereby; clasp low-born hands, ambitious one, in yours. And even to a slave, should he ask you—the cost is light—offer a gift. ... Believe me, make the humble people yours; let the gatekeeper always be one of them, and him who lies before her bedroom-door. ... But first take care to know the maidservant of the woman you would win; she will smooth your way. See that she be nearest the counsels of her mistress. ... She will choose a time—physicians also observe times—when her mistress is in an easy mood and apt for winning. ... You ask whether it profits to seduce the maid herself? ... see that you gain the mistress first, and let the servant follow: do not begin your love-making with the maid. ... Informing is taken away, when once she herself comes to have a part of the crime.

IV.ii, 84–90: Martial, *Epigrams*, IX.xxxvii, 1–6

Although, when you are at home, you are arrayed in the middle of the Subura [a crowded and disreputable district in Rome], your tresses, Galla, are manufactured far away, you lay aside your teeth at night just as you do your silk dresses, and you lie stored away in a hundred boxes, and your face does not sleep with you—yet you wink with that eyebrow which has been brought out for you in the morning ... [Jonson breaks off just as Martial becomes unrepeatably obscene.]

IV.vii, 12–18: Libanius, Declamation XXVI, 3–6 (pp. 1–4)

Do not throw me into a long speech, putting up with one of those clever speakers whose means of livelihood is speaking and counter-speaking.... I obey and put up with the din of the council chamber so as no longer to have to bear such a nuisance in the future ... because of the shouts of the speakers who are not able to keep silent. I very rarely enter the public assembly because of the many names of cases, phasis [Morel's Latin translation has *delatio*], endeixis [*accusatio*], apagoge [*abductio*], diadikasia [*petitio*], paragraphe [*praescriptio*: penultimate in the list should be 'graphe', which when restored gives a jingling conclusion similar to Jonson's 'convictions and afflictions'; Morel accidentally omitted the word from his Greek text, but translated it in his Latin, as *actio*], which even the people who have nothing to do with them love to name.

V.iii, 24–30: ibid., XXVI, 7 (p. 4)

Indeed that common formula of greeting ought to be banned from the assembly—heaven knows how it became customary—I mean saying 'chairein' [the Greek word for greeting which means 'rejoice': the Latin translation has *gaudere et salvere*]. I see no gain from the utterance. Anyone whose affairs are such as to merit grief will not find them improved by hearing 'chairein'.

V.iii, 47–57: ibid., XXVI, 6 (p. 3)

My father, gentlemen, advised me to collect and contain my mind, and not allow it to dissipate [lit. 'be poured different ways'], to see clearly what was essential in life, and what not, to adhere to the one and keep away from the other, to honour quiet and flee turmoils. This I have continued to do, gentlemen, not taking part in public meetings, not because I do not care about the good of the commonwealth, but because of the shouts of the speakers who are not able to keep silent.